Four-Season Harvest

ELIOT COLEMAN

Four-Season Harvest

Organic Vegetables from Your Home Garden
All Year Long

Illustrations by Kathy Bray
and photographs by Barbara Damrosch

CHELSEA GREEN PUBLISHING COMPANY
White River Junction, Vermont

Designed by Ann Aspell.

Printed in the United States of America.

20 19 18 17 16 15   11 12

First printing, September 1999

Library of Congress Cataloguing-in-Publication Data
Coleman, Eliot, 1938-
    Four-season harvest: how to harvest fresh organic
    vegetables from your home garden all year long / Eliot
    Coleman; illustrations by Kathy Bray; and photographs
    by Barbara Damrosch.—Rev. ed of: The new organic
    grower's four-season harvest. c1992.
        p.   cm.
    Includes bibliographical references (p.) and index.
    ISBN 1-890132-27-6
    1. Vegetable gardening. 2. Organic gardening. I. Title.
II. Title: Four-season harvest.
SB324.3.C64   1999
635.0484dc21   99013209

CHELSEA GREEN PUBLISHING COMPANY
P.O. Box 428
White River Junction, Vermont 05001
(800) 639-4099
www.chelseagreen.com

To Ian, Clara, and Melissa, who enjoy good food.

CONTENTS

List of Tables

FOREWORD

IT'S HARD TO ACHIEVE anything new in an endeavor as old as gardening, but Eliot Coleman has done it. After years of experimentation, he has reinvented the gardening year. The old seasons, and the iconography by which we know them, may soon be folklore.

Spring: A mischievous sprite, a warm breeze that moved housebound gardeners out of doors to happily waste themselves, despite whatever mercurial weather tested their commitment. Summer: A Rubenesque goddess who swelled the garden with far more bounty than anyone could tend, let alone eat, even with the help of rabbits and bugs. Fall: A scolding harpy who recited gardeners' failures to them as they picked their way through weeds and sprawling vines to glean tomatoes and squash before the apocalypse of frost. Winter: A wraith who hovered over what was once the garden, whispering, "Gone, gone. . . . Return to your VCR and supermarket vegetables."

Imagine, instead, a scenario in which spring work begins more gradually, summer spares time for other outdoor pleasures, fall is a gearing-up rather than a giving-up, and winter, best of all, is a time to reap a fresh harvest with almost no work. For most of us, "eating out of the garden" is a short seasonal pleasure, unless we live in a very warm place or can afford a heated greenhouse, and the canning-freezing-drying scramble never quite compensates for summer's loss.

The Four-Season Harvest presents a way to eat the best food—garden-fresh and chemical-free—all year long, with little effort or expense. Most dedicated gardeners know some season-extending techniques, but this book is not merely about season extension. It's about gardening and eating in a manner appropriate to each season.

I first learned something of Eliot's gardening methods through his first book, *The New Organic Grower*. It was refreshing to read someone for whom gardening is not a gladiatorial contest. Eliot makes nature his ally. Because his approach is biological, he focuses on plants and soil rather than high-tech structures. His tools are simple, refined to simpler, perfected as simplest.

Being a simpler-is-better sort of person myself, I was curious to see what Eliot was doing in his own garden, so on a trip to Maine to see my family, I paid him a visit. What I saw was a splendid, productive garden—the end result of twenty-five years of tinkering. Eliot's techniques may have been derived from age-old practices, but they had been customized and updated with modern know-how and, occasionally, modern materials. Nothing there was faddish. Just good, logical stuff: a more efficient cold frame; compost made in straw bale containers; subtly redesigned hand tools.

When I questioned Eliot it was obvious that his garden was not the result of his knowledge, but vice versa. He had paid attention to natural systems and they had taught him how to work with nature. This experience gave him enormous confidence in the natural world—the very thing so many gardeners seem to lack.

It became clear to me that Eliot's approach made his life a lot easier. I could see this in the project that was consuming him at the time: the practice of a year-round harvest which he shares in this book. Instead of trying to prolong his summer harvest, Eliot was growing a wide range of cold-tolerant crops (including some I'd never heard of) and then giving them the minimum protection they needed. He was doing this by taking the best cold-protection devices, modifying and recombining them into a system that enabled him to eat homegrown vegetables each day, a system that was inexpensive, easy to maintain, and fun.

Eliot's garden was a beckoning sort of place and he seemed to take constant delight in everything he did there. No wonder he wanted a garden that was "in" all the time, not just half the year.

I left Maine that summer with all sorts of good ideas, eager to try some of them in my Connecticut garden. That never happened. Soon after our meeting, I moved to Maine, and within a year Eliot and I were married. His garden is now "our" garden, though I am only vice president when it comes to the vegetables (he is vice president of the flowers). I can now attest to the joy and ease of eating a fresh, healthy, year-round harvest.

Should you take my word for it? Absolutely not. You'll need to try it for yourself. This book will start you off and steer you in the right direction.

Barbara Damrosch
Harborside, Maine

PREFACE TO THE REVISED EDITION

I INTRODUCED THE philosophy and practice of a year-round, fresh-food garden, no matter what the climate, in my 1992 edition of this book. The rewards of a twelve-month garden are so delightful that I have continued to develop it. As a result I have redesigned the layout of our home garden, added many new concepts, and simplified many practices. I gained an additional dose of inspiration and knowledge during a visit to French winter gardens in January of 1996.

Furthermore, nutritional science has continued to stress the importance of a home-garden-quality diet. Hardly a day goes by without another newspaper article about the health benefits of eating fresh vegetables. In light of this new emphasis on the importance of fresh vegetables to human health, and the newly simplified techniques for year-round backyard growing of fresh vegetables, it seemed a revised edition was in order. *Four-Season Harvest* now brings the winter-harvest concept up to date and, hopefully, will spark "the fresh food revolution" in everyone's backyard.

PREFACE TO THE ORIGINAL EDITION

THIS BOOK IS A product of three forces—inspiration, improvement, and impetus.

The inspiration came from seeing Scott and Helen Nearing's garden in the late 1960s. They were producing many crops beyond the typical growing season in the protection of a simple, lean-to greenhouse built into a stone wall. Their garden was my first exposure to the possibilities of extending a homegrown harvest.

The improvement came with my experience. Over time I learned to extend both the length of the harvest season and the number of crops grown. The qualities that have always served me well in the garden, informed hunches, stubbornness, and a bias toward low-tech solutions, helped create the productive system described in this book.

The impetus came from my friend Joan Gussow, a nutritionist who has investigated both the potential and the benefits of regional food production. A few years ago during lunch at an agricultural conference, I told her about my success with harvesting fresh vegetables all year-round, even in the chilly climate of New England. She encouraged me to write a book about it. And so I did.

INTRODUCTION

The traditional American vegetable garden begins in May and ends in October. For the rest of the year the frugal home-garden household must depend on shelves lined with canning jars and a well-stocked freezer. Our frugal household presents a different picture. We no longer can or freeze the summer vegetables so as to have them reappear all winter. By the time the season ends for our traditional summer garden, we are eating out of our untraditional winter garden, a garden that begins in October and ends in May.

We adore fresh food, what we call "real food," the fresher the better. We have never considered the many-month-old embalmed remains of last summer's harvest, whether canned or frozen, to be real food. Real food, the most pleasing to the palate and, as nutritional science increasingly reminds us, the most beneficial to health, means unprocessed whole foods like freshly harvested vegetables with all the crisp, crunchy, flavorful nutrition intact. So, when the summer vegetables are in season, we feast on beans, corn, tomatoes, and squash fresh from our summer garden. But, what about winter? What do we eat here in Maine when temperatures are frosty and snow is deep? Surprisingly, we keep right on eating fresh, home-grown food.

Our winter garden contains cold-weather foods such as spinach, tatsoi, scallions, and arugula that are as adapted to cold as the summer vegetables are to heat. The concept of a winter garden sits on the landscape like an undiscovered treasure. Undiscovered, because it seems impossible in a climate like ours where the sharp reality of winter cold intrudes. But some of us don't accept reality without pushing its boundaries. We started challenging Jack Frost years ago. We soon had harvests extending until late fall and harvests beginning by early spring. We wanted more. Could we continue until December? Could we begin again in February? What if we adjusted our planting dates? What if we added a little more protection? Each success led to another. Eventually, we brought the latest fall harvest and the earliest spring harvest together. Voilà, the end of winter!

The surprise of our winter garden (and yours, too) is how simple it is. Winter vegetables will thrive in any winter climate with a little protection from wind and weather. No heating or high-tech systems are necessary. The keys to success are a new attitude and new crops. To better establish these new concepts in the new world, we have consulted the old world where the French have a long tradition of winter gardens. This book describes fifteen years of experience with four-season harvesting in our own garden, plus the new inspirations we gained during a January pilgrimage to the winter gardens of southern France. That combination is a harvest of unparalleled bounty for fresh-food lovers across the U.S.

Eliot Coleman
Harborside, Maine
August 1999

Four-Season Harvest

The winter was not given to us for no purpose. We must thaw its cold with our genialness. We are tasked to find out and appropriate all the nutriment it yields. If it is a cold and hard season, its fruit, no doubt, is the more concentrated and nutty.

—Henry David Thoreau

CHAPTER 1

PRESENTING THE FOUR-SEASON HARVEST

A heavy wet snow is falling today. There could be a foot or more, said the radio, before its voice was silenced by a toppling tree that took out our power. It's a beautiful snow, clumping thickly on the evergreen woods that encircle our little house and bringing them in closer like a soft white duvet. This is the fourth snowfall so far this month, and it's the 10th of April. Being vegetable gardeners of great enthusiasm you would think we'd be dismayed, champing at the bit, eager to grow fresh food for the table again. But that is all in the past. We have managed to turn winter from deprivation to celebration.

We throw on our coats and go out to the cold frames to pick a salad for dinner. The cold frames are glass-covered, bottomless wooden boxes, eight feet long and four feet wide, lined up at the back of the garden along our gravel path, and a celebratory sight they are—as full of green bounty as the

Fig. 1

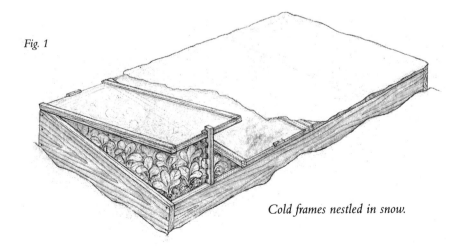

Cold frames nestled in snow.

1

produce aisle at the local market. Lifting up the glass lids and propping them with a notched stick, we are treated to a good whiff of moist unfrozen soil. While the snow sifts about us we get busy cutting tender leaves with small serrated knives, filling a towel-lined basket. Dressed with a good olive oil and a squirt of lemon, the salad will taste like renewal—a perfect accompaniment to the leek and potato soup simmering on the back of the stove.

This fresh daily harvest goes on all year, both from our traditional outdoor summer garden and our unconventional protected winter garden. The results are sumptuous. Dinner guests habitually exclaim about the freshness and flavor of our salads and always ask, "What all is in there?" In January, for example, our answer might be "a mix of frisée endive, baby leaf spinach, Chioggia radicchio, wild arugula, miner's lettuce, buckshorn plantain, and corn salad." We can almost anticipate the next question.

"From where?" they query, slightly conspiratorially, expecting us to confess to expensive overnight air delivery from exotic foreign suppliers. When we tell them we harvested the salad earlier that day from our unheated winter garden, the suspicion changes to stunned disbelief. "In winter? But it's too cold."

"Not for these crops. They don't mind freezing temperatures. These greens are the traditional winter peasant foods of southern France and northern Italy. Granted our winters are colder, but our simple protection makes up for the lower temperatures."

They nod in understanding but then pause again after a few more mouthfuls. "But you don't have enough sun way up here, do you? I mean, southern France is like Florida."

We acknowledge it may seem like that is so, but the truth is something different. "Based on daylength and sunshine, Miami, on the 26th parallel of latitude in Florida, corresponds with the city of Luxor, near the ruins of ancient Thebes, on the shore of the Nile River in southern Egypt. In contrast, the resort town of Cannes on the Mediterranean coast of France has the same winter sunshine and daylength as the city of Portland on the Atlantic coast of Maine."

"Maine? I can't believe it."

"It's true. Most of Europe lies further north on the globe than the U.S. does. Our farm on the 44th parallel in Maine is on the same latitude as Avignon in southern France and Genoa on the warm Ligurian coast of Italy. That means we have the same daylength and amount of sun they do."

The visitors' surprise and their response are not unexpected. We have received that same reaction from gardeners everywhere. In the first place, many people assume all vegetables will be killed by freezing temperatures in winter. Yet we habitually grow some thirty different crops that survive freezing temperatures with no problem when given a little protection from the wind, which is the real outdoor plant killer in winter. Secondly, many people assume there will not be enough sunshine during the winter months. Yet we get as much sunshine as regions of the world where winter gardening is traditional. That latter fact is probably the most surprising.

It is logical to assume that warm temperatures and sunshine go hand in hand. If France has a warmer winter climate, it must be sunnier. In truth, since Avignon has more cloudy winter days than we do, there is actually more winter sunshine in Maine. That raises an obvious question. Then how come the Maine climate and the French climate are so different? Just because we are on the same latitude doesn't necessarily mean we have the same climate. The climate difference between southern France and mid-coastal Maine is caused

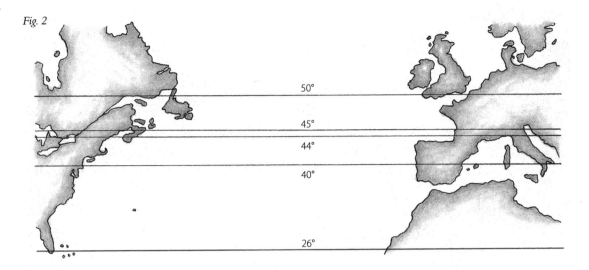

Fig. 2

by forces independent of latitude. Different climates are a result of different air and ocean currents.

Comparative latitudes.

Whereas masses of cold arctic air moving south across Canada give the northern parts of the North American continent a mostly frozen winter, the situation in France is different. The Gulf Stream, a massive flow of warm water moving northward across the Atlantic Ocean from the Caribbean to Scandinavia, ensures that western Europe's winter will be mostly cool and moist. Similarly, the warm Pacific currents on the west coast of the U.S. mean that Juneau, Alaska at latitude 57° has a warmer average temperature in January than New York City at latitude 41°. If judged on temperature alone, a gardener in Juneau should have a slightly easier time growing winter vegetables than a gardener in New York. But for winter vegetable crops, temperature is not the principal deciding factor. Daylength—the amount of available sunlight—is.

And that brings us back to latitude. Latitude determines daylength and the quantity of potential sunlight available to a winter gardener. Places around the globe at the same latitude will have the same daylength. Thus our Maine farm in the northeastern corner of the U.S. shares a "sun line" with those parts of France, previously mentioned, which lie on the same 44th parallel. Places to the north of that line, such as the rest of northern Europe, have less winter gardening potential than we do. And places to the south of that line, which includes 85 percent of the U.S., have better sun for winter vegetable gardening than Mediterranean France. We should make better use of it.

We are long-time devotees of four-season food production and, to tell the truth, we haven't been doing too badly making use of both winter and summer sunshine. We do this because we love to eat good fresh food and share it with our friends. Our four-season harvest is based on a simple premise. Whereas the *growing season* may be chiefly limited to the warmer months, the *harvest season* has no such limits. We enjoy a year-round harvest by following two practices: *succession planting* and *crop protection. Succession planting* means sowing vegetables more than once. Sowings at one- to three-week intervals during the growing season will extend the fresh harvest of summer crops for as long as possible. Midsummer to late-summer sowings of hardy crops begin the transition to the cool months. That is where crop protection takes over.

Crop protection means vegetables under cover. The traditional winter vegetables are very hardy. They will survive the fiercest cold under a blanket of snow. Since we can't count on snow cover, we substitute simple protective structures such as cold frames and plastic-covered tunnels. Many delicious winter vegetables need only this minimal protection to yield through the winter. All it takes are seeds of some familiar and unfamiliar hardy vegetables, a little crop protection, and a dose of innovative thinking.

The innovative thinking involves realizing that *only* the harvest season, and *not* the growing season, needs to be extended. The distinction is important because the harvest season can be extended with cool-weather vegetables and simple crop protection. Extending the growing season, however, involves adding or collecting heat, storing heat, adding insulation to protect that heat, and providing extra lighting for long-day summer crops. Growing-season extension is highly technological. Harvest-season extension is basically biological. It is also just plain logical. The harvest is what you eat.

We prefer not to define our simple crop protection method as "unheated," because that makes it sound as if we are not doing something—heating—that we should be doing. The reason our protection is unheated is because heating is not necessary. We often avoid the word "greenhouse" since many people assume that a greenhouse, if unheated, is a super-insulated technological marvel or a complicated heat-storage device. Ours is neither. The best short statement to describe our approach to the four-season garden is a quote from Buckminster Fuller in his book *Shelter* (1932): "Don't fight forces; use them." Instead of bemoaning the forces of winter and trying to fight them by adding heat, we have limited our intervention to the climatic protection provided by one or two translucent layers. Instead of trying to grow heat-loving crops during cold weather, we have said, "So it's cold, great! What likes cold?" The answer is some thirty or more hardy vegetables.

Fig. 3

Wild arugula.

Fighting force requires energy, and energy costs money. Our approach is to take advantage of everything that a translucent layer can get for free from the sun and the residual heat of the soil mass. In our minds, we have created an inexpensive "protected microclimate" and then found the plants that will thrive in that microclimate. The same applies in reverse during the summer. When those protected microclimates are extra warm, we don't fight that warmth with motorized greenhouse cooling systems. We use it to grow heat-loving crops.

Fresh harvesting all year round makes life simpler and easier in a number of ways. Since most of the fall, winter, and spring crops are planted in midsummer to late summer in spaces vacated by summer crops, this system results in year-round eating without year-round gardening. By extending the harvest, you also spread out the work. All the planting doesn't have to be done at once in the spring, and all the harvesting isn't crowded into the late summer. Instead of being a series of chores (putting in the garden, weeding the garden, harvesting, and canning and freezing) with rather rigid time frames, home food production becomes a part of the whole year. The four-season gardener doesn't have a date, such as Memorial Day (traditional in New England), to put in the garden. That's because there is no goal called "putting in the garden." The garden is in all the time. The goal is to eat well.

Is this more time-consuming? Not at all. It is certainly more pleasurable. The four-season harvest is a different arrangement of time and a different appreciation of the importance of quality food. It will free you from the chores of food preservation and trips to the market. You will always have fresh food in the garden—crisp and delicious. You will have set up a system that features many different vegetables in their respective

seasons rather than a limited list of vegetables suitable only for the summer season. The amount of work comes out about the same over the course of the year. The benefits are that the joys of a fresh harvest continue through all four seasons and the food is more nutritious and varied.

If this is such a great concept, why isn't everyone doing it? One reason could be that in many people's minds, the idea of supplying most of their food seems like a large, complicated chore outside of their experience. But the truth is that growing food is the most basic activity of human civilization, not some mysterious industrial process. You do not need a large-scale operation. Your food is now produced in bits and pieces around the year. You are integrating the garden into your life the same way you integrate other important activities, such as helping your children with homework, playing catch and talking with them, sharing in household chores, and helping out the neighbors. You don't hire others to do those jobs. You do them yourself because they are meaningful, joyful, and important to your family's spiritual welfare. Your food is of no less importance.

The impressive list of benefits from the four-season harvest is what motivates us to encourage others to give it a try. The first benefit is *freshness*. Nutritionists agree fresh is best and nothing is fresher than the home garden. All the vitamins and all the flavor the food is meant to have are there for you to enjoy. The carrots have crunch, the salad greens have crisp, the spinach is full of life. Week-old salads on the produce shelf can't compare with those that go from soil to salad bowl on the same day. Good chefs know this, the rare old-fashioned ones who shop the farmers' markets daily. And gardeners knew it long before the chefs.

The next benefit is *variety*. We love to eat with the seasons. Just as we have chosen to live in a place where spring, summer, fall, and winter are very different from one another, we like our menu to reflect this. Certain tastes and seasons go together—eating raw peas on the first sweaterless days; roasted corn at a beach picnic; pumpkin pie on a festive fall weekend; endive and mâche salad with roasted beets on a day when you're glad the wood stove is warm. As we have searched for new winter crops, we have been amazed at the wealth of choices.

The third benefit is *quality*. We are not vegetarians, but we eat a lot of vegetables and salads. They are our favorite foods. We want to know that what we eat has been grown on exceptional soil nourished with all the organic matter and minerals plants need. Since the government bureaucracy has displayed such dismal incompetence protecting us against the dangers of agricultural chemicals, we have decided to make the decisions ourselves. We no longer need to wonder, "Where has this lettuce been and what have they done to it?" Given the impressive statistics showing the nutritional importance of vegetables, we want to get all the minerals, soluble fiber, beta carotene, folic acid, and other positives without any regrets.

The fourth benefit is *simplicity*. We have been pleasantly surprised at how easy it can be to grow fresh winter food. The first step was to realize that we aren't gardening in winter, just harvesting. All the gardening was done in late summer and early fall when we planted most of these crops. Furthermore, biology is on our side. The crops that succeed in winter are those that like cool weather. Most fruiting crops such as corn, tomatoes, peppers, cucumbers, or eggplants need the heat of summer to do well. But the majority of the leafy crops need the cooler conditions of fall-winter-spring if they are to taste good. This is their traditional time of year. Most gardeners know how

quickly spinach bolts when warm weather arrives. The same is true for other cool-weather greens: arugula is very sharp-tasting in summer; radicchio and other chicories turn bitter; mâche won't germinate when the soil is too warm or days are long. Cold weather brings out the best in these leafy crops, making them tender and sweet.

Recently many of the traditional European cool-season crops, such as mâche, radicchio, Belgian endive, arugula, and dandelion, have been discovered by upscale restaurateurs. There is now a demand to have them available all year. How dull. We look forward to mâche and endive in the winter. That is their season, and they are fresh and alive, while corn and beans are limp specimens on the supermarket produce shelf or ice-encrusted in the store's freezer.

Doesn't this seasonality limit the meals? Not at all. Rather than being restricting, this garden larder is liberating and inspirational. Instead of canned or frozen peas in November, you eat fresh broccoli, crisp sugarloaf chicory, or a piquant sorrel soup. Instead of stale California head lettuce, your February salad is made from fresh mâche, Belgian endive, claytonia, and arugula. Canned corn in April? No way, when your garden offers fresh ingredients for creamed spinach, parsnip tempura, or a dandelion soufflé.

In our grandfathers' day, people celebrated the seasonality and variety of the home garden. They knew that one cabbage tasted best fresh in June and that another made the best sauerkraut. This was the pea for eating fresh and that the one for drying. They were familiar with fifty different apples and twenty kinds of pears. They knew when these were ripe and which blended best for cider or complemented the flavor of this or that cheese. We can recover such civilized living again.

Part of our search for such civilized living took us to Europe recently on a food and garden pilgrimage. We wanted to learn about winter gardening and winter foods in a part of the world with a warmer climate, but with the same winter daylength. We knew that with a little protection we could create warmer conditions. So we followed our "sun line" (the 44th parallel) across southern France. Our itinerary was planned out as a series of visits, usually one or two per day, between the Atlantic coast and the Italian border. We had old friends and contacts among European gardeners and gardening associations and with their help we had set up meetings with private gardeners, a few commercial growers, and any appropriate botanical gardens. We had also contacted some French seed companies. Who better, we thought, to ask about what worked best, in what areas, on what kind of schedule? Perhaps some regional varieties would be more appropriate than others. There might even be new crops to discover.

The time not scheduled for planned visits was allotted to chance encounters. We've found that no matter how well we plan a trip, it's often when we get sidetracked that we learn the most—and

Fig. 4

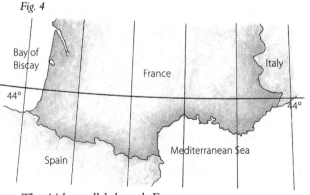

The 44th parallel through France.

have the most fun. This means keeping our eyes open as we drive, chatting with restaurateurs when we eat, asking questions of greengrocers when we shop, and never hesitating to stop and speak with anyone who looks interesting. In order to do this, we have had to overcome our normally retiring natures and polite reluctance to bother strangers. But we are rarely disappointed or rebuffed. And when the strangers are gardeners, a rapport and friendship always develops as soon as they find out that we too are gardeners who wish to exchange ideas. As a result of so many of these experiences, we've come to realize that all humanity shares a kinship when it comes to such a basic subject as growing and eating fresh food, and that the delights of the table are central to people's definition of themselves and what they enjoy in life.

For every convert drawn to our passion for four-season harvesting as a horticultural adventure, there are probably ten that are led there by their taste buds. A growing number of Americans are embracing the idea that fresh, locally grown food, eaten in season, is the best way to eat. But it is usually a six-month romance at best. To them, the prospect of fresh, local *winter* food comes as great news. And in fact, we find that whenever we talk to groups about this subject, it is our slides of enticing winter dishes, as much as those of our garden, that send the audience home full of determination to expand their gardens into all four seasons. So our tour of the 44th parallel was planned as a quest for delicious new crops as much as a quest for garden lore. We already knew the four-season harvest was good. We were determined to make it even better.

Earth is so kind—just tickle her with a hoe and she laughs with a harvest.

—Douglas Jerold

CHAPTER 2

GETTING STARTED

How do you begin a four-season garden? You can start on an area no larger than a tablecloth. Plant one or two short rows of a few salad crops. Then next week, plant a few more short rows of other crops. Now you're rolling. Less than a month after initiating the process, you will be eating radishes. There are also the early thinnings of spinach, beets, lettuce, and cabbage to add to your salads. Since you will plant many crops in succession, there will be plenty of thinnings. But since you are gardening for the table, there is no chore called "thinning the seedlings." There is only a sequence whereby you thin enough to add to a salad today, thin more for a stir-fry tomorrow, and thin yet again for soup

Fig. 5

Hand thinning seedlings.

8

the next day. The act of thinning not only feeds you but also enables future bounty by providing more room for the remaining plants.

As each crop stops producing, you clean off the area, spread a little more compost, and replant it with another vegetable suited to the advancing season. Thus, the warm-weather plantings are replaced by more cold-tolerant varieties and eventually by hardy winter crops. The vegetables for fresh winter eating and the earliest spring sowings are protected by cold frames or tunnels. Wintered-over crops and outdoor spring sowings pick up the process in spring. (See the specific tables in chapter 9.)

Once the year-round harvest has begun to flow, the productivity is unbelievable. Let's say you want fresh salads every day from your garden. There are about two dozen popular salad crops, all of them easily grown in the home garden. Some, such as tomatoes, cucumbers, peppers, and New Zealand spinach, are limited to the warm months. Others, such as lettuce, beets, cabbage, scallions, and Swiss chard, are spring, summer, and fall crops. Spinach, radishes, kohlrabi, mizuna, and peas do best in the cool months. Mâche, sorrel, arugula, escarole, endive, chicory, and claytonia will feed you daily from the winter garden even in the coldest climates. Carrots, parsley, onions, and sorrel can be harvested almost year-round. The edges of those categories will overlap depending on your climatic zone, but the message is clear: year-round fresh salads offer all the variety anyone could want.

If you don't have the space for that impressive salad bar lineup, how about growing your salad mixed? You can sow lettuce and other salad greens together, as in the popular *mesclun* combinations (from a French Provençal word indicating a combination of many ingredients). With mesclun, you harvest the leaves young on a cut-and-come-again basis to make a ready-mixed salad. This is a wonderful option for those who have less time and space to garden and wish to get more variety from each planting. Since the different mesclun mixes are adaptable to a wide range of temperatures and maturity dates, they will yield fresh salads over a good portion of the year from half a dozen succession sowings.

Not only is there a progression from one crop to another, but there is also a progression within crops. Beets become more than beets. They are appreciated as thinnings for a salad, young greens for steaming, baby beets for a cold summer borscht, and eventually large beets for pickling and winter storage. A multi-use pea, such as the sugar snap type, can be used as snow peas when young, as snap peas when mature, and shelled for green peas in between. Since short rows of many crops can be planted successively during their season, the process also repeats itself, like the singing of a round.

The Ever-Productive Garden

The potential for year-round garden harvesting is reminiscent of a story about wild-food gourmet Euell Gibbons leading a group of novices on a food-gathering expedition in New York's Central Park. The participants were astonished by what was available. It had always been there, but they had never looked because they didn't realize the possibilities. The same is true of your home garden. There may be a lot of food there already after the summer garden ends.

For example, if you grow Swiss chard, it should be edible right up until hard winter weather, and it should rebound in spring unless you live in the far north. After you cut the main head of a broccoli plant, many smaller side shoots emerge and will keep producing throughout the fall if you harvest them. Any onions that you missed at harvest time will sprout and grow tender greens in the spring. You might want to leave the small ones in the garden on purpose. A large number of common crops will survive the winter even in the coldest climates if there is consistent snow cover (snow is a wonderful insulator). They will certainly survive in the warmer zones.

During the January trip across France, we had an experience that emphasized the point. We were visiting the Jardin des Plantes in Montpelier, one of the oldest botanical gardens in France. Like many such venerable institutions, it was showing its age. Some of the walls were beginning to crumble and panes were missing in unused glasshouses. But we were not there for the architecture. We had come to see the "non-existent" vegetables. When we had called ahead to learn the winter hours and had inquired about the vegetable garden, the nice Frenchman on duty told us not to waste our time because the vegetable garden was "non-existent" in the winter. Ah, well, we had heard that song before. "There is nothing in the garden" is usually synonymous with "it doesn't look nice like it did last summer."

The vegetable garden at the Jardin des Plantes occupies one quarter of a parterre in front of the *orangerie*. Admittedly it probably did look nicer during the summer, but it was just what we wanted to find in January. Despite the disclaimers of the garden staff, this abandoned Zone 9 garden, which had probably seen no care since October, still contained ready-to-pick crops of chard, salsify and scorzonera, six different types of lettuces, radicchio, sorrel, mustard greens, turnips and turnip greens, kale, cabbages, winter radish, red and green scallions, leeks, and spinach. If that garden were our backyard, we would have considered it a source of fresh main course and salad vegetables for the rest of the winter. It was a cornucopian

example of a garden truth we have long noted— if you just look around in a post-season garden, you will almost always find something to eat.

All those disclaimers of "non-existent" vegetables are made by gardeners—not by gardens. The plants tell a different tale. With most gardeners there seems to be an end-of-the-summer mindset that says, "Oh dear, what a shame, it's all over till next year." It's almost as though a curtain had fallen. No one ever seems to have checked to see if it really is true or not. On the other hand, the end-of-the-summer reaction of most plants that tolerate cool weather is, "Days are getting shorter, nights are getting cooler, time to slow down." Not cease, just slow down. Yes, the warm weather annuals have ceased. The tomato, cucumber, corn, and pepper plants knew winter was coming and rushed to ripen their last fruits before frost. But the cool-weather crops are just beginning their second season.

Some of the cool-weather crops we saw were biennials such as the chard, salsify, scorzonera, radicchio, turnips, kale, cabbage, scallions, and leeks. They were planning to hang on through the winter so they could complete their cycle by producing seed next summer. Some were cool season annuals, including lettuce, mustard, radish, and spinach that were planted for a fall crop. They didn't have time to complete their growth the first year so they would also wait out the winter in order to produce seed next year. The only extra effort needed to make all these vegetables available in winter was to do some succession plantings during the late summer and early fall, as the Jardin des Plantes staff had obviously done.

The winter bounty that existed in the vegetable section of this parterre was simply hardy leftovers from the summer garden. They were not as pretty as they were before they hunkered down for the winter, but they were just as edible. However, such bounty can only be found if one looks for it. Sadly, the attitude has been not to look. Even the Jardin des Plantes security guard stationed next to the orangery, whom we were questioning about the garden, and who could see everything we could see, showed surprise that we had come in January "when there are no plants to see." Such determined blindness in the face of reality shows the power of preconceived notions to limit the four-season harvest. The end-of-season mindset prevents summer gardeners from exploring the winter feasts. But as the vegetable garden at the Jardin des Plantes made clear, succession crops from the summer garden, even uncovered and abandoned, are a sufficient treasure for the backyard gardener and there is almost no work involved.

The Inviting Garden

Too often the impediments to garden success are less in the garden than in the gardener's mind. The neglected end-of-summer garden can effectively inhibit your participation in harvest extension. It is what might be called a "subconscious garden negative." Anyone who has gone out to a summer garden in August or September knows the depressing feeling of the end of the growing season. The look of a spent garden is hardly uplifting. Neglected, untidy, and worn-out are all conditions we avoid. Perhaps we see some of our own mortality in the "death" of summer. But nature doesn't die off in the fall; some of its plants do. In the four-season garden, fall isn't an end but a place on the continuum. New possibilities open up for those plants that thrive in new conditions.

So here is a suggestion for gardeners wishing for an inspiring and enjoyable introduction to the four-season harvest. Go out to your garden at the end of the summer. Leave any plants that are pro-

ducing or will continue to produce, but clean up the rest of the garden and haul the crop residues to your compost heap. Rake or cultivate the surface into a clean seedbed. Next, pour into a bowl all the leftover varieties of vegetable seeds you can find in your seed drawer or in the sale rack at the hardware store. Then, with suitable Dionysian exuberance (he was the Greek god who represented the potency and teeming fertility of Nature), dance gaily about broadcasting the mixed seeds over the soil. Rake lightly to cover and irrigate where the soil is dry. If the neighbors haven't had you committed by this point, come back four weeks later to begin partaking of the new garden harvest.

Any warm-season plants you sowed are just there for a comparison. The young plants from the leftover eggplant and pepper seeds have no future except to let you know when the first frost occurs. In an exceptionally warm fall when the frost comes late there might be a small green bean harvest, and what a treat that would be. But this really concerns the cool-weather crops. Hopefully your seed smorgasbord included some lettuce, spinach, beets, kale, collards, or Swiss chard. Even in the colder zones you should be able to cut small leaves from all of those within four weeks after sowing. The small leaves are the basic ingredients for a classic out-of-season Nicoise-style mesclun salad. Round red radishes will take a little longer than the number of days-to-harvest printed on the packet, but they will mature and will be sweeter than you have ever known, due to the cooler temperatures and shorter fall days. So should baby carrots if you are in Zone 7 or southward.

Once you begin to enjoy these cool-weather harvests you may want to add other hardy crops next year that were not included in your standard seed purchases. Some possibilities are arugula, radicchio, claytonia, and minutina to accompany the more familiar mustard and turnip greens. With more possibilities of crops to harvest you may wish to be less Dionysian and sow them in rows for convenience. Once you do that you might be inspired, if you are in the colder zones, to ensure a longer harvest by adding a little climate protection for the plants. Your own four-season harvest has now become a reality.

Turning a one-season into a four-season garden invokes those marvelous human beings we all have been fortunate to know in our lives who, even in old age, keep themselves spiritually young. It is obvious why they are such refreshing company; they never stop participating, learning, producing, and contributing. That is exactly the spirit represented by the four-season garden. Specific seasons come and go, but the spirit perseveres throughout the year. In the future you can avoid the end-of-season feeling by cleaning up each crop as it matures and replanting that area. The four-season garden is perpetually renewed and always looks like spring and summer. Like those treasured friends, this garden is refreshing to be around, and it encourages your participation.

The Spacious Garden

Along with keeping the garden young at heart, I also suggest keeping it spacious. Like the companions we cherish, the spaces we willingly inhabit are those that welcome and comfort us. A crowded and tangled garden is as uninviting as a spent and neglected one. If the garden is not easy to enter and walk through, it will, subconsciously, keep you out. To that end, the distance between plants and rows in the garden should be less a function of the space requirements of the plants than a function of the space requirements of the gardener. Make the rows shorter and fewer or the beds narrower and the paths wider. Use succession plantings of zucchini, for example, and remove the large, sprawling plants when the new ones start to bear. Allow more comfortable space for picking, nibbling, planting, and cultivating. The highly intensive garden may be more productive spatially, but if it keeps you out, it is far less productive practically.

It is ideal to be able to pop out to the garden for that last-minute handful of basil, parsley, or chives, or to pull some radishes and baby carrots for snacks when company arrives. If your spur-of-the-moment garden visit requires any sort of balancing, tiptoeing, or rope swinging to reach the desired crops, the layout is too crowded. If the visit involves struggling with an old gate or being garroted by the clothesline, access is a problem. Very often, only by removing the negatives do you become aware of the powerful effect they have had. Try making your garden smaller, simpler, and

Fig. 6

The back-door kitchen garden.

more open. Additionally, you should try to locate the garden next to the kitchen door or as close to it as possible. Then the invitation to the garden larder will be not only pleasant but also close at hand.

The Guilt-Free Garden

Another subconscious garden negative is garden guilt. With year-round production, there are no mistakes or penalties to be paid for temporary neglect. This is the "don't worry, be happy" school of gardening. There is always tomorrow. If some other important aspect of your life calls you away and weeds dominate the beans or the new planting germinates poorly, just erase the problem and start again. Take a hoe and a rake, clean off the area, and replant it with whatever crop comes next in the sequence. Sure, one crop may be missing, but there are plenty of others. Even professionals who grow a wide range of crops will fail on a few of them every year.

This is no longer the old "I only had one chance to plant and I goofed" situation that you may dread. In the four-season garden, you have many chances and many seasons to come. Everything, even so-called failures, can have a purpose. Regard the weeds as the soil savers that they are—in essence a short-term green manure. Their roots have aerated the soil, and their tops will add to the bounty of the compost heap. Move ahead, get out the seed packets, and plant something new. This process has no penalties, only rewards; no disasters, only opportunities.

Let's dispense with another garden negative: produce envy. Do your yields measure up? Is your lettuce as big as the supermarket variety? Forget all that stuff. This is your garden, and the rules are your own. You don't need to do what the pros do, what your neighbor does, or what any book says. The commercial standards of industrial agriculture are meaningless in the home garden. Besides, they are achieved with innumerable chemicals that artificially expand and disguise poor produce by doping up the plant's metabolism. In addition to not wanting to eat such produce, you certainly don't want to emulate the techniques.

Enormous size should not be a criterion for garden success. It usually indicates overfertilization. If the vegetables look healthy and taste good, they are winners. Take lettuce as an example. If at the start you have trouble growing large heads of lettuce or prefer not to, plant two to four times as many, plant them closer together, and harvest them small. You now have baby lettuce (a gourmet item), which has taste and tenderness virtues all its own. In addition to enjoying greater variety, you will also experience far fewer pest and disease problems by harvesting your crops in their youth. Commercial standards are concerned with packing, shipping, and wholesale marketing, not flavor, tenderness, and eating pleasure. Ignore the commercial hype and concentrate on the standards that really count. Furthermore, if you follow the simple soil-improving suggestions in chapter 3, your vegetables will not take a backseat to anyone's.

The Organic Garden

Let's take a moment to discuss the benefits of organic gardening. No fearful tales are involved. I have no moral sermon. I have no plan to drown you in pages of factual data. Our home garden is organic, as it has been for thirty years, for a very practical reason. Organic methods are simpler and work better. That's right, they work better. Chemical agriculture is one of the great myths of the 20th century. The chemical salespeople swear that chemical fertilizers and pesticides are indispensable. In our experience, they are totally superfluous. They are necessary only as a crutch for the weaknesses of industrial food production.

Basically, organic gardening means a partnership with nature. Nature's gardeners are numerous and eager to help. Millions of beneficial organisms (everything from bacteria to earthworms to ground beetles) thrive in a fertile soil, and they make things go right if the gardener encourages them. The gardener does that by understanding the natural processes of the soil and aiding them with compost. The inherent stability and resilience of natural systems can be on your side if you work with them. Organic gardening is a great adventure, an expedition into a deeper and more satisfying understanding of vegetable production. You are now a participant rather than a spectator. You share creation.

A delightful bonus of organic soil care is the quality of the vegetables. To us, food is not a commodity to be produced as cheaply as possible. It is the living matter that fuels our systems. We agree with the conclusion of many other organic growers around the world that crops grown in a fertile soil are higher in food quality. It is not just the absence of the negatives—pesticides and chemicals—that makes the difference. It is also the presence of the positives. Whether the difference in composition is due to the amount of enzymes, the amino acid balance, trace minerals, unknown factors, or all of the above is yet to be determined. There are many theories. There is also increasing evidence that the biological quality of plants is vitally important because it determines the content of those plant substances which benefit human health. We are convinced that future investigations will confirm the value of food quality, just as present research has already confirmed the essential place of vegetables in the diet.

Since the key to vegetable quality is the quality of the soil in which the vegetables are grown, you want to have good raw material for the roots of your plants to forage in. Soil quality is influenced by the practices of the gardener. For a soil to be truly alive and productive, it must contain plenty of organic matter, plus the full spectrum of minerals. The soil can then feed the vegetables. A vital, alive soil will produce vital, alive vegetables. Very simple and successful backyard techniques for building a live soil are presented in chapters 3 and 4.

Once a product has been grown or manufactured, the next greatest effect on its quality is how it is taken care of or stored. A carefully crafted tool made of steel and left in the rain will soon rust and deteriorate. Vegetables are no different. Freshness influences both their nutrient content and their flavor. The nutritive value falls quickly after harvest. To preserve as much nutritive value as possible, all vegetables should be cooled and kept moist. It's best to harvest just before eating but if you can't eat your fresh garden harvest immediately, store it in the crisper drawer of the fridge.

In the pages to come, you will find an outline for a four-season harvest system for the home garden. It's the result of years of refining and adapting ideas from around the world. These techniques are tried and true enough to guarantee that they will work. If you have no preferences of your own, this is a good place to start. But don't stop with this model. You can do better. Always be curious enough to adjust and fine-tune. Over the years, you have put your own stamp on many other important activities you do regularly. Anything as much a part of your life as your food supply should be as personal as possible.

By dusk, on that winter day in France, it was closing time at the *Jardin des Plantes* and we chatted with one of the professional staff as, along with a few other last stragglers, we walked to the exit. We told him how much we had enjoyed seeing the gardens and inquired if he could recommend a good restaurant nearby where we might eat dinner. He sang the praises of one of his favorite bistros a few blocks away. We asked if he wasn't tempted to take home some of those fresh vegetables for his own dinner. "What vegetables?" he asked.

hollyhock and cucumber,
                    bean and marigold—
potato, zinnia, squash:
the opulence
            of everything that rots.
—Andrew Hudgins

CHAPTER 3

THE LIVING SOIL: COMPOST

So often, the obvious solution is right at our fingertips, but it looks so simple that we fail to notice. Generations of gardeners have consistently come up with the same chain of logic: a fertile soil is the key to growing garden vegetables; compost is the key to a fertile soil. The first step in the four-season harvest is learning to make good compost. It's not difficult. Compost wants to happen.

Compost is the end result of the decomposition of organic matter. It is basically a brown to black crumbly material that looks like a rich chocolate fudge cake. Compost is produced by managing the breakdown of organic material in a pile called a compost heap. Compost enhances soil fertility because fertile soil and compost share a prolific population of organisms whose food is decaying organic matter. The life processes of these organisms help make nutrients from the organic matter and the minerals in the soil available to growing plants. A fertile soil is filled with life. Compost is the life preserver.

Gardeners are not alone in their reverence for compost. Poets have found it equally inspiring. Andrew Hudgins, in a poem titled "Compost: An Ode," refers to the role of the compost heap in uniting life and death: "a leisurely collapsing of the thing into its possibilities." John Updike reminds us that since "all process is reprocessing," the forest can consume its fallen trees and "the woodchuck corpse vanish to leave behind a poem." Walt Whitman marvels at how composting allows the earth to grow "such sweet things out of such corruptions."

Good compost, like any other carefully crafted product, is not an accident. It comes about through a process involving microorganisms, organic matter, air, moisture, and time that can be orchestrated in anyone's backyard. No machinery is necessary, and no moving parts need repair. All you need to do is heap up the ingredients as specified in the next section and let nature's decomposers do the work.

Compost Ingredients

The ingredients for the heap are the organic waste materials produced in most yards, gardens, and kitchens. That is what is so miraculous and so compelling about compost. If you pile up organic waste products they eventually decompose into compost. There is nothing to buy, nothing to be delivered, nothing exotic. This acknowledged "best" garden fertilizer is so in harmony with the cyclical systems of the natural world that it is made for free in your back yard from naturally available waste products.

The more eclectic the list of ingredients, the better the compost. That is only logical. The plant wastes that go into your compost heap were once plants that grew because they were able to incorporate the nutrients they needed. So don't pass up any weeds, shrub trimmings, cow pies, or odd leaves you can find. If you mix together a broad range of plants with different mineral makeups, the resulting compost will cover the nutrient spectrum.

I suggest dividing your compost ingredients into two categories based on their age and composition. The two categories are called *green* and *brown*.

The green ingredients include mostly young, moist, and fresh materials. They are the most active decomposers. Examples are kitchen wastes such as apple peels, leftovers, carrot tops, and bread, and garden wastes such as grass clippings, weeds, fresh pea vines, outer cabbage leaves, and dead chipmunks. The average house and yard produce wastes such as these in surprising quantities. National solid waste data indicate that approximately 25 percent of household trash consists of food scraps and yard waste.

The brown ingredients are usually older and drier than the green ones, and they decompose more slowly. Examples are dried grass stems, old cornstalks, dried pea and bean vines, reeds, and old hay. The brown category is usually not well represented in the average backyard. To start, you may want to purchase straw, the best brown ingredient of all. Straw is the stem that holds up the amber waves of grain in crops such as wheat, oats, barley, and rye. After the heads containing the grains are harvested, the straw is baled as a byproduct. You can purchase straw a few bales at a time from feed stores, riding stables, or a good garden supply store.

The advantage of straw as the brown ingredient is that it will almost guarantee the success of your composting efforts. When home gardeners encounter smelly failures in their attempts to

Fig. 7

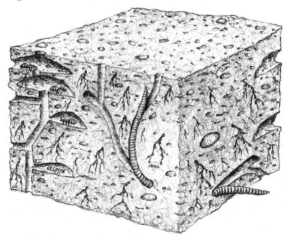

The living soil.

make good compost, the fault usually lies with the lack of a proper brown ingredient. In years to come, when you become an expert at composting, you may choose to expand your repertoire beyond this beginner's technique, but it is the most reliable method for beginners or experts.

Building the Compost Heap

Pick a site near the garden so the finished compost will be close at hand. Whenever possible, place the heap under the branches of a deciduous tree so there will be shade in hot weather and sunlight to thaw the heap in spring. A site near the kitchen makes it convenient to add kitchen scraps. Access to a hose is handy for those times when the heap needs extra moisture. If the site is uphill from the garden, the heavy work of wheelbarrowing loads of compost will have gravity on its side.

Build the compost heap by alternating layers of brown ingredients with layers of green ones. Begin with a layer of straw about 3 inches deep, then add 1 to 6 inches of green ingredients, another 3 inches of straw, and then more green ingredients. The thickness of the green layer depends on the nature of the materials. Loose, open material such as green bean vines or tomato stems can be applied in a thicker (6-inch) layer, while denser material that might mat together, such as kitchen scraps or grass clippings,

Fig. 8

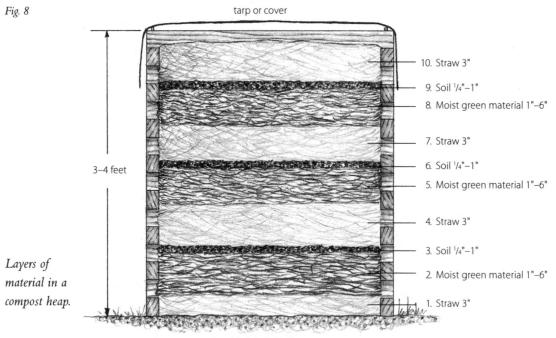

tarp or cover

10. Straw 3"

9. Soil ¼"–1"

8. Moist green material 1"–6"

7. Straw 3"

6. Soil ¼"–1"

5. Moist green material 1"–6"

4. Straw 3"

3. Soil ¼"–1"

2. Moist green material 1"–6"

1. Straw 3"

3–4 feet

soil lightly forked over

Layers of material in a compost heap.

18

should be layered thinly (1 to 2 inches). These thicknesses are a place for you to start, but you will learn to modify them as conditions require.

Sprinkle a thin covering of soil on top of each green layer. Make the soil ½ inch deep or so depending on what type of green material is available. If you have just added a layer of weeds with soil on their roots, you can skip the soil covering for that layer. The addition of soil to the compost heap has both a physical and a microbiological effect: physical because certain soil constituents (clay particles and minerals) have been shown to enhance the decomposition of organic matter; microbiological because soil contains millions of microorganisms, which are needed to break down the organic material in the heap. These bacteria, fungi, and other organisms multiply in the warm, moist conditions as decomposition is initiated. If your garden is very sandy or gravelly, you might want to find some clay to add to the heap as the soil layer. As an additional benefit, the clay will improve the balance of soil particle sizes in your garden.

Heap Dynamics

The reason for layering the ingredients is that the decomposition process is akin to a smoldering fire. If you use care in building the heap, it will "light" every time. The slow combustion of the compost heap is an exothermic reaction—that is, it gives off heat. The microorganisms create the heat by breaking down the organic material. Unlike the sticks in a campfire, however, these combustibles should not be dry. They should be slightly moist, like a muggy day. Sir Albert Howard, an early compost enthusiast, described the ideal moisture level as akin to that of a squeezed-out sponge.

The temperature inside an active heap can reach 140° to 160°F. In this microbiologically powered furnace, the brown ingredients provide the fuel. Straw, for instance, is a carbonaceous material with a high ratio of carbon to nitrogen. The green ingredients provide the fire. They are nitrogenous materials containing a higher ratio of nitrogen. All the millions of organisms in the heap use the nitrogen to help break down the carbon structure of organic material into a humus-like end product. The combination of green and brown materials provides the ideal balance between carbon and nitrogen for optimal breakdown.

As with any other fire, there is one more crucial requirement for the compost heap—air. The beneficial bacteria that create the heat, decomposition, and ultimate conversion of the ingredients into compost are aerobic (that is, requiring air). This explains why straw is perfect for successful composting. Straw stems, besides providing the carbonaceous fuel for this bacterial fire, also ensure aeration. They are hollow, like drinking straws, and tend to lie across each other loosely. That structure allows air to enter easily, in con-

Fig. 9

Hollow straw stems allow more air into the heap than does hay.

trast to a heap composed only of green material, which can mat together. When there is plenty of air, the aerobic bacteria can breathe deeply and multiply. When they are active in great numbers, decomposition proceeds smoothly and without odor. If composting fails, it is usually because the ingredients are packed into an airless mass and the activities of the aerobic bacteria are inhibited.

When the conditions for composting are less than optimum, the reaction of the heap will help you determine the problem. There are two common symptoms. The first is odor. A well-made compost heap is odorless. A bad smell indicates that something is amiss. When the heap is too wet or compacted the process becomes anaerobic (without air), and a different bacterial population takes over. The anaerobic bacteria create sewage-type odors. If the heap is made with too much fire (green nitrogenous material) and not enough fuel (brown carbonaceous material), it will have a strong ammonia odor because the bacteria are volatilizing the extra nitrogen. You can improve both situations by forking the material into a new pile alongside and piling it more loosely with additional layers of straw.

The second symptom is failure to heat up. If the heap is too dry, the bacteria are inhibited, as they thrive best under moist conditions. Normally the combination of ingredients will be adequately moist. But when the weather has been dry, you may want to add water. That is most easily accomplished with a watering can or hose sprayer. Add enough water to each layer as you build to ensure that it is moist. Remember the analogy of the squeezed-out sponge. Another reason the heap may fail to heat up is an excess of fuel (carbon) and not enough fire (nitrogen). In that case, you can try to stimulate the bacteria with an organic, high-nitrogen liquid fertilizer such as fish emulsion. Dissolve half a cup into a

watering can, make holes in the heap with a crowbar or pointed stake, and pour in the solution. In a pinch, you can use molasses (same proportions), sour milk diluted with an equal amount of water, or any other bacterial food. This should initiate the composting process by getting hordes of bacteria off to a running start.

It's worth noting these problems in case they arise. But if you follow the heap-building directions, your composting should run smoothly. When fire, fuel, moisture, and air are in balance, the heap will purr like a contented kitten.

Compost Bins

When making compost, it helps to enclose the pile in a container. A number of backyard compost containers are available. First are the ventilated bins made from recycled plastic. These are about 36 inches square. They are nice if you plan to make daily additions of kitchen scraps because the ingredients are protected from four-legged raiders by strong sides and a lid. Plan on having

Fig. 10

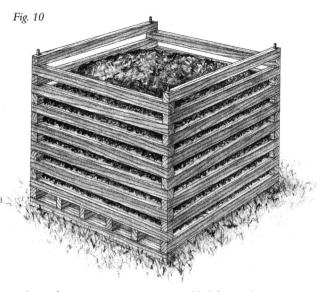

A wooden compost container, assembled from a kit.

Fig. 11

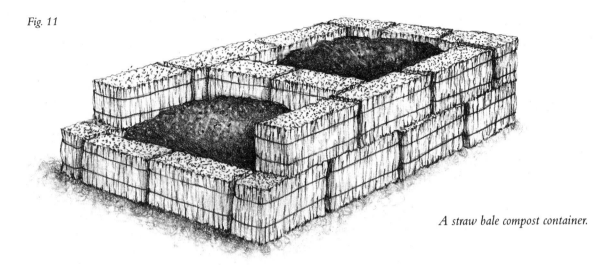

A straw bale compost container.

two bins so that one can supply usable compost while you are filling the other. Other models are made of wooden slats sawed from waste wood. The slats are put together like a Lincoln Log kit. They are held together at the corners with metal rods that fit into predrilled holes. Wooden-slat bins are about 3 to 3½ feet square. If you want a larger heap, buy two wooden-slat kits and make a hexagonal or octagonal structure with six or eight sides.

You can also make a heap by using bales of straw as walls. That way, you get double duty from the straw—first as a container and then as an ingredient. Lay the bales around an open center as if you were building a playhouse with large straw bricks. Leave small spaces between the bales for air to enter (see Fig. 11). Make the inside dimensions anywhere from 4 to 6 feet square. A heap smaller than 3 feet square won't have enough volume to hold heat and will decompose slowly. A heap larger than 8 feet square is too large for air to reach the center. Even with a 6-foot-square heap, we put a stake in the center while building the layers. We remove the stake when the heap is built to allow direct air access to the middle.

Build the walls progressively to a height of two or three bales. A heap with inside dimensions of 5 to 6 feet square requires sixteen to twenty bales of straw for a two-layer heap. After a year or two, when the bales begin to break down and no longer hold together as walls, they become ingredients in a subsequent heap. Bales tied with wire or plastic will last longer than those tied with baling twine. The straw becomes moist and partially decomposed while it serves as walls. That prepares it perfectly for its next role as compost ingredient.

Another advantage of straw walls is that the contents of the heap stay moist and warm right to the edge. As a result, the initial decomposition is

Fig. 12

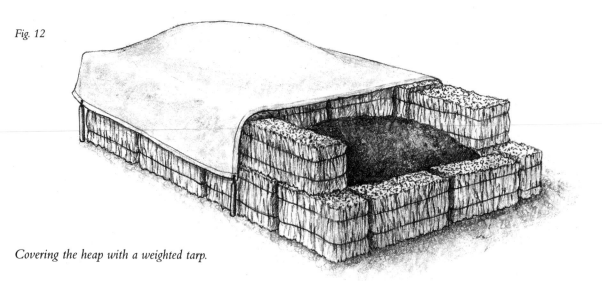

Covering the heap with a weighted tarp.

often so complete that the heap may not need to be turned (see below). The bales also provide insulation in cooler weather, which is useful for a heap made in late summer. The heating process can keep going longer into the fall. Both the store-bought bins and the straw bales will give you a heap that looks very neat, contains the ingredients successfully, and lets in plenty of air.

Ideally, you should build the heap over the course of a couple of months, but that schedule is very flexible. It is best if six or more layers can go on initially. Then there is enough mass for the heating to begin. Every few days afterward, you can add another couple of layers. The initial heating is stimulated by the continuous addition of new fuel, and the heat moves up layer by layer. The heap may seem to build quickly, but as the breakdown progresses, the material will settle. When you have reached three to four feet and the material is no longer settling, add a final layer of straw to complete the heap. Active breakdown will continue until the heat begins to decline.

A cover over the heap is a valuable addition at this point. The cover prevents excessive moisture from getting in during wet periods and keeps the heap from drying out during times of drought. Plastic bins include their own fitted covers. For wooden-slat bins or straw-bale heaps, use a tarp with a weight hanging from each corner so it won't blow off. If you think that the heap needs more moisture, remove the cover on rainy days. During winter, a wooden lid over our straw-bale heap keeps the snow out, yet is easily lifted for adding winter kitchen scraps interspersed with layers of straw.

The heat of composting reaches its peak a few weeks after the heap is completed and then dies down. By then the microorganisms have used up the easy fuel of the initial breakdown process. The gardener can speed up the subsequent breakdown by turning the heap. This remixing is akin to stirring a fire or using a bellows. By increasing the aeration, you get the combustion going again. The easiest system for turning compost is to erect another container alongside the first. Using a manure fork, turn the compost by forking the initial pile into the second container. Try to shake each forkful as it is dumped into the new space so as to loosen the material and allow more air to enter. If the outer edges of the heap are less decomposed than the center, try to place them in the middle of the new heap. Once the pile has been turned, cover it and start building again on the original site.

Autumn Leaves and Animal Manure

Autumn leaves, wood chips, or sawdust haven't been mentioned yet. They are in the brown category, but we don't use them in our compost heaps. Wood chips and sawdust take so long to decompose that we have never been happy with the resulting compost. Autumn leaves, on the other hand, are a wonderful soil improver, but they are not put in the compost heap because they mat together and can create airless conditions. Leaf decomposition takes place primarily through the action of fungi rather than bacteria. Thus, it seems to work better if leaves are piled separately. If a few leaves blow into your compost heap, they don't present a problem, but in quantity they are best used to make leaf mold, a wonderful product in its own right.

Leaf mold is the horticultural term for decomposed autumn leaves. You make it by putting leaves in a pile and waiting two to three years. A circular container 4 to 6 feet in diameter made of snow fence or stiff wire mesh holds leaves effectively. If the leaves are dry, wet them with a hose as you pile them. You can also stomp on them inside the bin to make room for more. Compaction doesn't hinder the fungal decomposition of wet leaves. Leaf mold has traditionally been used like compost as a general soil enhancer. We prefer to use it mainly for crops in the cabbage (Brassicaceae) and carrot (Apiaceae) families. It works like a health tonic for those crops. Leaves also can be a very effective soil enhancer if they are tilled directly into the garden in the fall.

Animal manure has been a favorite soil amendment for generations of horticulturists. Even before the horse and buggy was replaced by the automobile, however, gardeners who had no animals were looking for additional sources of organic soil amendments. Some of the early books on making compost from vegetable matter called compost "artificial manure." These early investigators learned that by composting mixed plant wastes, they got a product that worked better than the traditional rotted animal manures, because the ingredients were more varied and the moisture and aeration levels during the breakdown period could be managed more precisely.

If you have access to animal manures, by all means use them. Add them to the soil only when they are well rotted, not fresh. The nitrogen in fresh manure can be caustic to plant material. The soil-enhancing value of manure is especially good if the animals were bedded on straw rather than sawdust or shavings. The best animal manures are horse, cow, sheep, and goat. Rather than putting manure directly on the garden, add it as another ingredient in the compost heap. Try to limit the quantity to no more than 20 percent of the total. You can put a layer of manure on top of the brown or green layer as you build the heap. Be careful with poultry manure. It is very concentrated, and the nutrients are imbalanced. Sometimes poultry manure appears to cause more problems than it solves.

How Do You Know When It's Ready?

Compost has a number of stages of readiness, each one better than the one before. If the heap heats up properly, the compost is usable after the heap cools down. At this stage, you can still distinguish some of the original materials. Although not yet fully broken down, this is good compost. Further breakdown will take place in the soil after application. It is best to mix this rough compost into the soil at the end of the outdoor season so the decomposition can continue over the winter. You can use it as a top dressing at other times of the year. If you want finer compost immediately, you can sift this first stage compost through a wire mesh screen.

If you want all the compost to be dark, crumbly, and more thoroughly decomposed, you will need to turn the heap to initiate the second flush of heating and decomposition. This second stage of compost is a better product. Almost none of the original materials can be distinguished. Most of the compost is crumbly, very dark, and sweet smelling. This compost can be used almost anywhere.

The finest compost, like good wine or cheese, is a product of time. It needs to mature. To achieve full compost maturity, you must turn the heap a second time, cover it, and let the compost age until it is one to two years old. At that point, it will achieve a wonderful chocolate fudge cake texture throughout. A one- to two-year-old, well-decomposed vegetable compost is the definition of soil fertility. It comes as close as you can get to a miracle plant food. This is the quality of compost we prefer for all indoor and outdoor garden use. It is the secret to the success of the homemade potting soil mixtures described in chapter 9.

A specialist on composting would describe this mature compost as "well humified." Humus is the end stage of decomposition. It is the longest lasting, most effective soil organic matter. Humus in the soil provides stable and balanced conditions for plant nutrition and root growth. Gardeners have long known that a well-humified compost has amazing powers for enhancing plant growth and suppressing diseases. Research done at Ohio State University since the late 1970s has confirmed those conclusions and the researchers enthusiastically recommend compost specifically for its disease-controlling benefits.

The surest way to have plenty of mature compost available is to get started now, whatever the season. While you are waiting for the first heap to mature, keep making new heaps so you will always have more coming along. Then when the first heap is ready, you won't be stingy. Compost is such a wonderful medium for growing plants that once you start using it in the vegetable garden, you will want more for the flowers, shrubs, and bare spots in the lawn. To produce more compost, you will need more raw materials. Extra compost materials can be acquired in a number of ways, outlined in the next section.

Finding More Ingredients

An unused area of your lawn can be turned into a very attractive source of green matter for the compost heap by planting it to alfalfa and treating it like your own miniature hayfield. Alfalfa is a favorite forage with livestock farmers because it grows vigorously; has deep drought-resistant roots; and will regrow 12 to 16 inches tall after each cutting, allowing up to four cuts per season. Alfalfa will grow successfully in any sunny, well-drained site as long as the soil is not acidic. Alfalfa likes a pH of 7. (You can correct soil acidity by adding limestone.) Alfalfa is easy to establish. Just scatter the seeds on bare ground, rake them in, and keep the soil moist until germination. Planting alfalfa is no different from planting a lawn. Seeds for an alfalfa variety suited to your area can be purchased from your local farm supply store.

The most delightful way to mow your backyard alfalfa (or any other grasses or legumes for that matter) is with an old-fashioned scythe. Mowing with a scythe is pleasurable exercise and a wonderful skill to learn. If you take it up, the scythe will soon become one of your favorite yard tools and you will prefer it to a power mower or weed whacker for cleaning up those odd rough areas. It is quiet work because no mo-tor is involved, the air is clean because no fumes interfere with the sweet smell of the new-mown field, and the bodily motion involved in mowing is smooth, almost dance-like, and great exercise.

The best advice to beginners is to think of the scythe as one blade of a large pair of scissors. The other blade is the ground. Thus, the ideal motion is to move the scythe blade evenly just above the surface of the ground, taking a small slice of the uncut greenery with each large semi-circular stroke. The stroke of swinging the scythe is semi-circular because your body is the center pivot. Give it a try by standing up now, stand straight, let your arms hang at your sides and slowly twist your shoulders to the right, then to the left, and back again. Now position your arms as if they were holding a scythe snath and repeat. It is your strong abdominal muscles that make your body turn and they are the ones doing most of the work of mowing.

The job of your arms is to hold the tool so the blade lies parallel to the ground as it traces its circular motion. Your legs and feet balance you and also move you forward after each swing so as to position the blade for the next slice of the uncut greenery. Its important for a beginner to take small slices, say just an inch or two, off the "face" of the standing uncut material. You want to master the smooth flow of the swing without too much resistance from the stems being cut. Once you feel comfortable with the motion you can take larger bites.

If you are cleaning up small clumps of grass here and there, it is simplest to mow them as you come to them. But when you are ready to mow a larger area, the traditional technique is to mow around the perimeter of the area in a clockwise direction taking a slice off the strip in front of you with each swing. The follow-through of your stroke deposits much of the cut material in the

Alfalfa.

open area to your left, thus helping to move it out of the way of your next swing. The width of the "face" or strip that you mow each time around depends on your ability. As you become more proficient you can learn to mow a wider face with each stroke. You can grade your progress as a student mower by the evenness of the stubble and the number of lines or tags of uncut or partially cut stems. Master mowers take delight in the almost lawn-like appearance of the field after the harvest has been raked up and carted to the compost area.

There are two parts to a scythe: the handle, called the snath, and the blade. There are also two styles of scythe: the British and the European. The British snath is bent in a curve and the handholds, called nibs, are attached on the front side. The European style has a straight snath with the lower nib

Fig. 13

The key to success with a scythe is a sharp blade.

A European-style snath is lighter and more comfortable to use.

26

attached to an extended arm and with the nibs attached on the back side. We prefer the European-style scythe and recommend it to you. (See sources in appendix D.) It is a lighter tool and the mowing motion is more comfortable. But whatever your choice of tool, the key to success with a scythe, once the basic motion has been mastered, is to keep the blade sharp. As with any edge tool, the difference between sharp and dull is the difference between pleasure and drudgery.

There are many traditional scythe sharpening tools, including small hammers and anvils for peening out the edge on European blades. The simplest and quickest is a file—either a 10-inch mill bastard file or a diamond-faced file. Stand the scythe so the blade is up with the top end of the snath resting on the ground and the blade pointing toward you. Place your left hand on the back (dull) side of the blade to steady the scythe. Stroke along the edge of the blade with the file starting at the tip and moving toward the heel. Pay attention to the angle of the file vis-à-vis the blade so as to file the blade to a thin sharp edge. Turn the scythe around and file from the heel to the tip on the back side. If you find sharpening awkward while standing up, you can lay the snath on the ground with the blade upright and sharpen in that position.

We mow the alfalfa as needed for the green layers in the heap. The best management practice is to mow the area every time the first blossoms appear. The patch is more productive that way, and the regrowth will be even. Alfalfa has deep roots and is a strong feeder on nutrients from the lower levels of the soil. It is very high in minerals and is a valuable addition to any garden fertility-improvement scheme. Before planting, fertilize the patch with the rock minerals described later in this chapter. In good soil, an alfalfa planting can be productive for ten years or more. When the alfalfa thins out and other plants invade and lower the productivity of the patch, you should till the soil and replant.

You will become aware of many other sources of organic matter as soon as you become interested in composting. A time-honored source of compost materials is your neighbors' yards. "Hi, George, I'd love to have that pile of (trimmings, leaves, rotten apples) if you have no use for it." Many enthusiasts extend that search beyond immediate neighbors to the local area by carrying an empty trash container in the back of their car. The container is usually full of weeds, spoiled vegetables, or grass clippings when they arrive home. Weeds are a particularly valuable addition to compost, since they are vigorous, heavy-feeding plants with a high mineral content. It is best to collect weeds before they go to seed. If you see a particularly lush area of weeds, ask if you can cut them. Most people are delighted to oblige. You may acquire a reputation as an eccentric but, while you are neatly dispatching the greenery with your scythe, you can console yourself with the knowledge that you are setting a good example. Recycling is important. Nature is the classic recycler. If we use nature as a model, we won't lack for direction.

Using Compost

Once you have a quantity of dark, crumbly compost, what do you do with it? Rather than fork it in deeply, we recommend spreading it on top of the soil and just mixing it in shallowly. The quality of plant growth is superior if you duplicate nature's system of leaving organic matter on the surface to be mixed in by earthworms and other soil creatures. You can help out a little by mixing the compost into the top two inches of soil with a curved-tine cultivator (see appendix D). The one we prefer is about seven inches wide and has

Fig. 14

Curved-tine cultivator.

three large tines with the center tine offset from the others. Work the tool back and forth gently and shallowly like a lightweight, hand-powered tiller. It incorporates the compost without damaging the soil structure.

How much compost should you spread? Let's see if we can calculate an answer in a way that makes sense. One cubic foot of compost will logically cover a 12-square-foot area to a depth of 1 inch. If, for example, your garden dimensions are 900 square feet (30 by 30 feet), you would need 75 cubic feet of compost (900 square feet divided by 12 square feet) for a 1-inch-deep application over the whole garden. A compost heap 5 feet long by 5 feet wide by 3 feet tall would contain 75 cubic feet of compost.

Do you need to apply compost to a depth of one inch? Old-time commercial vegetable growers considered 50 tons per acre of manure to be a generous application. One inch of compost averages out to about 75 tons to the acre. Thus, a 1-inch layer of finished compost can be considered a very generous rate of use. But be generous at the start, even if that means purchasing rotted manure or peat moss. Peat moss alone is inadequate as a fertilizer but is an excellent source of organic matter for soil structure. Used in a half-and-half mixture with compost or manure, it will serve you quite well. Once you have enough compost, a maintenance application of ¼ to ½ inch per year should be more than enough to maintain and improve your garden's productivity.

How do you figure out the depth of compost you are spreading without using a measuring stick and wasting a lot of time? Let's say you have a garden bed 30 inches wide by 20 feet long. The surface area of that plot is 50 square feet, or 7,200 square inches. To put a 1-inch layer of compost on a 7,200-square-inch area would require 7,200 cubic inches of compost; a ½-inch layer would require half that. A 5-gallon pail holds about 1,200 cubic inches. Thus, spreading three 5-gallon pails of compost would give you 3,600 cubic inches, or a close approximation of ½ inch of compost on an area 30 inches wide by 20 feet long. Computations like these may seem complicated, but once you have the figures, they make your gardening more efficient and the results more predictable.

Mineral Amendments

In many situations, a good compost will usually provide all the nutrients necessary for a productive garden. We do, however, suggest adding three mineral supplements. The most familiar of these is limestone, which is added to the soil to counteract acidity. You may not be familiar with the other two supplements—phosphate rock and greensand. They are ground-up rock products that contain a broad spectrum of plant nutrients. You add them to the soil to make sure all the minerals necessary for healthy plant growth are available—a soil fertility insurance policy, if you will.

Limestone, or lime, is finely ground limestone rock, which contains mostly calcium carbonate. Lime is applied to acidic soils to raise the pH (pH indicates soil acidity on a scale of 1 to 14). The lower the number, the greater the acidity: 7 is neutral, above 7 is alkaline, and below 7 is acidic. Most of the natural processes in the soil that affect the growth of garden vegetables function optimally at a pH of 6 to 7 (slightly acidic). You can determine your soil's pH by purchasing a testing kit from a garden supply catalog or by having it tested professionally. The local extension service can help you find out where to get that done. If the soil is too acidic (below 6), add limestone by sprinkling it on the soil and mixing it in. Your soil test recommendations will suggest how much limestone to use. If the soil is too alkaline (above 7), adding extra organic matter such as an acidic peat moss is an effective solution.

Phosphate rock and colloidal phosphate are slow-release sources of phosphorus. They are mined from rock and clay deposits containing 20 to 30 percent phosphates. If phosphate rock is unavailable, bone meal is another slow-release source of phosphorus. Adding phosphate rock or bone meal is a good policy because phosphorus is the nutrient most likely to be deficient in your garden soil. When you start your garden, add phosphate rock to the soil at a rate of 10 pounds per 100 square feet.

Greensand is a mineral mined from old sea-bottom deposits. It is a slow-release source of potassium and trace elements. Potassium is an important nutrient for plant health and vigor. Trace elements such as zinc, copper, molybdenum, boron, and manganese, though required in very small quantities, are vital for plant and animal well-being. In most cases, if you add a compost of mixed ingredients to the soil, it should contain adequate amounts of potassium and trace elements. But just to make sure, we add greensand. Ten pounds per 100 square feet the first year is a reasonable application.

The mineral nutrients in these powdered rock products are not highly water soluble, unlike the treated ingredients in chemical fertilizers. They don't need to be, as the activities of microorganisms, which are nourished by organic matter in the soil, will make these nutrients available to plants at a balanced rate.

Initially, you should apply phosphate rock and greensand directly on the garden soil. After that, it's easier and more effective to sprinkle these products very lightly on the green layer of the compost heap. For our 40-by-40-foot garden, we add 25 pounds of each mineral to the compost each year. That is more than enough to make up for the minerals removed from the soil in the form of harvested crops. A number of scientific trials have determined that adding rock powders to the compost heap enhances their availability for plant use, since the soluble acids in humus formation begin to dissolve the rock nutrients.

In addition to the minerals mentioned, you may find one of the commercially available seaweed products useful. Seaweed is sold in a dried form to be added directly to the soil or in various liquid extractions for spraying on the leaves of plants as a pick-me-up. Although it can be expensive, the dried seaweed offers great benefits for some soils. If the soil fertility seems slow getting off the mark, seaweed is an option you may want to explore. Another possibility is crab shell or shrimp shell meal. As a by-product of their decomposition in the soil, the use of these meals has been found to help control nematodes. We find the calcium to be in a particularly effective form to benefit our naturally acid, sandy soil. The liquid extractions of seaweed can be sprayed onto plant leaves as natural plant stimulants. Their action has been described as "rescue nutrition" for below-par plants. They can be useful as palliatives in the soil-building years but shouldn't be needed once soil fertility is established.

The natural processes that you nurture by adding compost and rock minerals to your garden soil are the same processes that have been creating fertile soil and making soil nutrients available to plants for millions of years. If you wish to read a more detailed discussion of the subject, you can consult my book for small farmers, *The New Organic Grower* (Chelsea Green, 1995).

Phosphorus and toil
Are divine imperatives
Mix them and nature gives
The fertile earth to man

—Harry Elmore Hurd,
"To be New Hampshire Bred"

CHAPTER 4

THE OUTDOOR GARDEN: PLANNING AND PREPARING

Crisp 'French Breakfast' radishes with the dew still on them; baby beets—sweet, tender, and harvested just before dinner; tiny, crunchy carrots that taste like candy; the delightful aroma of herbs growing outside the kitchen door. With rewards like these awaiting the palate, nothing defeats the determined gardener. From the celebrated Aran Islanders layering seaweed and sand together to make soil on barren rock, to the deepest city dweller with pots of treasured vegetables on a windowsill, the urge to grow edibles is unstoppable.

The amount of work involved in creating a garden depends to some extent on where you live. If you are blessed with the perfect location and ideal soil, such as the deep, rich earth of the Midwest, you will have less to do when starting out. If your site was not blessed by Mother Nature, you will need to expend some effort making conditions hospitable for garden plants. But it's not a major project. You just have to supplement and modify what nature gave you.

Preparing the Garden Site

The initial test of our soil in Maine showed a pH of 4.3 (very acidic), and a note from the soil scientist warned that the ground did not seem suitable for agriculture. Well, every soil can be made suitable, and the first step was to spread limestone to make the soil less acidic. That got suitability for agriculture off to a running start. The soil was very sandy, so we added some clay from the house foundation and tilled it in thoroughly. (If the soil

31

had been too clayey, peat moss would have been the additive of choice. Because of the quantities involved, adding sand to a clay soil doesn't work as well as adding clay to a sandy soil.) This soil also contained too many stones, which have been gradually removed over time. The soil was low in minerals, so phosphate rock and greensand were called for. Like most gardens, the soil needed organic matter to make the biological processes work better. We live in farm country, so we added rotted manure for the first couple of years until our composting system was on track. If no manure had been available, we would have started by tilling in an inch or more of peat moss plus some organic fertilizer mix applied at the rate recommended on the bag. Once our own compost was available, it supplied practically everything we needed.

We also raked up autumn leaves and tilled them into parts of the garden. In the early years of establishing a garden, a rotary tiller can be a valuable aid in speeding up the transition to soil fertility. The action of the tiller tines is very effective at mixing organic and mineral supplements throughout the topsoil profile. If you overdo it and till frequently just to make the soil look nice, the tiller can destroy the soil structure. But when used to add organic matter and disperse minerals as a soil-building tool in the early years of a garden, a tiller is a useful tool to deepen topsoil, encourage microbiological activity, and create the foundation for long-lasting soil fertility.

Fig. 15

Tiller tines mixing in soil amendments.

It took a few years and some energy to convert that poor Maine soil into a bounteous vegetable garden, but success was inevitable. No matter what you start with, it is possible to build soil conditions for optimal plant growth. The work is really enjoyable. And, besides, the experience was a great teacher of all the soil fertility principles described in this book.

Garden Microclimate

In addition to a fertile soil, you should aspire to a few other ideal conditions for your crops. The aim is to create a beneficial microclimate. *Microclimate* is the term used to define the specific climatic conditions in a small area. We had two memorable experiences demonstrating the importance of microclimates during our trip to France. The first was on a mid-January evening when we stopped in the town of Roquefort—no relation to the cheese, but we chose it because even the name sounded delicious. After a light salad of radicchio, blanched escarole, and tiny heads of mâche, we took a moonlit walk through town. We saw gardens everywhere, some with and some without small plastic covers, sometimes both growing the same crops. Even though the ocean's moderating influence on temperature had waned sightly, Roquefort being about fifty miles inland from the Atlantic, some growers were able to take advantage of the influence of microclimates.

A microclimate is defined as the climate near the ground. It can exist in any small area—a corner, a yard, a field—where the temperature is warmer or colder than the norm because of shelter, exposure, or other climatic effect. We've found that one way to find microclimates is to wander with bare head and arms, as we were doing on this cool evening. Human skin is sensitive to temperature changes and you are instantly aware of the warmer and cooler spots. So, wandering in your yard, or sitting still to gauge the effects of wind, are good ways to find those little warm zones. You might also observe the areas where snow first recedes in spring, and where plants show the earliest green. Those are the places worth remembering when it comes to siting a garden.

We found the warmest microclimate in Roquefort below a magnificent Romanesque church, where stone stairways led down into a narrow ravine. All along the walls, as we descended, were tufts of many different wildflowers, in full bloom. At the ravine's bottom lay the little river that ran through town—and more gardens, including one belonging to the church. The crops growing there, in fertile alluvial soil, were comparable to those growing elsewhere in town, except that here the salad crops were growing without the shelter of plastic covers. The effect of running water and the vapor it gives off provided these river gardens with extra protection against freezing temperatures.

The church's garden, set at the base of a south-facing stone wall right next to the river, was the warmest of all, because the wall, at night, radiated the sun's heat it had stored during the day. It was a beautiful illustration of a fact known for centuries, that the warm microclimate within five or six feet of a masonry wall is a boon to the gardener. English monasteries often ripened peaches and grapes by espaliering them against the south side of stone walls in a climate with cool, foggy summers, where fruit in an open situation would never have matured. A good lesson with which to end our day, we thought: the south side of a stone or brick building, if you are lucky enough to have one, is the perfect place to start a winter garden.

A few days later as we were heading toward Perpignan, we saw a lot more examples of natural climate-enhancement techniques. Many of the gardens growing winter crops were located in obvious "warm and sheltered spots." By that I mean the same type of protected location a person would choose if sitting outside on a cold day. These were either naturally warmer sites, such as the south face of a hillside, or wind-sheltered locations, such as on the lee side of a hedge or building. We began analyzing garden sites by these sheltered-spot criteria and soon became aware just how many gardens were taking advantage of them. We are sure this understanding of slopes and hedges comes instinctively to observant gardeners in all parts of the world. It certainly seems to have long historical precedent, as evidenced by the numerous references in Roman gardening literature.

The effects are subtle but pervasive. Every increase in degree of slope of the land to the south improves the soil-warming effects of the sun over similar land on the flat. Along the 44th parallel, a garden on soil sloping 5° to the south has the same solar climate as flat land 300 miles further south. As the angle of the soil tips toward the sun, the rays strike more directly and the soil absorbs more heat during the day, which is radiated back at night. According to our 1921 *Larousse Agricole,* French gardeners even have a word, *ados,* to define garden beds where the surface has been deliberately inclined toward the sun. Sometimes this was even done on whole fields by shoveling the soil up into a saw-toothed pattern of east-west ridges, giving each one a small southern slope.

More often the *ados* slopes, also known as *côtières,* were formed by sloping the soil up against a south-facing wall. The usual slope was 4 inches of rise for every foot of run giving an angle of 15° to the south and increasing the warming effect of the low-angle winter sun on the soil by more than 20 percent. The south-facing wall behind the sloped bed would enhance the effect even more because its absorbed heat would be radiated back at night. This simple combination of wall and sloped soil, one step beyond what we had seen next to the river in Roquefort, contributed just that much more climate modification for winter garden plants.

Gardens located on the natural slopes of hillsides gain another out-of-season advantage. On frosty nights, the cold air, which is heavier than

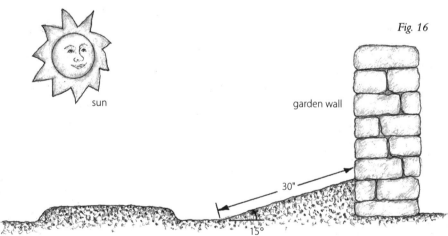

Fig. 16

sun

garden wall

30"

15°

Sloped beds, called ados *or* côtières *in French.*

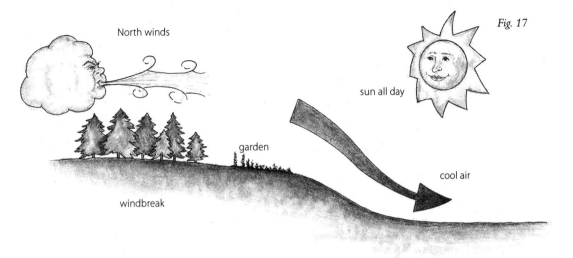

North winds

Fig. 17

sun all day

garden

cool air

windbreak

warm air, will tend to flow down the slope, just like water would, and collect in the valley at the bottom. A garden situated on the upper half of a slope will often escape all the light freezes because there won't be a long enough duration of the cold air to "fill" the valley to the level of the garden. Those who live in such situations have often noticed in the early morning that the white frost line on the vegetation in the valley below only comes up the sides of the valley to a certain height and the whole area above that is frost-free. Wise gardeners on slopes have often enhanced that effect either by cutting an air flow channel through woods below their garden so the trees could not "dam up" the flow of cold air, or by planting a hedge above their garden to divert the cold air flow to either side as it passes downhill.

Airflow around a garden site.

That same hedge is also valuable as a windbreak at any time of year, but especially in the winter. Cold winds can reduce soil temperature dramatically. Even on a sunny day, if air conditions are dry, a cold wind alone can be more damaging to plants than low temperatures. In addition to battering the plants and pelting them with soil particles, the wind almost seems to suck out the life juices. A windbreak as simple as some evergreen boughs placed vertically (a possible way to recycle the Christmas tree) or a temporary section of snow fence has been shown to make a difference of 2° to 5°F warmer temperatures in the protected area. Even a horizontal windbreak is effective. Evergreen boughs laid on top of fall-planted spinach as a wind-protective mulch have increased plant survival by 90 percent compared with unprotected plants.

As we reached the outskirts of Perpignan, we passed a number of commercial market gardens where large fields of outdoor winter crops were protected by artificial windbreaks. These were temporary fences made of an 8-foot-tall material which looked like a strong black mesh screen. The supports were 6-inch-diameter posts, slightly taller than the material, and set about ten feet apart in the row. A strong wire ran across their tops. The material was attached to the posts at intervals and also to the cross wire. The windbreak rows were 50 feet apart. A windbreak, whether a natural hedge or an artificial fence, provides some wind protection for a distance downwind equal to twenty times its height. The protection diminishes with increasing distance from the windbreak. The best protection exists in a downwind area six times the height of the fence, and these fences were obviously placed to optimize that effect.

We didn't see any single winter garden where all possible combinations of these ideas—windbreak, southern exposure, hillside location, *ados*, stone wall—were used together, but it was easy to imagine. Especially since these are simple home garden techniques that improve upon conditions already functioning in the natural world. If, in addition to selecting an ideal site, the garden soil were enriched every year with a well-decomposed compost, conditions would be better yet. Not only would the soil be fertile, but the darker soil color resulting from the organic matter would absorb more sun heat and warm up sooner in the spring. Where natural forces are at play, each simple, positive step complements the next and contributes to the synergy of the whole.

Many gardens will benefit from some of these modifications, and a few may need all of them. But there is one overriding consideration for the four-season garden: if you are going to participate daily in your garden, it helps to have it close at hand—just like the cupboards and the refrigerator. Ideally, it should be right outside the kitchen door or as close as you can manage. It is worth sacrificing some other feature (except sunshine)

for the benefits of proximity. If a back-door site is not possible for the whole garden, try to have a small plot for crops such as lettuce, parsley, and chives. Your garden site should be based on the needs of both growing and eating. The better the location, the better both needs will be met.

Planning the Home Garden

Nature programs on television often feature indigenous food gatherers from remote parts of the world who successfully use the jungle or desert as their supermarket. Whatever the season, they instinctively know where to look and what to choose for the ingredients of their diet. Ideally, your home garden can be a similar food jungle—not necessarily in the sense of wild and unrestrained (although if you prefer to garden that way, go for it), but in the sense of a dependable, year-round, sustainable larder waiting to be brought to the table.

Many possible garden layouts can give you access to that larder. The easiest ones are usually the best. Organizing and maintaining your garden should be simple, pleasant work. The process of growing and harvesting the food should be just as joyful as the process of preparing and eating it so that you will look forward to both.

We like to have two distinct areas in the garden: space in which to walk and space in which to grow. A direct benefit from this arrangement is improved plant growth. When you walk on garden soil, you exert a pressure of around six to ten pounds per square inch. That pressure closes the soil pores and seriously inhibits root expansion. Compacted soil contains less air. As with the compost heap, air is an important ingredient for optimal soil health, root growth, and microorganism activity. Roots are the invisible yet vital foundation for the aboveground parts. When root growth is below par, the whole plant suffers. It is always best to confine your foot traffic to paths between the growing areas.

Our present garden dimensions can serve as an example. Overall, our garden is 43 feet wide east to west and approximately 40 feet north to south. The walking spaces are 12 inches wide and the growing spaces (beds) are 30 inches wide. A ground-level view of the growing garden looks like this:

The 30-inch-wide growing spaces in our home garden are narrower than the 48-inch width used for commercial production. The wide commercial beds are keyed to tractor-based tillage, planting, cultivating, and harvesting equipment. For the home gardener, a 30-inch-wide bed is more sensible. It is easier to step over (from path to path), to straddle if you need to work above it, and to reach across when planting or harvesting.

In our garden, the beds are 20 feet long because that size fits neatly in the 43-foot dimension (the two 20-foot lengths are separated by a 3-foot-wide center path: see table 3). The beds run east to west for best sun access.

Fig. 18

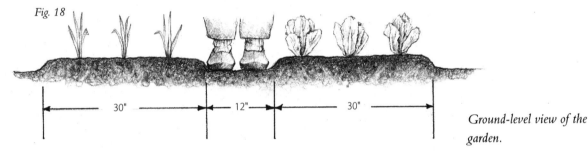

Ground-level view of the garden.

The 30-inch bed width allows ideal spacing for most vegetable crops. If you run rows down the middle of the bed, you can plant hills of corn, double rows of trellised peas, trellised cucumbers and tomatoes, brassica crops, potatoes, zucchini, and so forth. Large storage beets, celery, celeriac, parsnips, and other crops of similar size have adequate space when planted at two rows to the bed. Lettuce, storage carrots, strawberries, and onions are among the crops that grow well at three rows to the bed. You will find specific spacing directions for each crop in appendix A.

You can run many short rows across the bed or along the bed for frequently sown crops or for seedlings that will later be transplanted. These short rows are an easy way to maintain year-round succession plantings. It takes almost no time at all, say once a week, to sow a few short rows of radishes, mesclun mix, carrots, beet greens, arugula, spinach, or lettuce wherever there is an empty spot (see table 1).

This garden layout is offered as a point of departure for those with no preferences of their own. The dimensions, shape, and scale of this layout are comfortable and efficient. If you feel more comfortable working with ovals, triangles, squares, circles, pentagons, or spirals, use those shapes in your garden layout. The idea is for you to create a garden in which you will want to spend time.

But there is one strong suggestion to be made with respect to layout. Your cropping area, whatever its shape, should be easily divisible. You want to encourage the small succession plantings that characterize a four-season garden. They are the best way to maintain a continual supply of vegetables. Thus, in the space where you have recently harvested some lettuce, you can remove any roots and weeds, mix in a little compost, and plant three or four short rows of carrots. If you have no need for another vegetable planting, you can sow small areas of a legume such as clover or vetch to protect the soil and improve its fertility. See "Green Manures" later in this chapter for more information.

Garden Soil Structure

Figures 18 and 19 show a garden that may look like it has the raised beds with which many gardeners are familiar. However, we do not spend hours with spade and fork laboriously trenching and fluffing the earth. What you see instead of raised beds could best be called trodden paths. The soil is compacted only where we walk and it remains loose and friable elsewhere.

But isn't it necessary to turn and fluff the soil to keep it loose and friable? Isn't that what raised beds do? Well, that's what they try to do, but the techniques don't succeed as well as advertised. In fact, soil compaction studies have shown that disturbing the natural soil structure by fluffing and turning the soil with spade and fork is not beneficial. Undisturbed, the natural crumb structure that characterizes the work of microorganisms, earthworms, and other soil inhabitants actually has more air spaces than disturbed soil. Applying compost to the surface of the soil aids the natural

---

TABLE 1

SUCCESSION PLANTING

I succession-plant many outdoor crops for a continuous harvest during the growing season. I cease sowing based on the latest dates for my area (see table 5). Even if you think your area is too hot or too cold for these suggestions, give them a try. Experiment with heat- and cold-resistant varieties. You may be pleasantly surprised by the results.

Beans—Every two weeks

Beets—Every two weeks

Carrots—Every two weeks

Celery—Twice: early spring and three months before fall frost.

Corn—I usually sow a number of varieties with different maturity dates rather than sowing succession plantings.

Cucumbers—A second and third planting at monthly intervals will keep fruit quality high.

Lettuce and salad greens—These are the most important crops for succession plantings. I sow short rows of lettuce, chicory, arugula, mizuna, and claytonia every week or two during the growing season.

Peas—Twice: Early spring and midsummer.

Radishes—Sow every week and harvest promptly for the crispest roots.

Spinach—Sow short rows every week during spring and late summer.

Summer squash—See remarks under Cucumbers above.

Fig. 19

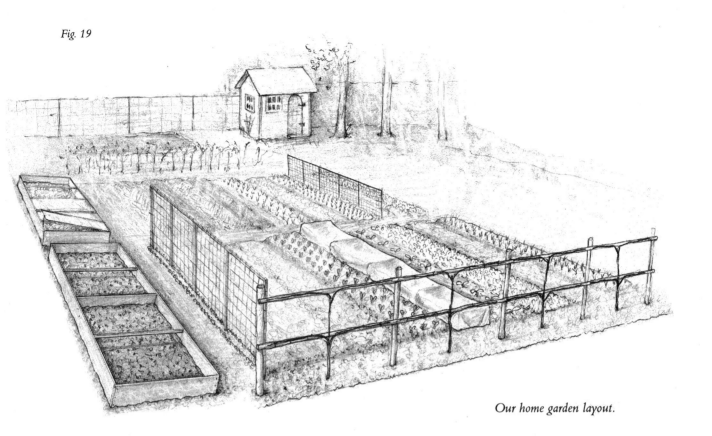

Our home garden layout.

process. The surface organic matter is slowly incorporated into the topsoil by the actions of earthworms and their coworkers. Further decomposition of organic matter by fungal and bacterial action goes on continuously underground. All these processes create and maintain a soil that allows air and moisture to enter, roots to grow and find nourishment, and an atmosphere that favors the life processes of all the soil inhabitants, roots included.

The subsoil is less aerated and less fertile than the topsoil but serves as a continuous source of raw materials for soil building. When the subsoil has been brought to the surface, as on a building site or other disturbed location, the best soil-building technique, if you want a garden on that

spot, is to add organic matter to the surface and encourage the natural processes. Nature's system of soil layers is very successful and it is best to leave them as they are. In fact, not only should the topsoil be on top and the subsoil below, but it's also best not to mix them within themselves. We have found the most success in gardening by following the design and intention of nature's processes.

We haven't always acted this wisely. In springs long past, we dug and spaded with a vengeance. It felt purifying, as if the hard work was somehow ennobling. But if you ever dig an area that has been undisturbed for a few years, and look closely at the soil, you will marvel at the beautiful crumb structure that has resulted from the decomposition of organic matter by microorganisms and the equally beautiful interlacing worm tunnels—nature's underground handiwork. "Wow, what a lovely soil structure! Why destroy this?"—a question that is hard to answer. We no longer dig the garden. We spread compost on the surface and mix it in shallowly (an inch or two). Crop yields and quality are noticeably improved. It is a valuable lesson: soil disturbance should be to correct the gardener's faults, not to correct nature.

Soil Aeration

Do we as gardeners have a problem with soil aeration as long as we don't walk on the soil of the beds? There is one fault worth correcting. Vegetable gardens grow mostly short-season annuals rather than perennials. By so doing, they miss a key factor in natural soil structure and aeration: the roots of perennial plants. The root systems of perennial herbs, grasses, shrubs, and trees in a truly undisturbed soil are more fibrous and permanent than the roots of annuals in a garden. Although you may have added extra organic matter with compost, the soil still lacks the additional aeration provided by the perennial roots. To get that extra aeration without breaking up the soil structure, it would be nice to just lift up the soil, without turning it over, and allow air underneath. Fortunately, there is a wonderful tool designed to do just that.

Fig. 20

Using the broadfork.

Once a year, we aerate the soil in our garden with a broadfork. This is a 24-inch-wide, five-tined fork with two handles (see Fig. 20). It is used to lift and loosen the soil without mixing the layers. The gardener holds a handle in each hand, presses the tool into the soil by stepping on the crossbar, pulls back on the handles to gently lift the soil, pulls out the tool, moves it six to eight inches back, and repeats the process. You can do the same thing with a standard garden fork in smaller bites, but the broadfork is more fun. Like any classic hand tool designed for a specific job, it is a pleasure to use. With its two handles and wide crossbar, the motion is effortless. Helpers in our garden, especially kids, always enjoy using the broadfork, first because it is a simple tool and makes them feel athletic and coordinated, and second because of the sense of accomplishment it gives. People instinctively feel that the tool makes sense.

A gardener with a broadfork is doing by hand what large-scale organic farmers do with a winged chisel plow. One belief organic vegetable farmers in many parts of the world share is the value of gentle soil-lifting from below without turning. They regard it as a key practice for enhancing long-term soil productivity.

Crop Rotation

In our four-season garden, as shown in figure 19, there are eighteen beds (each 30 inches wide by 20 feet long) and four cold frames. The garden is divided in half east and west by a central path. The cold frames occupy the north edge. Usually, taller or trellised crops are planted in the northern half and lower-growing crops to the south. That way the taller crops won't shade the shorter ones. An advantage of dividing the garden into a number of growing areas is that it simplifies a valuable age-old garden practice: crop rotation. That means not growing the same crop in the same spot year after year. With eighteen beds, and two sides to the garden, there are many options for change.

Most annual crops do best if they grow where something else grew the year before. Ideally, that something else should be an unrelated crop. For example, potatoes and tomatoes are related (both belong to the Solanaceae, or nightshade family), so one should not follow the other in rotation. But potatoes can grow where sweet corn (unrelated) grew last year, or tomatoes can follow zucchini (also unrelated). Crop rotation avoids exhausting the soil, since different crops remove different nutrients. It also avoids the pest and disease buildup that occurs when one crop is grown year after year in the same place.

In the year-round garden, where some beds will be planted with more than one crop per year, it is worth applying the principles of crop rotation not only as crops change year to year but also within the same year. This need not be complicated. It means that if you harvest a bed of early lettuce, you should follow it with beans, carrots, or corn rather than more lettuce. The next lettuce plantings could go where early beet greens were

TABLE 2

CROP FAMILIES

Apiaceae	Cucurbitaceae
Carrot	Cucumber
Celery	Melon
Celeriac	Pumpkin
Parsley	Squash, summer
Parsley root	Squash, winter
Parsnip	**Fabaceae**
Asteraceae	Bean
Artichoke	Pea
Chicory	**Liliaceae**
Dandelion	Asparagus
Endive	Garlic
Escarole	Leek
Lettuce	Onion
Radicchio	**Poaceae**
Brassicaceae	Corn
Arugula	**Polygonaceae**
Broccoli	Sorrel
Brussels sprouts	**Portulacaceae**
Cabbage	Claytonia
Cabbage, Chinese	Purslane
Cress	**Solanaceae**
Kale	Eggplant
Kohlrabi	Pepper
Mizuna	Potato
Mustard	Tomato
Radish	**Tetragoniaceae**
Rutabaga	New Zealand spinach
Totsoi	
Watercress	
Chenopodiaceae	
Beet	
Orach	
Spinach	
Swiss chard	

TABLE 3
EXAMPLE OF CROP ROTATION

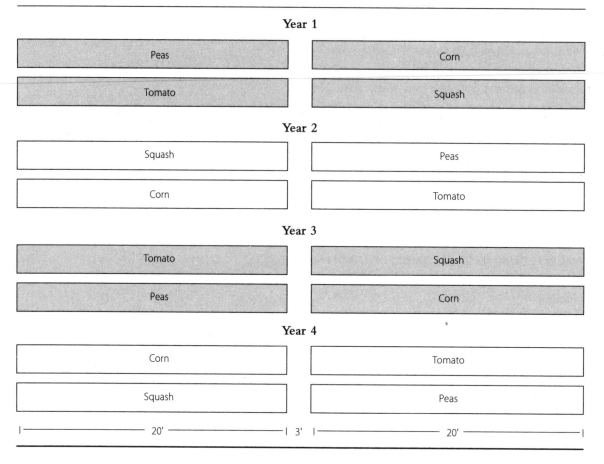

Year 1

Peas	Corn
Tomato	Squash

Year 2

Squash	Peas
Corn	Tomato

Year 3

Tomato	Squash
Peas	Corn

Year 4

Corn	Tomato
Squash	Peas

|———— 20' ————| 3' |———— 20' ————|

harvested. A three-year hiatus before a crop returns to the original spot is better than a two-year hiatus, four years are better than three. A general view of the trellised beds in my garden will serve as an example of a four-year rotation. The representative crops are peas (which could be pole beans), tomatoes (or peppers and eggplant), squashes (including winter squashes, cucumbers, and melons), and corn (which is not trellised but is tall, so it fits in this section). Over a four-year span, those four crops would rotate among the trellised beds as illustrated in table 3.

A map of your garden plots is a useful aid. Of all the tried-and-true garden management practices, crop rotation is one of the most beneficial and economical. It costs nothing more than a little planning and imagination. There are few absolutes; it's variety that counts. So think variety when you move crops around. If you would like to read a more detailed explanation of crop rotation, consult *The New Organic Grower*.

Green Manures

Many farm crops such as clover, alfalfa, and vetch can be rejuvenators for your garden soil. They will cover and protect unused areas and store nitrogen for future use. When planted specifically to take advantage of their soil-enhancing qualities, these plants are called green manures.

Farmers and gardeners since the beginning of agriculture have been aware that legumes can improve the soil for the following crop. But it wasn't until the late 1800s that science understood the mechanism involved. Specific soil bacteria live in association with the roots of legumes. Through this symbiotic (mutually beneficial) association, the bacteria provide the legumes with access to the nitrogen in the air, while the legume roots provide nutrition to the bacteria. The captured nitrogen is stored in nodules on the roots.

Whether the legumes that you grow for soil improvement are turned under, killed by winter temperatures, or mowed and composted, the nodules remain in the soil for other plants to use. Since nitrogen is an important food, this natural process adds plant food to the soil. If you have not grown a specific legume in your garden before, it is a good idea to purchase inoculant bacteria when you purchase the legume seeds. The inoculant comes in the form of a dry powder that looks like fine compost and contains the symbiotic bacteria specific to that legume. You mix the powder with the seeds before sowing. This is just one more example of how gardeners can work with the built-in processes of the natural world to enhance the fertility of their garden soil.

You can sow legumes for green manure in any empty space in the garden. You can even sow them with the crop in anticipation of the bed becoming empty in the future. That practice is called *undersowing*. It is like planting a deliberate but noncompetitive weed. Most garden plants are sufficiently well established by a month after planting so that the competition of small plants underneath will not hinder them. In fact, you can even let weeds grow after a month and still get a reasonable yield. Instead, we choose to plant legumes as deliberate weeds.

About a month after well-spaced crops such as broccoli, cabbage, corn, squashes, beans, and eggplant are established, sprinkle the legume seeds on the soil under the crop and mix them in shallowly. The legume will grow in the understory of the crop. When the crop is harvested and the residues removed to the compost heap, a bed of green manure is already growing. Undersowing is a fun option. You get to grow the crop and initiate soil improvement simultaneously.

Fig. 21

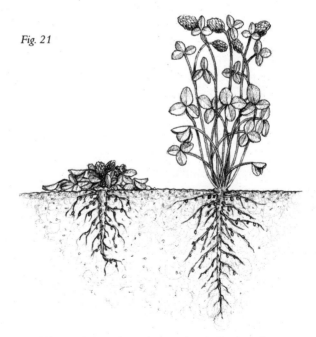

Nodules remain in the soil even after the legume dies.

Dwarf white clover is the most popular under-sown legume but alsike, red, and sweet clover are also suitable.

In general, green manures are planted like small patches of lawn. Broadcast the seeds on bare soil, rake them in, then tamp the soil lightly with the back of the rake to make sure the seeds are in contact with moist earth. You can do this any-where you want a green manure as the next crop in the rotation, although it is not worth the trouble if it will be growing for less than six to eight weeks. A green manure will protect the soil over the coming winter, shade it during a hot period be-tween spring and fall crops, or help renovate the soil in a bed that needs some extra care.

Once you have grown a green manure, you have to bury or remove the greenery to obtain a clean seedbed for the next crop. You can incorpo-rate the green manure residues by turning over the soil shallowly with a spade. If you do that, you should wait three weeks before planting or trans-planting because the early stages of the decompo-sition process after residues are incorporated into the soil can inhibit seed germination and root growth. Alternatively, you can cut the crop off as close to the ground as possible and leave the greenery as a mulch to smother regrowth. Or, if you want to add the greenery to the compost heap, chop the surface clean with a hoe to prevent regrowth, rake the bed smooth, and spread a little compost on the surface. The bed is then ready for transplants or large seeds. Smaller seeds that need a finer seedbed may be at a slight disadvantage.

There is one other effortless system for man-aging green manures: freeze them out. This sys-tem will still protect the soil of the outdoor gar-den through the fall and winter, but it will save work the following spring. Choose your green manure cover crop from among those legumes that grow well in the cool weather of late sum-mer, fall, and early winter but are not hardy enough to survive the winter in your area. Even though the plants are killed, the residues will pro-tect the soil for the remainder of the winter. Our choices for winter-killed green manures are oats, common vetch, and field peas (*Pisum sativum* var. *arvense*), either sown singly or mixed together. Gardeners in more southern climes will want to ask at their farm store for even more frost-sensi-tive candidates such as cowpeas (*Vigna unguicu-lata*) or crotolaria. In spring, rake the bed clean and add the rakings to the compost heap. Then you're ready to plant.

We have as much fun fitting green manure crops into the garden plan, whether undersown or seeded on their own, as we do growing veg-etables. Green manures are another part of the process. When the soil is not needed for human food, it makes sense to plant it to soil food. To benefit the soil of all the beds, you will want to move the green manure areas around the garden as part of your crop rotation. We usually prefer to sow legumes as green manures, but grasses such as rye, oats, and barley are also effective, especially before leguminous vegetables such as peas and beans. Mustard, oil radish, phacelia, and buck-wheat are other non-leguminous green manures. Different green manures have particular uses in the garden, just as different vegetables have spe-cific uses in the kitchen.

Rye, Oats, and Barley—Rye can be planted later in the fall than most other green manures and will grow a lot of bulk. It is hardy enough to survive the coldest winters. We don't use rye in our gar-den because it requires so much work to get rid of the following spring. You have to spade it un-der thoroughly, or it will regrow. If you wish to use a grass family green manure, try growing ei-ther an oat or barley variety that is not winter

TABLE 4

Green Manures

Legumes	Non-Legumes
Hardy	
Hairy vetch	Rye
Red clover	Wheat
Sweet clover	
White Dutch clover	
Half-Hardy	
Austrian winter pea	Barley
Berseem clover	Mustard
Black Medic	Oats
Crimson clover	Oil radish
Lupine	Phacelia
Purple vetch	
Rose clover	
Tender	
Cowpeas	Buckwheat
Crotolaria	
Guar	
Sesbania	

hardy in your region. This generally applies to gardeners in Zone 6 and north. Cleaning up the residues of winter-killed oats or barley is as simple as raking the surface clean—much easier than trying to get rye under control.

Buckwheat and Others—Although buckwheat will be killed by the slightest frost, it is useful during the summer to smother weeds on new ground. It grows quickly once the weather is warm, and its leaves rapidly shade out weed competition. You have to cut it down and turn it under or compost the residues once it begins to flower. If it sets seed and self-sows, buckwheat can become a weed in its own right.

British gardeners favor mustard as a fast-growing, short-term green manure (except before cabbage family relatives). They find that both its root structure and rapidly decomposed tops stimulate beneficial microorganisms in the soil. Any home-garden variety of mustard can be used. A favorite green manure in Holland is phacelia (*Phacelia tanacetifolia*), originally a California weed. My Dutch friends regard it as one of the best all-around green manures and a real benefit to any subsequent crop. German gardeners often include oil radish in their green manures. It has a deep taproot that loosens the subsoil and is also reputed to have a beneficial effect on microorganisms. At present, neither phacelia nor oil radish seeds are easily available in the United States, but keep your eyes open.

Green manures will care for your garden when you can't. If travel or business calls you away for long periods of time in spring, summer, or fall, you can sow the whole garden to a soil-enhancing crop before you leave. The soil in a neglected garden will eventually cover itself with weeds or other wild vegetation unless you take action and plant your choice of "weed." Planting an intentional soil-improving cover crop will help keep out the unwanted weeds and make it much easier to resume gardening upon your return.

You know, James, the wonderful thing about quality is it's an option that's renewable.

—Siegfried to James in the final episode of *All Creatures Great and Small*

CHAPTER 5

SEEDS FOR FOUR SEASONS

If compost is the life source of the garden, seeds are the life spark. What a marvel that a carrot, a bunch of celery, or a cabbage can be hidden in a tiny speck. Yet that small seed is a powerhouse of performance. Take the tomato, for example. Do you want return on investment? One tomato seed, yielding at least one thousand to one in four months, makes even the highest fliers seem paltry. How about impregnable packaging? Tomato seeds are known to remain viable through the most thorough sewage treatment technologies and emerge unscathed to sprout all over the sludge heaps. Are you fascinated by design and miniaturization? The finest computer is but a crude makeshift device beside a tomato seed. To top it all off, if those seeds are sown in your well-composted home garden, the results will be equally impressive in flavor, tenderness, and eating satisfaction.

We purchase seeds principally through seed catalogs. We like the broad selection of old favorites, the yearly introduction of newcomers, and the prompt service. There are enough seed catalogs available to fit every climate and to fill the space limitations of a small pickup if you were to send for all of them. Be discriminating. Over the years, we have settled on a few favorites (see appendix D) that allow us more than adequate climatic and culinary latitude without overwhelming the mailbox.

If you intend to garden in four seasons, you have to plan ahead. When the seed catalogs arrive in midwinter, don't procrastinate. Check the seed drawer in the cupboard to determine what's left from last year. If seeds are stored in a cool, dry location, you can usually count on them to be adequately viable the second year. Then check your garden notes (yes, you will benefit greatly from keeping garden notes) to see which ones you wished you had ordered more of, which new varieties were successful, and which varieties you decided to replace. In our notes we also include the fruits of observing the garden in action. Comments like "does much better in fall than spring" or "grew exceptionally well planted in clumps" are invaluable for future varietal selection.

Then, begin with the catalogs. Reordering the dependable standards is straightforward. Hunting for replacements requires more careful perusal. At times you may be seeking a specific virtue (a variety that stores longer or gives better hot-weather performance); at other times you might like to find a variety with superior adaptability to your soil conditions (some varieties do better in sandy soil, others in clay). Even if the catalog description doesn't specify those qualities precisely, you can learn a lot by reading between the lines. For example, "drought-resistant" varieties often do well in sandy soil; "quick-growing" varieties will respond to extra compost, moisture, and warmth. At times we are simply tempted by a particularly enticing phrase: "exceptionally delicate flavor," "eye pleasing," "wonderful heirloom," "a personal favorite." Our variety selections for each vegetable are listed in appendix A.

It may be necessary to rein in the contagious enthusiasm of the moment and restrain yourself somewhat. The writers of seed catalog descriptions are a sales force, and we are all susceptible. You may suddenly find that your passion has created a monster of twenty-five hundred finely tuned varieties requiring a staff of nine to manage. We avoid that by limiting ourselves, for the most part, to one or two varieties of each vegetable. So instead of buying seeds for a low-growing, very early pea, another with good flavor and lovely chartreuse blossoms, and another that is tall, late, and "highly recommended by Sir Cedric," we have settled on 'Maestro' for early frame production and the dependable, very flavorful, long-yielding variety, 'Lincoln', for the garden. That way we enjoy both the vegetable and the ease of management.

Once you determine what and how much you need for the next year of gardening, order promptly. Time, tide, and the garden wait for no one. All of a sudden, there may be an early thaw. You notice an empty space and have an opportunity to plant. Your inspiration, experience, or planting schedule tells you a specific seed variety could be planted at that moment. What comfort to know it's waiting in the seed drawer.

Where Seeds Are Born

The fifth day of our 1996 journey through France turned out to be an alpha and omega experience. But there was no good or bad involved. Both of the extremes were superlatives. We would be visiting the largest and the smallest, the most modern and the most old-fashioned, the most liberal and the most conservative seed companies in this region of France. In the spectrum of things horticultural, where scale runs from industrial to

Fig. 22

Seeds and catalogs.

artisanal, where technology runs from complicated to simple, and where cultivation runs from chemical to biological, our preference has always been with the simpler end of the scale. Yet, as our French seed company experience confirmed, when you get right down to it we are principally captivated by excellence. In a world where shoddy work is all too commonplace, either option can be done poorly. When something is done well, as long as the limits of the planet are respected, we are impressed. And this day we were doubly impressed. We don't believe our two hosts had ever met, but if they had, we are sure their mutual appreciation of each other's work would have been as strong as our appreciation of both of them.

Our morning visit took us to a small village south of Avignon for a tour of Graines Gautier, a premier French seed house. We had gotten an introduction from a friend who had dealt with this company for many years. It was an eye-opening experience. The highly professional, meticulous care we could see throughout the visit was the best reassurance possible that the future of large-scale vegetable seed breeding, variety evaluation, and seed storage and germination testing is in competent hands.

The phrase "seed house" rather than "seed catalog" usually refers to those companies involved principally in breeding and developing new varieties for the seed trade. The beautiful Gautier catalog reflected that bias. It was obviously not aimed at sales to home gardeners but toward sales to catalog companies and to professional growers. This is a highly capitalized and competitive business where companies specialize in varieties for specific regions. Since Gautier's focus was the Mediterranean areas of France, right along our 44th parallel path, their seeds were of special interest to us.

Graines Gautier is renowned for their winter varieties of endive and escarole; for their fall-planted cabbage for spring harvest, 'Pointu de Châteaurenard' (especially adapted for southern France), which would be worth growing for its name alone; for their many cauliflowers adapted to *récoltes échelonnées* (successional harvests) from February until May; for the small, round, sweet winter-harvested turnips that French chefs love to serve; for cold-tolerant winter lettuces; for red onions sown in fall and harvested in early summer; for parsley and radish varieties adapted to winter greenhouse culture; and for leeks, with *très*

Fig. 23

Pointu de Châteaurenard and 'Musquée de Provence' pumpkin.

bonne resistance to cold and to *maladies* of the foliage. For the region's summer crops they have developed a long-keeping, delicious-tasting pumpkin 'Musquée de Provence' which looks as if it were the model for Cinderella's coach; zucchini for both standard-size harvest and for the small, very French *courgettes;* green filet beans of exquisite slimness and delicacy; and, of course, melons, from the smooth to the netted, from the very French 'Charantais' varieties to the Spanish and Persian types.

The catalog cover announces the company's focus on *semences maraîcheres*—seeds for market gardeners. Significantly, the word *maraîcher* derives from *marais* meaning swamp or bog, demonstrating the long understanding of the relationship between soils of high organic matter content and successful vegetable culture. Originally, the "muck" soils of important vegetable-growing areas in all parts of the world were brought into cultivation by draining swamp land. But the high-organic-matter soils of the *maraîchers* around Paris, whose efficient production (amounting to over 110 pounds of vegetables per year for each person in Paris) made the intensive vegetable-growing industry famous in the 19th century, were maintained as a by-product of horticultural practices. The *maraîchers* used the heat from fermenting horse manure as the heat source for their winter cold frame production, and subsequently used the spongy mold resulting from the decaying horse manure as the principal ingredient of their soils. The horse manure itself was a by-product of that era's transportation system. The horses of Paris produced approximately one million tons yearly of what was regarded as the premier vegetable fertilizer. Wagon loads of fresh vegetables went into the city and wagon loads of fresh horse manure returned to the farms. How nice if today's transportation systems could yield a by-product that was, at the least, equally benign if not equally useful.

As soon as we finished inquiring as to which of their winter vegetable varieties would be adaptable to our system, and had acquired samples of numerous Gautier varieties to trial in our winter garden, we bombarded Gautier's melon breeder with questions. His answers indicated the high quality of work being done by seed houses like Gautier and, also, by the agricultural researchers of the French agricultural services. Provençal melons are a renowned crop and Gautier's varieties 'Bastion' and 'Orus' are two of the best. Melons grown around the town of Cavaillon, twelve miles east of Avignon, hold a French regional *marque* (or specialty, like Vidalia onions). A visit there is like a trip to Mecca for European melon lovers.

We were interested in melons because in addition to our pampered outdoor melon crops (grown on plastic mulch and under mini-tunnels), we grow them in our greenhouse during the summer when it becomes a "hot house." It seems logical to take advantage of that extra heat especially for crops such as melons, sweet potatoes, and eggplants that don't thrive unprotected in our cool Maine summer temperatures. The sweet potatoes and eggplants had been a great success but not the melons. Despite reading many specialized books on intensive melon culture, books filled with pictures of sweet tasting, aromatically scented, trellised melons hanging seductively in serried rows like an epicures dream, our efforts had not looked like that. Fruit set had been spotty and although the few we did get were delicious, they were not particularly early.

We knew our techniques for the trellised melons were amateurish, because we often got to the plants too late. But we had followed French pruning instructions for the non-trellised melons carefully because the French had melon pruning down to a fine art. Each melon variety had a recommended "pruning numeral." These were expressed in code as a series of digits written like 2-4-3 or «243»—indicating how many leaves on the young plant were allowed to grow before the growing tip would be pinched out. For example, the first digit, 2, indicated that the plant was to be pruned the first time after two true leaves had formed. Pruning encourages the growth of side branches from buds at the base of the leaves. The female blossoms which bear the fruits are formed on the side branches. To focus the plant's resources on the fruits, the side branches were subsequently pruned after a specified number of leaves (4 in the example above), and then the branches arising from them were pruned (after 3 leaves in this case), hence the «243» code. Other codes might have been «246» or «260», the 0 indicating that no pruning was to be done at that site. Although we had no specific numerals for the varieties available

to us in the U.S., we thought we had been making reasonable choices.

Ah, but things had changed. We were told our information only applied to the old-time varieties. The melon research from the 1960s, the source of our information, had been superseded by new techniques beginning in the early 1980s. Although the changes were horticultural, the driving force was economic. The rising cost of labor had made pruning too expensive. (It takes about fifty hours of labor per acre on a commercial operation to do a «243» pruning.) Melon germplasm had offered other options. Monoecious varieties were now available which formed their female flowers sooner and thus did not need pruning. In fact, pruning could seriously reduce yields of the new cultivars. Furthermore, all our attempts at trellising had been misplaced because, as we were now told, the old techniques were most suitable for extra-early heated crops in specialized greenhouses. So much for what we thought were our well-informed attempts at growing modern melons with old-time techniques. A humbling experience, but full of hope for the future.

Still, we felt that the extent of our failures were yet to be sufficiently explained, and we were right. There was more to come. Greenhouse melon growers had traditionally relied on hand pollination to attain a good fruit set. Pollen was transferred from the male to the female blossoms with a fine, soft-bristle brush. This, too, was now cost-prohibitive. Present techniques relied on hives of specialized bumble bees for pollination. Bumble bees do not get disoriented under the glass or plastic covering of a greenhouse as honey bees do. Being lazy, we had never hand pollinated. Instead, we had relied on our native wild bumble bee population which, we were now told, might need to be encouraged to visit the greenhouse area by nearby outdoor flower plantings, a practice we

Fig. 24

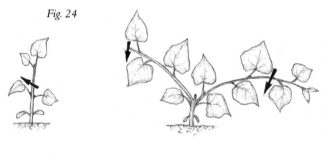

«243» pruning.

have since adopted. But, not to lose hope. We could join the new world order. We now had seed samples of Gautier's latest melon-breeding efforts and we promised ourselves to pay more attention to summer greenhouse management in hopes of truly succeeding with this tastiest of all crops. However, we still planned to get seeds of the renowned old varieties from seed-saving groups so we could grow them with the old techniques and have a basis for flavor comparison. We left with dreams of Cape Rosier becoming as hallowed as Cavaillon in the pantheon of melon devotees. (See appendix D for the address of a French seed catalog that sells a wide range of varieties and will ship to the U.S.)

When the morning ended we went for a delicious lunch with our hosts. It is significant how much of our delight in this trip and joy in what we learned corresponds with the meals. But that is a reflection of the French genius for eating with the seasons. We may have been fantasizing about melon crops for next summer, but we were not eating them. We were eating the very winter foods that were in season at the moment.

An hour after lunch and fifty kilometers further east we were at the other end of the seed industry spectrum. The seed business of Jean-Luc Danneyrolles, *Le Potager d'un Curieux*, is tiny and non-technological. He jokingly referred to his catalog as the smallest in the world—not because it lacks variety, there are plenty of cultivars offered—but because of its small 4-by-6-inch format and the minimalist philosophy of its proprietor. The selection of seeds in its twenty-eight pages, self-published on peach-colored paper, runs to hundreds of varieties. But these varieties, rather than reflecting the breeding and crossing and hybridizing of seed industry technology, reflect the traditional selecting that resulted in old-style gardens of the past and Jean-Luc's continued

selecting of wild plants yet to be truly domesticated. Thus the catalog features both the well-known and the obscure vegetables he thinks are the most flavorful, plus the wild Provençal herbs and edible plants he thinks should be better known.

The selection in his seed catalog reflects Jean-Luc's passion for good food and beautiful surroundings. The 1996 edition listed twenty-five salad greens (or I should say salad *leaves* since not all are green), fifteen aromatic herbs to season them, twenty-seven heirloom tomatoes to serve alongside, in addition to unique root crops like skirret *(Sium sisarum)*, Hamburg parsley *(Petroselinum crispum* var. *tuberosum)*, rampion *(Campanula rapunculus)*, and scolymus *(Scolymus hispanicus)*. Also included are perennial vegetables (Good King Henry, Russian comfrey, Chinese rhubarb), garlic and shallots, a wide selection of specialty herbs including medicinal ones, and an extensive collection (some fifty varieties) of unique flower seeds. There is even a "research" page with names of a dozen odd crops he would like to include in future catalogs but has not been able to find. He encourages readers to let him know if they are aware of seed sources. The page ends with the phrase, *"Toute curiosité pour le potager . . ."*

We had heard about Jean-Luc from three different sources. All were his devoted customers at the local market where he sold his mesclun salad and other crops. He was renowned in the region as a grower with a passion for the highest quality and most uniquely varied ingredients in his salad mixes. The customers were wildly enthusiastic. All had agreed that his salad was "The Best." Beyond that, it was alive. This liveliness stemmed not only from being freshly harvested, cleanly washed, artistically presented, and imaginative with its appealing mix of flavors, colors, shapes, and textures, which are the hallmarks of a memorable salad, but also because of the obvious realness of the ingredients. Somehow one could tell that these were fully nutritious, old-time varieties grown on a nurtured soil by someone who cared about the end result.

It was obvious from the moment we entered his cozy house that we had almost not left home. Here was an artisanal soul mate. Here was a fellow vegetable "loony" (one of our correspondents had respectfully referred to Jean-Luc as the *maraîcher fou,* the crazy market gardener) who shared our enthusiasm about just how good vegetables can be in the hands of a grower who cares about the subtleties of soil fertility, variety selection, time of harvest, and all the other quality concerns that affect the final product.

The possibilities for improving flavor have always been understood with wine and cheese. Volumes have been written about the influence of the numerous quality factors on the nuances of the finished product—how soil and climate affect the grapes, how the cow's diet affects the milk. But vegetables are not traditionally included in that exalted company. In fact, the United States Department of Agriculture and its nutritionists, in contravention of common sense, have followed a party line stressing just the opposite. This myth of vegetable homogeneity has been encouraged by a supermarket-dominated food system where mass marketing requires standardized thinking. The public has been led into a mistaken belief that a carrot is a carrot no matter where it comes from or how it is grown.

Nothing could be further from the truth. There are just as many nuances—in flavor, texture, and suitability of use—to be enjoyed both with carrot varieties and the methods by which they are grown as there are with wine and cheese. This is the carrot for cooking, this one for juicing, this

Fig. 25

The seed catalog, Le Potager d'un Curieux.

one for eating fresh. In addition, this strain is best for cool conditions, this for warm weather, and this for winter culture. This type thrives best on clay soil, another on muck soil, or sandy soil, or a deep loam. But in today's world this information is mainly ignored because it is only of use to the few growers who concentrate on "quality" products for a local market. Large-scale growers, producing bulk for the supermarket, choose varieties for yield and standardized appearance.

The same has happened with most commercial fruit, only worse. When fruit is picked green for shipping it is never able to develop its flavor and nutritional potential, even if the variety possessed those qualities to begin with. Research has shown that the health-enhancing compounds naturally present in plant foods, popularly called phytonutrients, are only produced during the ripening process. Produce picked green to stand up to long-distance shipping and storage is thus just a shadow of the "real food" it could be. Our conversation with Jean-Luc kept returning to the importance of focused local production for an epicurean food supply.

Epicurean vegetables? Absolutely. It was a joy to be discussing these ideas with someone who shared our passion for the subject. Vegetables can be so much more compelling than people think. And if they are properly grown, they will be eaten with gusto. New studies are frequently reported by nutritional researchers confirming that Mom was right when she told us to eat our vegetables if we wanted to be healthy. But despite the urging of countless nutritionists, doctors, and government agencies, this advice is rarely taken. People are mostly uninspired about eating vegetables because most supermarket vegetables are uninspiring.

No so for Jean-Luc's customers. We mentioned above those who had told us in what high regard they held this "crazy market gardener" because the flavor of his produce was so compelling. Jean-Luc modestly confirmed that his produce was *très populaire.* Our own experience mirrors his. Customers of our commercial farm produce have told us our "sweet winter" carrots are so tasty they are almost addictive. Their children ask for them. They tell us our baby-leaf salad mix (which incidentally, because of the variety of nutritious leaves, contains six or more times the vitamin content

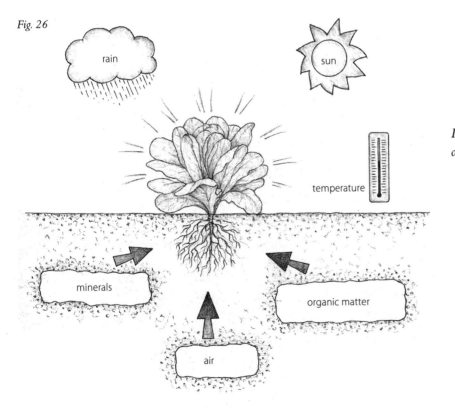

Fig. 26

Influence of soil and climate on vegetable quality.

of a salad of head lettuce) seems to disappear from the drawer in the refrigerator because it is a "healthy fast food" which looks so inviting you want to eat it, and so easy to put a handful into a bowl and add dressing that you do just that. When vegetables have flavor and freshness they become snacks as well as main courses. For Jean-Luc's customers and ours, eating the right foods for good health is no longer a chore to be urged on the unwilling. It becomes positively epicurean—done as a voluntary action because it is so pleasurable.

How far can this sense of epicurean vegetables lead us? Famed chef Alice Waters, who insists upon fresh, local, organically grown vegetables for her Chez Panisse restaurant, was on the right track when she said in a recent talk, "The sensual pleasure of eating beautiful food from the garden brings with it the moral satisfaction of doing the right thing for the planet and for yourself." Can four-season gardens help to bring that level of enlightenment and understanding to everyone's back yard? Well, if cabbages and carrots can sprout from such small specks of seed, why not ideas that change the way we eat and think?

Since seeds are where it all begins, it was reassuring at the end of the day to feel that both the conventional and the alternative seed resources we had visited were in good hands and working toward a more delicious future. Will we feel the same ten years hence? Or will the entire seed industry have been taken over by square tomatoes, bland lettuce, and genetic engineering? I suspect it depends on all of us. If we create the demand with our seed purchases for varieties that grow the most flavorful vegetables, there will always be plenty of competent professionals and passionate amateurs to supply them.

CHAPTER 6

THE OUTDOOR GARDEN: PLANTING AND CULTIVATING

Seeds are determined to grow. The gardener's role is to help them do so. The first step in plant growth is seed germination. Three factors that affect the success of seed germination are soil temperature, seed depth, and moisture. If you have chosen and/or modified your garden site to enhance the microclimate, the outdoor soil temperature conditions will have been improved already. The other factors, the depth at which the seeds are planted and the moisture level of the soil after planting, can be more directly controlled by the gardener.

Sowing Seeds

Seeds are planted in either a hole in the soil or a furrow (a long, shallow opening) and then covered. The covering of soil keeps the seeds moist, warm, and protected while they germinate. As a general rule for depth of planting, cover the seeds to three or four times their diameter. Thus, a small seed, such as a carrot, which measures about $1/16$ inch in diameter, should be covered with ¼ inch of soil. Plant a ¼-inch-diameter pea or corn seed 1 inch deep. In a heavy clay soil, the three-times factor is more appropriate. As general rules go, this one is quite dependable for most garden seeds. If sowing large seeds, such as peas, beans, or corn, when the weather is warmer and drier than usual, you may want to plant them slightly deeper to ensure adequate moisture for germination.

When planting small seeds, you can make accurate shallow furrows with the edge of a board. We use a 30-inch-long 1x2 for planting rows across the beds. Lay a sharp edge of the board on the soil where you want

Fig. 27

Making a furrow with a board.

Fig. 28

Sowing seeds with a creased seed packet.

the furrow and wiggle it in a little to move the soil aside. When you lift up the board, it leaves a shallow, level, V-shaped furrow. Then drop in the seeds and cover them lightly by pushing soil over them with your fingers. For larger seeds, such as pea and bean, you can make a furrow with the edge of a hoe. For corn and squash seeds, poke a hole with your finger to the desired depth.

When you sprinkle the seeds in furrows, take the extra time to space them evenly. Aim for the distances suggested in appendix A. It is worth spacing seeds carefully. The thinning, if any is necessary, will be less destructive to the plants to be left if they are not tangled together with the ones to be removed. An easy way to sow is to crease one side of the seed packet and use the V of that crease to align the seeds as you tap them out one by one. With practice, this can be a very efficient technique. If you have a large garden you might be interested in one of the rolling seed sowers sold in seed catalogs, but in many cases, after fiddling and adjusting and refiddling with them, you may conclude that it's simpler to sow the home garden by hand.

Once you have planted the seeds at the proper depth, you must keep them moist. When the weather is dry, we water the seed rows daily until the seeds germinate. Just make a quick pass down the row using a watering can with a fine rose or a hose and sprinkler nozzle. This is especially important with small seeds, such as carrot and parsley, that are planted shallowly and take a while to germinate. By watering those rows once or twice a day until the seedlings emerge, you can guarantee a full stand with no gaps in the row.

When conditions are really dry, planting with the old-time "Cavex" hoe will help a lot. The Cavex hoe has a blade in the shape of a skinny football. First you use the broad rounded edge to skim ½ inch or so of dry soil off the surface for the length of the row to be planted. Next you use one of the pointed ends to make a small sharp furrow of the proper depth down the center of the first shallow rounded furrow and into the moister soil below. The seeds are planted in the small furrow and covered with soil to a depth appropriate to their size. The shallow rounded furrow serves as a basin to hold in the moisture from a once- or twice-daily trip down the row with a watering can. The dryer the weather, the more seed germination depends upon the seeds staying moist, and this double furrow technique works wonders.

Transplanting

Transplanting is like seeding except that you set out young plants (seedlings) rather than seeds. Whether you acquire the seedlings by purchasing them from a garden center or growing your own, the techniques for moving them to the garden are the same. (Information on growing your own seedlings is given in chapter 9.) Before transplanting, make sure the soil around the seedling roots is very moist. That is their best protection against the stress of drying out while they are becoming established. After the seedlings are in the ground, water the whole bed. Within a few days, they start rooting out into the soil around them and are then treated like any other plant in the garden.

To reduce the effort of measuring the spacing for the transplants, you can use homemade marking jigs. Two simple ideas work well. First, you can make lightweight wooden frames the width of the bed with pegs screwed in at the spacing desired. When you press the frame and pegs against the prepared soil, the pegs leave marks so you know where to make the hole and set the transplant. Second, we have made pegs that fit over the teeth of our 30-inch-wide garden rake.

We slide the pegs on at whatever spacing we want and mark the bed both lengthwise and widthwise. Where the lines cross is where the plants are to go.

For many people, a standard garden trowel is uncomfortable to use when making holes for small transplants because of the strain it places on the wrist. A better solution is a transplant tool that allows the gardener to jab and pull with the wrist straight. There is an excellent design on the market called the right-angle trowel (see fig. 31), or you can make your own tool by following the instructions in the next paragraph.

Purchase a bricklayer's trowel with a triangular blade (2 by 5 inches) and a strong attachment between the handle and blade. Use a hacksaw to cut 2 inches off the end of the blade. Clamp a vise

Fig. 29

Water daily until seedlings begin to emerge.

Fig. 30

Homemade marking jig.

Fig. 31

Right-angled trowel.

firmly just above where the handle meets the blade. Bend the handle back until it is parallel with the blade and then a few degrees farther. You hold the resulting tool like a dagger. Just jab it into the soil, then pull it back toward you, and you will have a hole the right size for your transplant.

Trellised Crops

Many space-demanding crops will fit into our 30-inch-wide beds if we grow them vertically. Climbing peas, pole beans, and tomatoes all benefit from trellises for vertical support. Trellises are not a garden necessity but a choice. You should not feel any obligation to trellis your crops if it seems too complicated. All vegetable crops can be grown without support. Just be sure to choose low-growing varieties. For example, 'Sugar Snap' and 'Alderman' peas grow six feet tall and need support, but other varieties with vines under thirty inches (such as 'Bounty' or 'Knight') can be grown on the ground. The seed catalog description gives that information. With beans, choose bush varieties over pole varieties if you don't plan to stake them. Similarly, there are varieties of bush cucumbers and bush squashes if you don't have enough space for trailing vines. Tomatoes for ground culture should be determinate rather than indeterminate (see appendix A). Again, catalog descriptions will inform you.

For those of you who are intrigued by the idea of trellises, you can grow many trellised crops in addition to peas, beans, and tomatoes. Among these are cucumbers, melons, winter squashes, and even a vining zucchini. New Zealand spinach *(Tetragonia expansa)* is a hot-weather green that can be grown vertically. The advantages of trellising are numerous: two to three times higher yields from the same garden space, more efficient use of sunlight for optimal photosynthesis, easier picking with no bending over, and cleaner produce because there is no soil splatter from rain or watering.

We build the same basic trellis for all vertically growing crops. It consists of upright poles every 5 feet with a crossbar on top. You can use poles cut

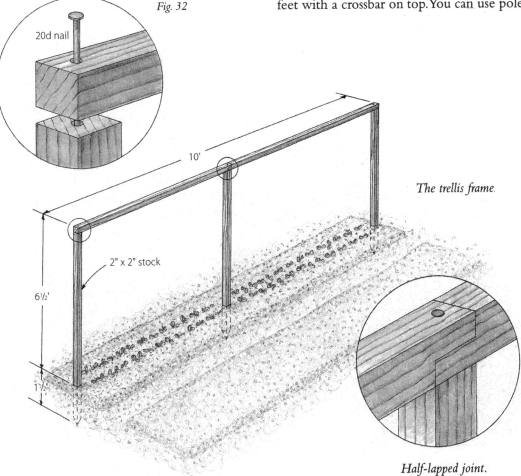

Fig. 32

20d nail

10'

2" x 2" stock

6½'

1½'

The trellis frame.

Half-lapped joint.

Fig. 33

"Sewing" the crossbar through the netting.

in the woods, or 2x2s from the lumberyard. A standard 2x4 ripped lengthwise will yield a pair of 2x2s. We don't use treated wood for our trellises because we prefer not to be around the chemicals it is treated with. You may want to apply an environmentally friendly wood preservative yourself (see appendix D). If you have access to a scrap yard, you can make this simple trellis out of metal pipe.

The upright poles are 8 feet long, and sharpened to a point for driving into the ground. Since our beds are 20 feet long, we use 5- or 10-foot crossbars. Each one has a half-lapped end so they can both sit on the same upright where they meet. Place an upright at one end of the 20-foot-long bed and then lay the crossbars on the soil, positioned as they would be on top of the uprights. The middles and ends of the crossbars determine the positions of the second upright and

so on to the end of the bed. In my sandy soil, I drive the uprights one and a half to two feet deep for solid support. That leaves six feet or so aboveground. If you make a preliminary hole with an iron bar, they will be much easier to drive. In heavier soils that provide support, you can cut the uprights shorter or not drive them in as deep.

The crossbars sit on the uprights. I drill a $7/32$-inch hole through the crossbar at the ends and the middle and into the top of the upright. Then I can drop a galvanized 20d nail in the hole to hold the crossbar in place. This makes a simple, attractive structure that will not blow over and is strong enough to support the weight of the crop. It needs to be strong. You may be surprised at how many pounds of fruit are carried by a row of trellised beefsteak tomato plants.

The six-foot height works well for all trellised

Fig. 34

Securing the netting with a notched peg.

crops and is also the height of the tallest pea netting available. The best pea netting is made of nylon or plastic and has a large mesh with 6-inch-square holes (see appendix D for sources). Hang the mesh from the crossbar by "sewing" the crossbar through alternate holes in the top edge of the mesh. Then place the crossbar on top of the uprights and drop in the nails. Drive in garden stakes (1 inch square and 12 inches long) with a slight notch near the upper end to hold the netting taut at the bottom. This is the simplest, strongest, and most versatile trellis we have ever used.

You can use trellis netting as the climbing support for peas, cucumbers, melons, squash, vining zucchini, and New Zealand spinach. Untreated garden twine is the best support for tomatoes and pole beans. The 4- or 5-ply strength is best. Tie the twine to the crossbar and then down to a garden stake driven into the soil next to the

tomato plant or hill of beans. The beans will climb the string on their own. Prune the tomatoes to one stem and support them by taking a turn of the string around the stem every so often as it grows. That provides enough friction between string and stem to hold the plants upright. At the end of the season, compost the string with the vines. (See appendix A for more detailed pruning and tying instructions for tomatoes.)

This same trellis frame will support a sheet of plastic to make a temporary A-frame greenhouse to protect your tomatoes into the first cool weeks of autumn. Bury the edges of the plastic in the soil of the path on each side. Close in the ends by clipping with clothespins. This temporary structure is not secure against strong winds, but it will provide an excellent level of frost protection at night.

You can leave the uprights in the ground permanently if you wish. You would then rotate the trellised crops to a different trellised bed each year. Actually, you can grow any crop you want in a trellised bed. If you remove the crossbars, the

Fig. 35

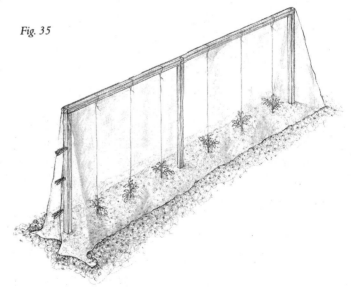

The temporary A-frame greenhouse.

uprights cast almost no shade and are not in the way of planting, harvesting, or using the broadfork. If you plan to leave the uprights in place permanently, the wood should be a rot-resistant species such as cedar, or coated with one of the environmentally friendly wood preservatives. If you remove the uprights at the end of the season, let them dry, and store them under cover, they will last many years with no preservative.

Weeds

Weeds probably discourage more potential gardeners than any other single problem. "Oh, the garden was overgrown with weeds and we finally gave up" is so common a statement that it is almost considered a normal reaction. It doesn't need to be that way. Have you ever heard anyone say, "Oh, the living room finally got so dirty that we just stopped using it"? We don't stop enjoying the living room because of dust. We simply vacuum or sweep every so often to keep the room clean. The same applies in the garden. Furthermore, just as dirt in the living room can be minimized by placing a mat outside the front door or asking people to remove their shoes before entering the house, weeds in the garden can be prevented in a number of ways. All of them make less work for the gardener.

First, don't dig the garden. Let buried seeds stay buried. Most weed seeds germinate only in the top two inches of soil. When starting a new garden, you can encourage that germination by shallow rotary tilling. The combination of air, moisture, and exposure to light creates conditions that stimulate weed germination. Wait a week after tilling and till again to eradicate all the newly germinated weeds before you plant. Once the upper-layer weed seeds are exhausted (it takes a number of years, so be patient), very few new weeds will appear unless you bring them up from below or you don't pay attention to the next suggestion.

Don't let weeds go to seed. Nature is prolific. Each plant can produce an enormous number of seeds. The old saying "One year's seeding means seven year's weeding" holds. You won't get any debate from me, because I have seen it. The results of carelessness are cumulative: the more seeds you have, the more weeds you have. But the results of care also are cumulative. If weed plants are removed from the garden to the compost heap before they go to seed, their thousands of seeds are not added to the garden lode: no seeds, no weeds. As the years progress, there will be fewer and fewer seeds left to germinate. Of course, your life will be even easier if you follow the final suggestion.

Dispatch weeds while they are small. Tiny, newly germinated weeds are the easiest to deal with. A sharp hoe drawn shallowly through the soil between the crop rows will quickly dispatch small weeds. That minimum effort yields a maximum benefit. It not only cures the weed problem but also makes the garden look neat and cared for. Because it looks nice, you will spend more quiet and relaxed time there keeping it that way. This is not weeding, which is work, but rather cultivating. Cultivating is the gentle, shallow stirring of the soil's surface that uproots newly germinated weeds before they become a problem.

If a hoe is to be effective when "drawn shallowly through the soil," that hoe must be sharp; angled for drawing, not chopping; slim, so as not to bulldoze soil onto the vegetable plants; and accurate, so as to pass between the crop rows without damage. It also must be comfortable and fun to use, or you will find some other way to spend your time. Years ago I could never find such a hoe, so I made my own. Let me explain the process.

I was after a draw hoe, not a chopping hoe. I wanted an efficiently designed tool, not a crude bludgeon. I wanted a hoe I could use standing upright (no back strain) and draw toward me shallowly just under the soil's surface. Since that meant I would be holding it with my thumbs up the handle, as with a broom or leaf rake, I had to find the ideal angle between the blade and the handle for a shallow, skimming action. Seventy degrees turned out to be ideal. I made the blade as thin and narrow as possible so that it would cut and skim without gouging and bulldozing. Since the blade was narrow, I could put the cutting edge in line with the centerline of the hoe handle so that it could be aimed accurately and cut weeds rather than crops. Finally, I sharpened it like a razor so that the cutting edge was next to the soil. A sharp hoe allows you to work shallowly and not disturb the roots of the crop plants. Voilà, the hoe of my dreams.

Using a draw hoe with the proper angle and a thin, sharp blade is like dancing with a skilled partner, and just as enjoyable. Hold it in a ballroom-dancing position, with your thumbs upward. Stand comfortably with your back straight. The hoe blade draws effortlessly through the soil

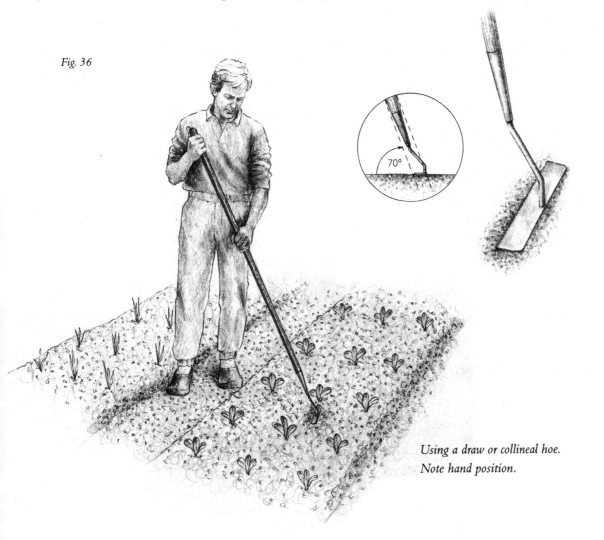

Fig. 36

Using a draw or collineal hoe. Note hand position.

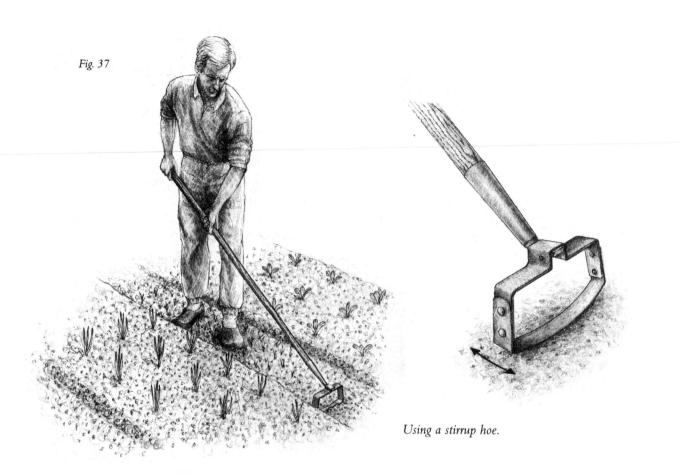

Fig. 37

Using a stirrup hoe.

of the growing areas. This is a very pleasant activity. Hoe when weeds are very small, keeping the garden shallowly cultivated. Go out to the garden on a summer's evening, put a Strauss waltz on the stereo, and dance with your hoe. Weed control has never been so civilized.

Your evening dancing partner is called the collineal hoe (collineal means "in the same straight line"). Various interpretations of this design are sold by a number of garden tool catalogs. It is designed for skimming in soft, fertile soil rather than for chopping compacted earth. The only compaction in your garden should be in the paths. For those areas, another hoe will make your life easier.

This is called a stirrup hoe because it has a thin, curved blade held by a square frame some- what in the shape of a stirrup. The stirrup is hinged where it attaches to the handle so it swings back and forth slightly. The blade is sharpened on both edges. The hinged action changes the angle of the blade to the soil just enough so that it cuts smoothly whether you are pushing or pulling. This hoe is held with the thumbs pointing down the handle so that a lot of power can be applied. It can cut effectively just below the soil's surface or go deeper if you wish. The cutting blade is curved and fits nicely in the paths between the beds where your feet have passed. We use this hoe while moving down the paths backward, working the hinged action of the hoe back and forth in the compacted soil. It neatly cuts off all weeds and leaves a fresh, aerated surface.

CHAPTER 7

GARDEN HELPERS

Before we leave the outdoor garden, there is one more ingredient to discuss. Back in the 1950s, cartoonist Al Capp created the Schmoo, a roly-poly little creature that inhabited his Li'l Abner comic strip. Schmoos were friendly animals who provided all manner of food and services willingly and joyfully to the inhabitants of Dogpatch. We think there is a real-life Schmoo that might interest gardeners; a creature that can provide a daily source of fresh eggs, devastatingly effective bug and slug control, and charming garden companionship. The real-life backyard Schmoo is the duck.

We are long-time fans of the duck. We keep three or four of them as companions and helpers in our yard. Over the years we have raised several breeds: Australian Spotted Bantams, Welsh Harlequins, and Indian Runners. Each breed has its virtues and it is difficult to recommend one over the other. Ducks are the perfect backyard livestock because they are so well behaved. Ducks need water only for drinking, not swimming, although they do appreciate the water from a sprinkler in hot, dry weather, just as the garden does. They don't scratch and fight like chickens do, they aren't noisy like chickens are, and they lay their eggs at night so the basis for a fresh omelette awaits us most every morning when we let them out of their night shelter. They lay more eggs than chickens, and the eggs are richer and better tasting. Best of all, ducks lay eggs at a reasonable rate during the winter without fancy housing or supplementary light. Even if fed on a homegrown diet of garden and kitchen scraps, instead of the expensive mixed feeds that chickens require, ducks will lay at about 60 percent of the summer rate. But we are fond of them more for what they eat than for what we eat. One of their favorite foods is the common garden slug.

The cool, damp conditions within a winter cold frame or tunnel, so pleasing to the winter vegetable crops, are also very attractive to slugs. The ducks take care of the slug problem with almost magical efficiency. In mid-summer when the cold frames are empty of crops, we let the ducks in to harvest any slugs already in residence. With meticulous thoroughness they use their bills to explore in, under, around, and through all the places we could never get to. Not having found an existing word to describe this duck-bill action, an almost belligerent back-and-forth head motion with the bill deep in crevices while small beady eyes search for snacks, we have christened it "snarfeling." Whether practiced in the frames, the garden, or the lawn, snarfeling is a highly effective pest control practice.

Once we begin planting the winter crops, the ducks have full access to all the ground outside the winter harvest areas. Any new slugs arriving in search of winter housing must first cross "DUCK COUNTRY," and the ducks don't miss much. During the whole of this past winter we found only two slugs in the tunnel greenhouse and none in the cold frames.

To protect young vegetable seedlings, the ducks are fenced out of our summer vegetable garden by an 18-inch-high temporary fence from mid-April, when we begin planting, until early October. By then the remaining outdoor crops are too large for them to bother and the fall cold frames have begun to provide our salads. Other than that temporary exclusion, they have the run of the yard, the gardens, and the perennial flower and shrub borders throughout the year. In the course of their activities they occasionally do something that irritates us. They sometimes eat the early yellow crocuses, they have nibbled on a few annual flowers, and they like borage so much we now grow it in the fenced garden. But considering the larger picture, any minor damage they do is insignificant compared with the benefits they provide and the delight we take in their company. Friendly, curious, and often hilariously ridiculous, they possess enough dignified reserve that they never become bothersome.

Not only are ducks popular with us but also, to their great misfortune, they are popular with seemingly every predator on the planet. At one time or another we have lost ducks to foxes, dogs, raccoons, skunks, hawks, and ravens (a young duckling). It is easy to imagine wolves, bears, and bobcats lurking in the shadows. Having learned what to expect we know that the duck's nighttime housing, although not fancy, needs to be secure. But in achieving security we haven't wanted to create an unsightly fortress or create awkward or excessive work cleaning out duck manure. We also wanted a house the ducks could live in from the day they arrived as day-old ducklings. Based on our experience with movable chicken houses, we designed and built what our son immediately christened "Duckingham Palace." The Palace has two parts.

PART 1: THE TOP

The top looks like a small gable-roofed house 32 inches wide by 36 inches long by 30 inches high. It has a lightweight frame made of 2x2s that is sheathed with overlapping clapboards on the roof and sides. The gable ends are open and covered with hardware cloth for ventilation, as are the spaces on either side of the entrance door. The door, hinged at the bottom, also serves as an access ramp.

PART 2: THE BOTTOM

The bottom is a simple 32-inch-wide by 36-inch-long rectangle made of 2x4s covered with half-inch hardware cloth. The top is held to the bottom with removable bolts.

Fig. 38

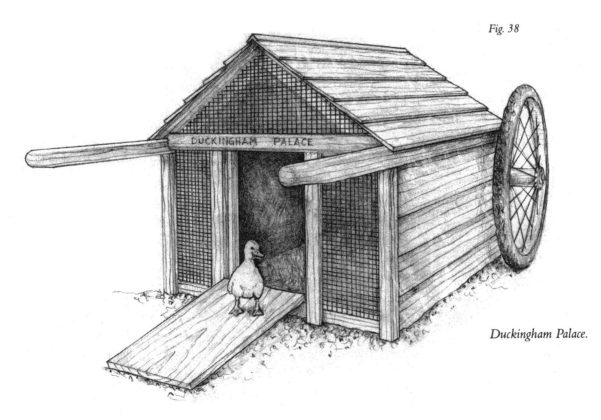

Duckingham Palace.

Two features make Duckingham Palace unique. The 2x2s used for the top plate of each wall extend three feet out to the front (the entrance door side) like the handles of a wheelbarrow. A pair of cart wheels separated by an axle are attached to the back wall by a double bracket, which holds the axle in a lower position when the house is being wheeled and in an upper position so the house can rest securely on the ground.

The house looks pretty enough to sit out on the lawn where, each evening after the ducks are shut in, it is moved one house-length further along. The duck droppings, which fall through the mesh floor during the night, provide just the right amount of lawn fertilizer before the house is moved a further length the next night, and so on. Twice a year we unbolt the top from the bottom and hose off the bottom to keep the mesh clean and prevent any manure buildup along the edges.

The house is large enough to give night protection to eight ducks but we usually keep only three or four. As might be expected, Duckingham Palace's inhabitants over the years have been given Royal Family names such as Henry VIII, Anne, Katherine, and Jane. But then how can one not find nobility in an animal that fertilizes the lawn, eats bugs and slugs, lays eggs, and delights the eye of the beholder?

Raising Ducklings in the Palace

The best way to begin with ducks is to purchase ducklings from one of the specialist hatcheries. When they arrive by overnight air mail in their special travel box the postmaster always calls and we can usually hear them cheeping in the background. Before the due date, we scrub down the house and prepare it for their needs. We tack plastic over the hardware cloth in the gable ends and on either side of the door to prevent drafts. We put a few sheets of newspaper on the floor and cover them with a layer of wood shavings. A single infrared heat lamp is hung from a hook in the ceiling. The 30-inch height of the house positions the lamp at the ideal height above the floor. We place a waterer in the corner to one side of the door and a feeder in the corner to the other side. We wheel the house into the garage, the greenhouse, or the shed (i.e., wherever sheltered space is available) and plug in the lamp.

After the ducklings have had a few days to adjust, we wheel the house into the yard and run an extension cord to the heat lamp. We choose a spot where the grass can be cut very short. We place a temporary low fence around an area about twice the size of the house and let the ducklings out. They are timid at first but soon venture forth, then run back inside when they feel cold. Access to short grass is the best vitamin pill and health insurance for young poultry. And you can tell they love it.

Every few days we move the house and the pen. If the weather is predicted to be unseasonably cold at night, we wheel the house back into shelter. As the ducklings grow and need less heat we progressively uncover the hardware cloth areas. Once the ducks are grown and no longer need the heat lamp we remove it, add the newspaper and wood shavings to the compost heap, and proceed as described above.

French Ducks

Ducks attract our attention whenever we see them, so the large flock of black and white ducks grazing across an incredibly green pasture caught our eyes immediately as we drove south of Agen, just north of the 44th parallel. We had not planned to research ducks on this journey but when the sign at the entrance to the duck farm also advertised their in-house foie gras museum we couldn't resist. The *foie gras* or fat liver of ducks and geese that have been artificially fattened are a quintessential gourmet food and the southwest of France is the center of this particularly French culinary tradition. Although the production of *foie gras* is traditionally associated with raising geese, especially the Toulouse goose, it seems that the duck has come to the forefront for the present. The black and white ducks on the pasture were a hybrid cross between the Barbary and the Pekin or Rouen. Their offspring grow into a particularly large, heavy duck that is ideal for producing *foie gras*.

A charming French farmer showed us around and we asked about the system for fattening the birds. The fattening, or, to be honest, the force-feeding process, known as *le gavage*, is done three times a day for four to five weeks with geese and twice a day for a month with ducks. Goose fattening begins when they are five months old and duck fattening at three months. A funnel is used to literally stuff extra grain down the birds' throats. This over-feeding results in the fatty carcasses and enlarged livers that are the staples of the industry. The farmer assured us this can all be done humanely and we believe he was sincere. Yet like any lovers of fine food who learn the realities of the production techniques (veal lovers should visit a veal farm), we wished the same culinary perfection might be achieved by gentler methods. There are farms in France that provide lodging for students who wish to come for a few days to learn the hows and wherefores of *le gavage*. Thus far, we haven't signed up.

As we toured the very professional displays of the Musée du Foie Gras, read its informative wall plaques, viewed a video of the process from baby duck to finished product, and perused its farm-shop shelves laden with foie gras preserved in duck fat, confit preserved in duck fat, and jars of

Fig. 39

The real-life Schmoo in the garden.

just plain old duck fat, it was impossible not to laugh aloud at human dietary confusion. In an age when it has become politically incorrect to say anything positive about dietary fat, here was the counter-revolution in full swing. Of course, it is not a counter-revolution, it is the way it has always been and we were not the first to be intrigued by what is called *le paradoxe français.* The French paradox goes something like this—if cholesterol is bad, then how come the French, who eat large quantities of fat, continue to have far less heart disease than all the fat-phobic cultures? An article on the wall of the museum added to the paradox. It cited the results of long-term medical statistics which found that the southwest of France, where they eat the most fat, has the least heart disease in all of France in addition to the greatest longevity.

Many attempts have been made to explain away this "paradox." The most popular theory, whether accurate or not, holds that red wine, consumed in large quantities by the French, contains heart-protective factors. In its most up-to-date version, this theory recommends an intake of three to five glasses of red wine daily to provide the greatest benefit. Although I will admit to enjoying red wine, this answer seems a little simplistic. In a similar vein, the Mediterranean Diet Theory gives the place of honor for the heart health of southern European populations to consumption of olive oil. Surely there have been healthy populations of humans where no red wine or olive oil was available. I have no intention of becoming embroiled in this controversy, or of extolling the health benefits of duck fat (which was exactly what the medical research cited in another article on the museum wall proceeded to do), but I have my own theory to explain *le paradoxe française.* It fits right in with the essential message of the four-season garden. The French, like the other Mediterranean peoples, eat a lot of fresh vegetables all year round. The key for maintaining human health is consumption of the fresh vegetables that can easily be grown in anyone's backyard.

French fresh vegetable consumption was amply demonstrated later in the afternoon. We had stopped to purchase some of those delicious French tangerines called Clementines. We like to munch them while we drive. As we stood in line at the counter of the small village store, we couldn't help but notice the ingredients in the baskets of the three shoppers, two beret-wearing older men and a middle-aged woman, who were in line before us. There was *no* junk food, *no* canned goods, *no* frozen foods, *no* TV dinners, *no* soda pop. The baskets all contained fresh local bread, one had a soft cheese, another a hard cheese, and the rest was fresh vegetables. One had leeks (obviously not a winter gardener), two had escarole, and then there was broccoli, sugar-loaf chicory, carrots, chard, and large red beets.

Cast back in your mind and picture the ingredients in the carts of any three typical customers in line before you at the local supermarket. This was not Main Street USA where, whether because of intense advertising, rushed lifestyles, or inadequate familiarity with "real food," consumers have somehow been duped into accepting dead, over-processed, refined, and embalmed foods as their steady diet. The French paradox ceases to be a puzzle when credit is given to the health benefits of a diet rich in fresh vegetables. Researchers seem to miss that obvious connection as they look for more complicated answers. In our rapidly improving French we talked with the man next to us about the exquisite quality of the escarole at this time of year.

I know nothing so pleasant to the mind, as the discovery of anything that is at once new and valuable—nothing so lightens and sweetens toil as the hopeful pursuit of such discovery. And how vast, and how varied a field is agriculture, for such discovery.

—Abraham Lincoln

CHAPTER 8

ENVISIONING THE WINTER GARDEN

A most striking introduction to the winter harvest is provided by making two visits to our protected garden—one at dawn after a cold night, and the other a few hours later. During the dawn visit all the crops are frozen solid. The garden is a spectacle of drooping, frost-coated leaves bleak enough to convince anyone that this idea is foolhardy. Yet a few hours later, after the sun (even the weak sunlight of a cloudy day) has warmed the protected area above freezing, the second visit presents a miraculous contrast. Closely spaced rows of vigorous healthy leaves stretch the length of the growing bed. The leaf colors in different shades of greens, reds, and maroons, stand bright against the dark soil. It looks like a perpetual spring.

Over the course of devising, developing, and improving our winter-harvest garden, we have amassed a collection of technical studies on hardy crops and the effect of freezing temperatures. Copies of research papers fill our file cabinets. Yet none of them offer as much information (or inspiration) as those two visits. In the natural world, hardy crops like spinach and chard inhabit niches where resistance to cold has been a requirement for survival. Winter annual crops, such as mâche and claytonia, have found their space to grow by germinating in fall, growing over winter, and going to seed in spring. Whereas the outdoor winter climate here in Maine is too harsh for even the hardiest of them, the tempered climate in our protected garden offers them conditions within the range in which they have evolved. But, admittedly, it does seem illogical that this can happen during the months when North Americans have traditionally not gardened.

The Winter Garden in France

It is interesting how unaware of winter we were those January days in France. We noticed a different sense of winter almost immediately after inaugurating the trip by dipping our toes in the Atlantic as close to the 44th parallel as our crude calculations and road access could get us. A few miles down the road, we saw our first garden, a large community garden filled with winter vegetables, and stopped to check it out. Standing in such a productive garden, it struck us how much the "look" of the season shapes one's gardening instincts. What a negative effect our winter climate obviously has on the will to garden! Even though there is no difference in sunshine between home and here, the sun at home just plain seems lower and the days shorter with deep snow on the ground and the temperature below freezing.

Despite the community garden's obvious popularity and the large number of plots, it was empty that weekday morning except for a single individual—a short, stocky gentleman in his late sixties, wearing a beret. He had just harvested a bunch of leeks for supper and placed them on the concrete stanchion that protected his irrigation line, and he was busily working the dark soil with a spading fork. His plot, about thirty feet by fifty feet, was exceptionally tidy and well kept. We wandered over to introduce ourselves, praise his efforts, and explain the nature of our quest.

"We're delighted to see a garden full of winter crops," we said, "but surprised that there are no plastic tunnels or cold frames protecting any of them." "You don't need them in a climate as mild as this," he explained. "The only disadvantage of winter," he continued," is that crops take longer to mature because the days are shorter, so the gardener has to plan ahead." He pointed to the healthy rows of peas and fava beans he had planted back in November for a harvest in April. They would mature a month earlier than the ones he was planting now. The ground he had just forked over would soon be growing early potatoes.

The variety of his winter crops was everything we expected, and more—Brussels sprouts, sugar loaf chicory, parsley, radicchio, escarole, lettuce, garlic, cabbage (both Chinese and regular), kale, chard, and leeks. There were even tidy rows of flowers—pansies and some little, low-growing daisies in pastel colors—that were new to us. "Those are *paquerelles,*" he told us. "You'll find white ones growing all over the countryside in winter; this is a garden form of them." Then he showed us an adjoining plot where a neighbor of Portuguese descent was growing *couve tronchuda,* a tender and delicious open-headed Portuguese cabbage which thrives in our cool Maine summer climate and seemed equally at home in winter here. We asked about other hardy winter crops

Fig. 40

Leeks on an irrigation post.

such as mâche and arugula that we didn't see in his garden. He said he didn't grow them because they weren't his "traditional" salads. We told him we were amazed to see so much going on in these gardens, because even in areas of the U.S. with a similar climate, we rarely saw winter vegetable gardens. His simple reply: "That is probably because they have no tradition."

He was right, of course. Gardeners everywhere prefer the crops they know, and he was just as conditioned to the traditional salads of his region as Americans are to theirs. But at least he was growing his. In the U.S., most of the traditional salads are made from summer crops—usually supermarket head lettuce, unripe (green) peppers, and anemic tomatoes—that must be imported from places warm enough to grow them. For some reason, the European winter gardening and eating traditions never carried over to the New World. Perhaps the cold climate in the Northeast, where so many of the first immigrants arrived, convinced them that winter gardens were no longer a possibility. Even after moving to warmer climates they never regained the initiative. Or possibly, since many of the early immigrants arrived from northern European countries where the winter light levels are very low, they didn't recognize the huge growing potential of the longer American days. (Even Thomas Jefferson, always the up-to-date gardener, did not employ cold frames to extend his harvest at Monticello, though the technology would surely have been known to him.) Trying to understand how the winter gardening tradition might have been lost and how it could be regained was a recurring theme in our many conversations with gardeners on the trip.

There were some winter vegetables in every one of the community garden plots. Even in those that looked weedy, because they were not actively maintained at the moment, there was a lot to harvest. We told our guide that his plot showed exceptional care not only because it was neat and well kept, but because it was even more bounteous than the rest. Yes, he admitted proudly, others in the garden called him "the perfectionist." Well, he continued, he was retired and the work was enjoyable, even though it was not necessary to be so meticulous in such a generous climate and with these cool-weather crops. As long as they were planted on time, they would produce well in the winter. "When is the proper time to plant the winter garden?" we asked. The dates he gave us, in August and September, were almost identical to those we use in Maine. Obviously the parallel of latitude has the final say. Our premise was already being confirmed: the sun and not the climate is the principal determining factor for the winter garden. And we are fortunate—we have the sun.

Adapting to Nature

A few days later when the waiter at lunch recommended a local red wine, a Chateau de Rozier, we ordered it at once. By chance we had encountered a connection between our New-World farm in Maine and the Old-World European culture that had discovered it. Jean Rozier, chronicler and cartographer on a voyage with the explorer George Weymouth in 1604, gave his own name to the six-square-mile rocky peninsula where our farm lies near the mouth of the Penobscot River. It remains Cape Rozier to the present day. Could it have been the same family? After lunch we happened upon the vineyard itself. Since it advertised tastings for the public, *degustation*, we drove in for a visit.

The quality of work in the fields was impeccable. All the vines were precisely pruned and well cultivated. But what impressed us most was the soil, or should we say the lack thereof. The vines on either side of the magnificent entrance road to the walled grounds appeared to be mulched heavily with stones. The stones, from golf ball to baseball in size and yellowish-orange in color, were especially striking against the dark brown trunks of the heavily pruned grape vines. When the owner came out to greet us ("Visitors in January! *Quel rare!*") we inquired immediately about the mulch.

"*C'est ne pas du mulch, c'est le sol.*"—"That's no mulch, that's the soil." His amused expression indicated we were not the first to ask the question. "The last glaciation left it here. It covers much of this region of the Costieres." He admitted that it certainly looked daunting and took some getting used to, but the determined farmer was never at a loss for options. It turned out to be the perfect soil for these grapes and also for the pear, apricot, and nut varieties grown by his neighbors. "All those plants like it deep and airy. They have the ability to get their water from way down below. When conditions for certain crops are just right, those are logically the ones to grow."

For every crop there is a soil—and, we would add from our passion, a season. We had been seeking out perfect vegetables for winter conditions. Our perfect crops were those that thrived not only in moist conditions, but also in cool to cold to colder temperatures, and would not mind the shorter daylength of the winter months. The vegetable varieties we had selected were adapted as successfully to the winter cold frames and tunnel greenhouses on Cape Rozier as these grapes were adapted to the gravel-pit soil of Chateau Rozier. It was an apt metaphor because, on first glance, this soil looked no more hospitable to plant survival than our winter weather does. The key to success in any new garden endeavor can be found by exploring Nature's broad genetic resources. Nature has plants for any horticultural challenge.

The Quality of the Winter Harvest

The generous resources of Nature's plant cupboard caught our attention again later that afternoon. We were driving through the Alpiles, a series of low, craggy limestone hills south of Avignon. As we neared a plateau on the scenic, twisting road we spied a solitary figure, bending over and then standing again, as he wandered the open low woodland of the park-like landscape. We pulled over, parked, and headed off in his direction, making our way past luxuriant bushes of wild rosemary and thyme. Just the other side of a little knoll we found our figure—another stocky, elderly gentleman, also wearing a beret, but in this case harvesting wild greens into a plastic bag. We struck up a conversation and asked politely what he was finding. He smiled broadly, obviously delighted and surprised that two foreigners would be interested in such matters.

The plant he was harvesting looked like a small fuzzy-leaved dandelion possessing a very dandelion-like tap root. With a small knife he harvested each plant with a bit of the root attached, "so it won't wilt." We asked the plant name but his Provençal accent made it hard to understand. The best we could distinguish were the words *mur* and *cochon*. A wall and a pig. Pigpen weed, possibly? We gathered one to take with us so we could seek identification help elsewhere. We asked if he had a home garden. "*Bien sur!*" he replied. *Of course!* Were these wild greens as good as what he could grow in his garden? "*Bien sur!*" But they were also different than garden greens and offered a new variety of flavors and textures. He had enjoyed them since childhood.

We too were delighted and surprised, for this was a serendipitous meeting. Even though we had not been actively searching for someone harvesting wild winter foods, the possibility that we might encounter such a person was part of the inspiration for this trip. Edible wild foods, growing outside, are the most natural of winter foods. They are eagerly sought by human consumers, and obviously by wild creatures such as deer and rabbits and some birds that eat greenery. Like the crops in our winter garden, these plants have adapted to the cooler winter temperatures by modifying their systems. According to investigators we have interviewed, these modifications, such as higher levels of soluble proteins and reducing sugars, would appear to make winter greenery even more nutritious and digestible than hot-season plants. But no specific studies have been done. We had also searched the literature on wildlife winter-diet research but had similarly found no studies there that dealt with the nutritional aspects of these temperature-induced modifications. We considered this an important subject because of questions we had been asked.

Whenever one is pioneering new ground, as we are with winter harvesting, there are always plenty of naysayers who claim it can't or shouldn't be done. In our case the naysayers claimed winter foods produced in our winter daylength would be unnatural or imbalanced or not as nourishing as those imported from sunnier southern regions. The principal objection was that any green leaves we harvested would be high in nitrates because, without enough hours of sunlight, the growing plants could not adequately metabolize the nitrogen they absorbed from the soil. Studies of lettuce from Dutch winter greenhouse production had shown that to be a problem. But the daylength in Holland was a good deal shorter than ours since they were growing at latitudes above the 52nd parallel. They were also forcing their crops with artificial heat and high levels of soluble fertilizers. Not so with our crops.

We have made every effort to harmonize our winter garden production with natural processes. A generous annual application of homemade compost is our tried and true soil amendment. We sow the crops out-of-doors. We sow them early enough so they make their growth during the longer days of late summer and fall, yet we sow them late enough, according to each crop's timetable, so they will not have time to mature and then go to seed. We want them at their prime eating condition when the shorter days and cooler temperatures of November tell them to slow their growth.

At that point we protect them with a cover to maintain their quality during the colder weather to come. The protective layer, like putting on a windbreaker, helps bring our Maine climate closer to the naturally milder conditions in a climate like that of southern France. On this trip we had already met home gardeners and commercial growers along the 44th parallel who had no doubts about the quality of their winter produce. But here was the real test. In this wild garden Nature was fully in charge. We had always wanted to talk to a knowledgeable human being who represented the peasant wisdom of centuries of eating from Nature's garden.

Our newfound friend was obviously versed in the time-honored food traditions of this region and knew the wild foods of winter. So we asked the key question. Did he think these greens were less nutritious now than they would be later in the year when there was even more sun? His reply was classic peasant wisdom. "But they are not as edible later in the year. This is what Nature is serving now, so now is the time to eat it." Obviously a charter member of the seasonal-foods appreciation club and a man after our own hearts.

The delight in his voice articulated better than words his love for these seasonal foods. As he closed his bag and prepared to depart he told us these plants would be used that evening to make a *salade verte*, lightly dressed with a vinaigrette. Not just any vinaigrette, but one made with a *"très bon"* olive oil and plenty of garlic. The flavor of this particular salad, he continued, complemented his favorite aperitif, the dialectical name of which we missed entirely. It may have been a local or even a homemade specialty, as are so many of the often aromatic before-dinner drinks so common in France. We said our goodbyes and headed back to the car, plucking bouquets of wild rosemary and thyme to place on the dash. We envied this sweet old gentleman his proximity to all this. How could such a land fail to produce people who loved real food year round? How could we plant the same passion in the U.S.?

As we drove down out of the hills toward Avignon, where we had a reservation for the night, we talked about how traditional wild foods, in the areas where they are available, should be a wonderful winter resource. The Native Americans of Maine may have foraged for winter greens but we can find no mention of the practice in the accounts of the early explorers. But then our native forbs offer little scope for such activity. The wild foods so popular with authors such as Euell Gibbons *(Stalking the Wild Asparagus)* are principally species introduced from Europe. Well, why not encourage those species then? Instead of a trendy wild *flower* meadow, how about establishing a wild *salad* meadow? Cool-season cultivated species such as claytonia, dandelion, mâche, minutina, sylvetta arugula, and sorrel were weeds themselves not too long ago and could easily be wild once again. What a fascinating experiment for those gardeners in the mild winter climates to take a hospitable piece of unused land and see how many of these hardy greens might naturalize.

Then, equipped with nothing more than a knife, a collecting bag, and possibly a beret, they could seek them out in their proper season. Of course, they would want to make sure they had some first-class olive oil handy and a bottle of . . . what *was* the name of that liqueur?

When it's cold outside, I got the month of May.

—"My Girl," R. White and W. Robinson

CHAPTER 9

THE COVERED GARDEN: COLD FRAMES

It is the middle of winter on the coast of Maine, and we are harvesting crops for dinner. We can choose from some twenty vegetables, garden-fresh in our cold frames. We may harvest a salad of mâche, endive hearts, and claytonia. (See appendix A for specific information on these and other hardy crops.) We could serve the salad with a mustard vinaigrette and raw carrot and celeriac slices on the side. In addition, how about some spinach for a duck-egg soufflé, some leeks to prepare sautéed with butter, and some parsley to garnish the potatoes from the cellar? Planning ahead, we might decide to have sorrel soup, au gratin Swiss chard, or a tatsoi and scallion stir fry the following night. Not bad for fresh garden harvesting in Zone 5.

Noticing a few empty spaces where crops were harvested earlier in the winter, I shift from chef to gardener and make the first early-spring plantings of radishes, arugula, mizuna, spinach, and two or three varieties of lettuce. Germination will be slow, but they will be off and growing in a month or so as winter retreats. Nearby is a bed of September-sown lettuce plants that will be ready to eat by early March. Outdoor beds of parsnips should be ready to dig later that month. You will notice that none of the crops mentioned are the typical heat-lovers of the summer garden. And therein lies the secret.

The popular crops of summer—beans, corn, cucumbers, eggplant, peppers, and tomatoes—are "chilling sensitive," which is to say they do not appreciate temperatures below 50°F. When temperatures go below freezing, they are killed. They are not candidates for the winter harvest unless protected by highly technological systems. But we have no interest in messing with foam insulation or space-age phase-change materials because that is not our style. This book won't discuss heat pumps, thermal mass, solar gain, or R factors because they are too complicated. They make the simple joys of food production seem more industrial than poetic. Given the option, we choose poetry. We take our design clues from the natural world, where simple systems with biological diversity are the most successful and enduring. We have a prejudice that simpler is better, especially where simpler has been time-tested.

For our kind of winter harvest, we obviously need to focus on "chilling-resistant" vegetables. "Which ones are they?" many gardeners will ask at this point, and understandably so. According to a National Gardening Association list of vegetables ranked in order of popularity in home gardens, the warm-weather crops dominate the top ten. Only one of our crops, carrots, is ranked in that select group, at number seven. Two other winter garden successes, spinach and chard, finish twenty-fourth and thirty-second respectively and that is it. The remainder of our crops don't make the cut before the list of forty vegetables ends.

Because of that, the seeds for a winter harvest are probably not available on every garden center seed rack. In the rare cases where they are on the rack, the rack has often been stored away come August or September, the months when planting of the winter garden begins. Probably more important than seed scarcity is culinary unfamiliarity. Everyone's favorite foods are their "traditional" foods. "Don't know them, don't grow them" is a familiar garden attitude. And, because the arrival of cool temperatures in fall has always denoted the end of the warm-season crops, end-of-summer has come to be synonymous with end-of-garden. That concept is so deeply ingrained that most American gardeners have never realized how the chilling-resistant crops, with very little work and great reward, can be next on the garden agenda. Although we occasionally see a few leeks or Brussels sprouts or kale plants hovering forgotten in American vegetable gardens as the days shorten, we rarely see the bounty we know is possible; the bounty American gardeners will find irresistible once they give it a try.

Most of the chilling-resistant crops (some of which, like arugula, have become yuppie food in fancy American restaurants) are traditional winter peasant food in Europe. However, in much of the continental United States our normal weather is harsher and more changeable than the cold but more evenly tempered regions where the cool-season plants originated. Thus, we need to moderate the winter climate to be able to harvest even the hardiest of winter foods. But we don't need to provide warmth. In fact, too-warm temperatures can be detrimental. All that's necessary is to take the edge off the harshness of sudden change. There is an old saying in New England that if you don't like the weather, just wait five minutes. Very often a rainy day with a temperature of 55°F during a midwinter thaw will change to a clear, cold night with strong winds and a -5°F thermometer reading. Such extremes are true for much of the country.

Hardy plants don't mind cold, but they are affected by those alternating freeze/thaw, wet/dry, and gale/calm conditions. Such extremes are as stressful to plants as they are to humans. The aim of crop protection in the winter garden is to lessen those climatic extremes and consequently to lessen plant stress. The first step toward lessening plant stress is to cover the plants. The simplest cover is a cold frame.

The Magic Box

Gardeners should dedicate a monument to the cold frame. It is the simplest, most flexible, and most successful low-tech tool for modifying the garden climate. It's simple because it is basically a box with a glass top and no bottom that sits on the soil. It's flexible because it can be made as long, as wide, or as tall as the gardener wishes. And it's successful because it is a tried-and-true garden aid that has been used in one form or another since ancient times (sheets of mica predated glass). The cold frame was the foundation for the early development of intensive commercial horticulture.

My first experience with cold frames occurred when I was a child, long before I began growing plants. A gardening neighbor had a small cold frame in which she grew hardy flowers for early and late blooms. I can remember going over to her yard every so often to see the "magic box." The drab tones of fall and winter prevailed in the outdoor world, but inside the frame, a riot of

bright colors and green leaves existed. It was like looking into a warm, friendly house on a cold, snowy night. I never knew what flowers she grew in there—possibly calendulas and chrysanthemums, strawflowers and anemones—but their beauty stuck in my memory. I experience that same fascination today when I look into the green and growing world of our vegetable cold frames. The magic is created with a single sheet of glass and the careful selection of hardy cultivars.

Comparative investigations of different cold frame designs back in the 1970s showed that the standard old-time model—a bottomless box made of 2-inch-thick planks, 12 inches high at the back and 8 inches high at the front, and covered with glass frames—was still the best. Our cold frames look just like that and would be familiar to a gardener of one hundred years ago.

Since growing in cold frames is nothing new, it's interesting to ponder, as we did so often on our trip to France, why the idea of a winter garden has never caught on in the U.S. For those gardeners without a "tradition" of winter gardening, it may be that the timing involved takes some getting used to. You can't wait till winter to plant the winter garden. Most of the crops must be planted in late summer and early fall. That's because the rate of plant growth diminishes with the shortening days of fall until it almost stops around November 15. If you don't plant till then, it's too late. By then the plants need to be grown to the size for harvesting. They will hibernate successfully in the shelter of the cold frame. A friend has described this process as storing them in a large translucent refrigerator crisper drawer. The vigorous growth that took place in the fall, plus some slow winter regrowth, provides plenty of food to harvest until February, when the days have lengthened enough for serious new growth to begin again.

Occasionally, gardeners have told us that by fall they are just tired of gardening and glad for a break. But that is the best part. You can have your break and eat it too. There is little gardening—soil preparation, sowing, cultivation, etcetera—taking place after late summer and early fall. Furthermore, the weeds aren't growing and the pests aren't pestering in the winter garden. Just some watering of the frames until November and then no more of that until spring. It is necessary to vent the frames to prevent overheating in fall and spring, but ingenious, temperature-activated ventilating arms can be installed to look after that for you. We aren't gardening in the winter, just harvesting, which in the final analysis is the aim of all this activity anyway.

Back when I started with winter gardening, I soon realized that success lay not in technology, but in biology—in the selection of the crops. Surprisingly, the successful crops, many of which may seem exotic to gardeners today, would also have been familiar to gardeners of one hundred years ago, since Fearing Burr's 1863 classic, *Field and Garden Vegetables of America,* describes all of them and gives cultural directions. I didn't know which of the cool-season crops would work best at first so I began by experimenting. Nothing scientific. I just planted selected crops and observed how long they could be harvested. The results were judged at the dinner table.

Spinach was a first choice. Gardeners often sow spinach in September and protect the young plants over winter with a mulch of straw or evergreen boughs. When uncovered in spring the result is an extra early crop. What would spinach do if covered with a cold frame? It would yield all winter, that's what. I also tried scallions. I remembered once chopping scallions out of the frozen ground in a sheltered spot in the garden and being surprised that they looked as good as new when they thawed. They were even better from the cold frame. I had always done a last planting of carrots on August 1 and enjoyed a delicious late harvest of tender baby carrots. Why not cover them with a cold frame? Another success. With a layer of straw as insulation inside the frame they could be pulled fresh all winter. Best yet, the cold soil storage turned some of their starch to sugar. They became known as "candy carrots." Swiss chard was another success. Many times Swiss chard will revive in the garden during a January thaw only to succumb to the rest of the winter. When I covered the hardy cultivar 'Argentata' with a cold frame, it was still going strong in spring.

Full-size lettuce was a failure. After too many freeze-thaw cycles in the late fall, heads of lettuce turned to mush. Young lettuces, however, which are much hardier, can be successfully wintered over for a spring harvest. But we needed a midwinter salad staple. The answer was mâche, also known as corn salad or nusslisalat. This traditional European midwinter crop is not only far hardier than lettuce, but it is also the only salad green we found that could be harvested while frozen solid and still look beautiful after it thawed. The others, even good old hardy spinach, needed to be harvested when they were unfrozen. But that was really no problem because the protected area of the cold frame will rise to a temperature above 32°F on most average winter days, even if the sky is cloudy.

Following on the heels of the mâche discovery we looked to Europe for more winter salad ingredients. Frisée endive proved quite hardy, as did radicchio. Other favorites were cultivated weeds. *Montia perfoliata,* known in the U.S. as "claytonia," started life as "miner's lettuce," a California weed which was eagerly consumed in gold rush days. The Europeans took it across the ocean and domesticated it to what they call "winter

Fig. 41

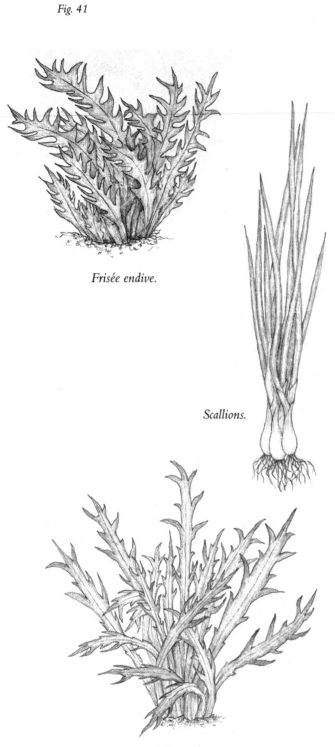

Frisée endive.

Scallions.

Buck's-horn plantain.

purslane." *Plantago coronopus,* a relative of the plantain weeds in your lawn, is popular in Italy as "minutina" and occasionally known in the U.S. as "buckshorn plantain" (so-called because of the multi-branched shape of its leaves). And in the arugula family we found *Diplotaxis tenuifolia,* a wild arugula known as 'Sylvetta', which can be planted thickly to yield abundant quantities of delicious, tender, dark green, indented leaves which survive the coldest winter.

Not all of our attempts were successful but the eventual list is surprisingly extensive. In addition to those mentioned above we found that dandelion, escarole, leeks, mizuna, mustard greens, parsley, sorrel, tatsoi, and turnip greens also met the chilling-resistant criterion and contributed to the fresh larder for all or part of the winter when protected by a cold frame.

Over the course of the winter the amount of variety available from the winter harvest depends on where you live and the severity of the weather. Southern gardeners in Zones 9 and 10 where the winter climate is mild will need nothing more than a list of winter crops, a source for the seeds, cultural directions, and suggested planting dates. Once they become familiar with the hardy winter crops and the ease of winter gardening, they'll be hooked. Gardeners in Zones 7 and 8 may need nothing more than a low tunnel over their winter garden (discussed later in this chapter). They will be amazed how effectively just that thin layer moves the protected crops one and a half zones to the south, thus ensuring a safe winter harvest. Gardeners in Zones 5 and 6 will want to protect their crops from the colder blasts of winter with the more substantial snow-supporting cover of a cold frame. And the hardy souls in Zones 3 and 4 will be amazed that they can harvest anything at all. In the frigid mountains of Vermont (Zone 3) only five crops—spinach, scallions, mâche, claytonia, and carrots—will be dependably harvestable all winter from a cold frame, and only mâche during the coldest periods. However, the rest of the crops take only a two-month hiatus and will be yielding again soon enough as spring returns. Any crops that don't bounce back can be removed and the area replanted, as you will want to do with empty spaces all along.

How the Cold Frame Works

The cold frame lessens climatic stress in a number of ways:

Temperature. A single layer of glass creates a microclimate in which the nighttime temperature inside the frame can be as much as 20°F warmer than the temperature outside, although the average difference is 7° to 10°F. The daytime temperature inside the frame, even on a cloudy, early spring day, will be 10° to 15°F warmer than outdoors. On a sunny spring day, the temperature can rise high enough to cook the soil and the plants if you don't vent off the extra heat. Both daytime and nighttime temperature differences depend on the time of year, the angle and intensity of the sun, the rate of outdoor temperature change, and the initial temperature in the frame.

Moisture. Much of the havoc that freezing can wreak on winter vegetables is a function of how wet the plants are. High humidity helps protect plants from cold but plants sitting in a puddled soil just soaked by a rain before freezing will be more stressed than one that is drier. The glass roof of the cold frame protects the crops inside from pounding winter rains.

Wind. The wind can make a cool day feel very cold. Weather forecasters always mention the windchill factor. The same conditions affect plants. Wind cools by removing ambient heat and evaporating moisture. The stress of winter wind alone can mean the difference between life and death for hardy vegetables. Even the slightest windbreak will help. That was proven by two beds of spinach planted a few Septembers ago to winter over outdoors. One was covered lightly with a mulch of pine boughs and the other left uncovered. Even though you could look through the thin layer of pine boughs and clearly see the spinach, that minimal amount of wind protection was significant. Ninety percent of the protected spinach survived the winter, compared to ten percent of the unprotected crop.

Building the Cold Frame

As previously mentioned, a cold frame is a bottomless box that sits on the soil and has a glass cover. Thus, there are two parts—the sides (the box) and the top (the glass). The sides can be made of almost any material—boards, concrete blocks, bales of hay, logs, and so on, all of which have their virtues. From our experience, we suggest making the sides out of boards. This will give you a frame that is long-lasting, easy to construct, easy to use, reasonably light, and movable.

The top covering is called a *light*. In the old days, lights were 4 to 6 feet square and made of overlapping panes of glass. They were heavy and required two people to carry them. Today's home gardeners often use old storm windows as lights. Storm windows are easy to find and the size is right for covering cold frames. Modern lights can be glazed with translucent materials other than glass, such as plastic, polycarbonate, or fiberglass. Depending on its size, a cold frame is covered with one or more lights.

A cold frame can be any width that the lights

will cover and any length or height. Traditional home garden cold frames measure 4 to 6 feet front to back and are 8 to 12 feet long. They are laid out with the long dimension running east to west. The frame should be just tall enough to clear the crops you plan to grow. In the standard design, the back wall is 12 inches high and the front wall 8 inches high, so that there is a slight slope to the south.

Some experimenters have built frames with the lights at a 45° angle facing south to maximize midwinter sun input. Such frames don't work as well as the traditional low-angle models for two reasons. First, you don't need maximum heat in midwinter for hardy crops. All they require is the protection of the frame. Second, there seems to be some benefit to having the glass roof near the plants as if it were a covering of snow. The environment inside the traditional low-angle frames better meets the needs of hardy crops.

The Cold Frame Box

Any cold frame design that protects plants will serve you well. To be enjoyable to use, however, the design must be simple, attractive, pleasant to work with, and dependable. Having tried them all, we settled on the traditional design. The simplest cold frame is a rectangular wooden box, 8 feet long and 4 feet front to back, with a slight slope to the south. We build them out of 2-inch lumber to make them strong, but 1-inch stock would be adequate. Three 8-foot boards are necessary: two boards 12 inches wide and one board 8 inches wide. One of the 12-inch-wide boards is used for the back wall. The 8-inch-wide board is used for the front wall. The second 12-inch board is cut into two 4-foot pieces, which are each cut diagonally lengthwise so that they are 8 inches wide at one end and 12 inches wide at the other.

It is easiest to put the frame together with the boards sitting on a flat surface and the diagonal cut edge of the side walls facing up. When you do this, you will notice that the bottom edge of the frame is flat, whereas the upper edge has a slight discontinuity where the diagonal cut meets the front and back walls. In order for the lights to sit on the flattest surface, you should turn the frame over before using it. Any discontinuity of the other edge is then hidden by contact with the soil. The frame will slant slightly to the south, allowing more light to enter.

Attach a 4-foot-long 2x2 to what is now the top. This piece extends across the middle of the frame, running front to back. You will want to cut notches in the top of the front and back walls so this cross piece sits flush with the top. (See drawing.) This helps keep the sides spaced and also provides a handle that one person can use to lift the empty frame and carry it to a new location. If you use 1-inch wood, you might want to place more of these stiffeners across the frame.

We use standard pine or spruce for our frames. We purposely do not use treated wood, nor do we treat the frames with a preservative. Even the supposedly safe products should not be used in close proximity to food crops. Wood rots where it is in contact with the earth, however, so we attach a strip of scrap wood about 1 inch thick to the bottom edge of the frame where it touches the soil. In a few years, when this strip begins to rot, we replace it with another. The rest of the untreated wood frame will last for many years.

We also do not paint the frame. Yes, if the interior were white, it might reflect a little more light than the gray weathered wood, but paint is just one more complication. Rather than having to scrape and paint every few years, it's best to keep things simple.

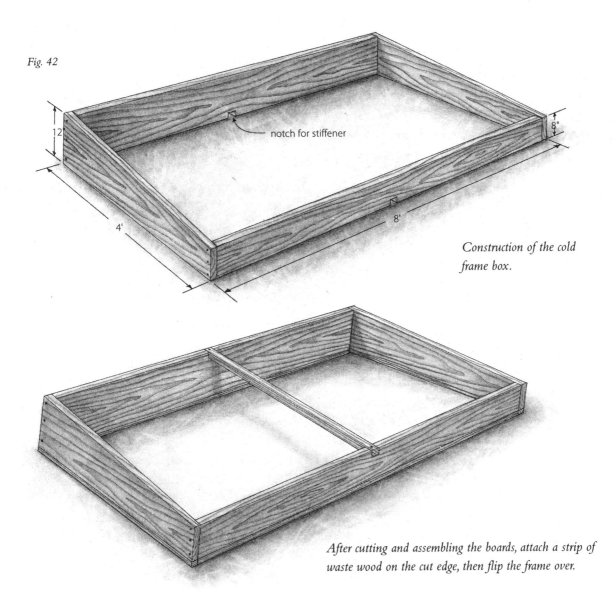

Fig. 42

notch for stiffener

12

8"

4'

8'

Construction of the cold frame box.

After cutting and assembling the boards, attach a strip of waste wood on the cut edge, then flip the frame over.

The Cold Frame Light

The light sits on top of the frame just like a lid on a pan. If it is glazed with plastic or another light-weight material, you will want to use clips or hooks and eyes to hold it on when the wind blows. The advantage of lights glazed with glass is that they are heavy enough not to be blown off under most conditions. If your garden is in a par-ticularly windy spot, you may still want to take precautions. The simplest method is to fasten a raised border around the outside of the frame so that the wind can't catch under the edge of the light.

If instead of using old storm windows you wish to build your own lights, the best design is one used for many years in Holland. Glass cold frames were a traditional feature of Dutch commercial horticulture. Recently, they have died out in favor of huge greenhouses, but a few old-time market gardens probably still use the traditional technology. The feature that makes them worth copying is the simplicity of the Dutch lights. They were made specifically for horticulture and avoid the problems that arise with storm windows.

Storm windows are meant to be used in a vertical position. When used horizontally, as on a cold frame, the wooden crossbars that hold the panes inhibit the flow of water off the frame. The trapped water can weaken and rot the crossbars and loosen the putty that holds the glass in place. As the putty deteriorates, the lights may drip water on the crops below.

The Dutch lights are designed for horticultural use. They consist of a simple wooden rim, approximately 2½ by 5 feet, with slots on the inside edges into which a single pane of glass is inserted. A small wooden stop at each end prevents the glass from sliding out. With the exception of the small stops, there are no crosspieces above the glass surface and thus nothing to inhibit the free flow of water. No putty is used, since the glass is held by the slots in the frame. Simple systems are always the most fascinating and satisfying. The Dutch design for lights is a classic example.

Hemlock was the wood traditionally used for framing the lights. We make our light frames out of Maine white cedar. Any good western cedar, southern yellow pine, or spruce also should be suitable. The lights are not in contact with the earth and, if carefully stored when not in use, they will last a long time.

Although the traditional Dutch lights are 5 feet by 2½ feet, they are a little too heavy for many people to handle without practice. Therefore, we suggest that most home gardeners make them smaller, say 2 by 4 feet. Our cold frames are separate from our 30-inch-wide garden beds, so

their size is not contingent on garden layout. If, however, they were planned to cover the 30-inch-wide beds, then both frames and lights would be made to fit those dimensions. Conversely, if you already have some 36-inch-wide storm windows and wish to use them in the garden, you could make your garden beds 36 inches wide.

To construct Dutch lights, you will need four pieces of wood to make the rim that holds the glass. Let's say you wish to make the lights 2 by 4 feet. The two sides (each 4 feet long) are made from 2x2 stock (actual dimensions 1½ by 1½). A slot ¾ inch deep, cut with a table saw (called a kerf) runs the length of each piece. Make that cut 1 inch above what will be the bottom edge of these side rails. The two ends of the wooden rim are cut from a 2x2 to an actual dimension of 1 by 1½. They are 21 inches long. They hold the rails apart and support the glass at either end. Attach them at the corners with 4-inch galvanized drywall screws. The finished wooden rim of the light has outside dimensions of 2 by 4 feet.

The glass for that light is a single pane measuring 46½ by 22¾ inches. It slides into the kerfs in the side rails and rests on top of the end pieces. (You need to determine beforehand whether the kerf made by the saw blade is wide enough to accommodate the edge of the glass. If not, run the side piece through the saw again at a slightly different setting to widen it.) The glass quality should be *double strength*. Even better if it's tempered. Tempered glass is more expensive but is ten times more resistant to breakage. Attach a small piece of wood measuring ¾ by ½ by 3 inches in the middle of each end piece as a stop to hold the glass in place.

If glass breakage is a major concern for you or tempered glass seems too expensive, you could use one of the rigid greenhouse covering materials such as Lexan or Polygal. You can purchase these double-layer glass substitutes from greenhouse suppliers and cut them to size with a saw. The two layers are held apart by internal ribs. From an end view, they look like many square tubes glued side by side. If you use these materials for Dutch lights, you will need to cut a wider kerf into the side pieces, as these materials are thicker than double-strength glass.

Almost any of these options, and others yet to be conceived, will work. If you can find good storm windows, use them. If you can't and are fascinated with simple design, you can build lights according to the Dutch model. Or you can purchase one of the many cold frames sold by garden catalogs. If you are more ingenious still, you will come up with an even better and simpler design and pioneer the next step in cold frame development. The evolution of this classic horticultural technology has resulted from the ideas of gardeners in the past and will continue through the inspiration of gardeners in the future.

Other Options

One of those evolutions took place when plastic first became available in the late 1940s. Numerous growers, looking for a less expensive alternative to cold frames, began using lengths of plastic sheet supported by wire arches to make small plastic covered tunnels. These are popularly called *low tunnels,* usually only one and a half to two feet tall. To make the wire arches insert the ends of a 6½-foot length of number 9 wire into the ground on either side of a 30- to 36-inch-wide bed. These wire arches are placed every four feet. In the typical models, the plastic sheet is held down over the arches by burying its edges with soil along either side and also at the ends. That gives you a solid, wind-stable structure, but two problems inhibit its use for the winter harvest.

First, access to the protected area requires the buried edge to be unburied, a difficult and awkward process to go through every time you want

Fig. 43

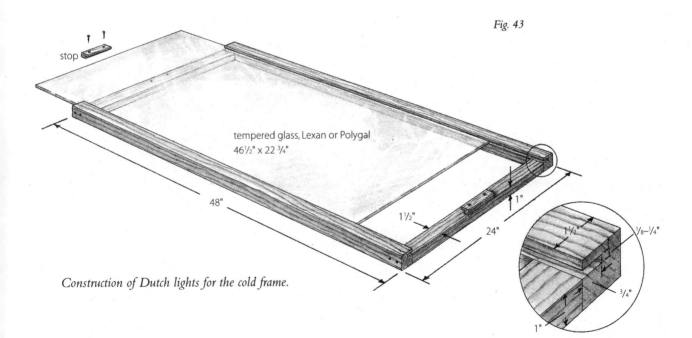

stop

tempered glass, Lexan or Polygal
46½" x 22 ¾"

48"

1½"

24"

1"

1½"

⅛–¼"

¾"

1"

Construction of Dutch lights for the cold frame.

to harvest and impossible once the soil freezes. Second, there is no easy way to vent off extra heat. When using these low tunnels to protect spring crops, gardeners solve the venting problem by cutting ever larger holes into the plastic cover (to vent off more and more excess heat) as the spring advances. That works adequately although the frost-protection potential is progressively lessened if a late spring frost comes along. It would obviously not be a suitable technique for over-wintering where some venting is needed in the fall but none in the winter.

The new agricultural fabrics for season extension, known as *floating row covers,* solve the venting problem by being porous to air and, thus, are reasonably self-venting. They also allow early season gardeners to dispense with the wire arches because these fabrics are light enough to be laid directly over the soil and be lifted by the growing crops. Although they could be laid over arches to provide self-venting winter protection, they are no more accessible than the plastic-covered low tunnels because they are still secured by burying their edges with soil.

While visiting a French organic farm in the valley of the Lot River we saw a low tunnel design ideal for a winter garden. The farm specialized in growing winter salads under plastic tunnel greenhouses. As we would note often on the trip, the commercial scale of an operation rarely hindered our learning worthwhile information for the home garden. Most of the good ideas seem to be scale-neutral (they apply to large scale as well as small scale) and that was certainly the case here.

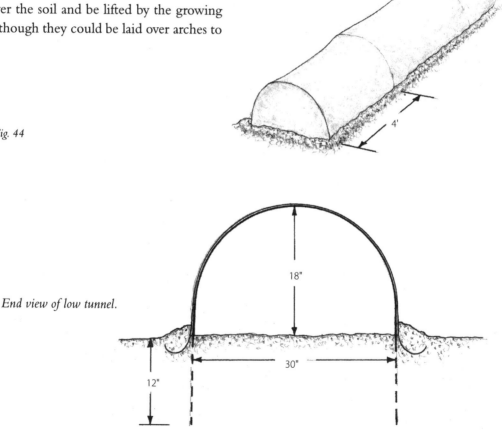

Fig. 44

4'

End view of low tunnel.

18"

30"

12"

In addition to the large plastic tunnel greenhouses, crops were growing under numerous low tunnels (36 inches wide by 18 inches tall). Low tunnels are called *chenilles* (caterpillars) in French. Fields of them look like large chenille bedspreads.

The French chenille design made venting possible by securing the plastic differently. Instead of a sheet of plastic wide enough so its edges could be buried, the sheet was the exact width to fit ground-to-ground over the top of the wire arches. In addition, the plastic was tensioned lengthwise, by being tied to a stake at either end and pulled tight. The plastic was further secured against the wind by a length of garden twine running diagonally back and forth over the top to hold it down onto the arches.

The twine was secured by a novel twist in the arch design. When constructing a low tunnel the ends of the wire arches are pushed about a foot into the ground. Most gardeners do this by eye. However, on these arches that 1-foot distance was marked by a 1-inch-diameter loop where the wire had been twisted once around in a circle. The twine was attached through these small loops at soil level. The process was started by tying the twine to one loop of the first arch and then crossing it diagonally over the plastic to the opposite loop on the second arch, and then back diagonally to the third and so forth. With the plastic pulled tight at either end, the arches provided upward support for the plastic, and the twine tensioning held the plastic down. It was then possible for the gardener to vent these chenilles by sliding up the bottom edge of the plastic along one (or both) sides. The friction between the arch and the twine held the plastic up at whatever venting height the gardener chose. At night the plastic pulled snugly down to the soil level again.

We asked about wind security and were told that this design was not quite as windproof as the buried-edge models, but as long as the plastic was stretched tightly when tied off to the stakes at either end, the structure would be secure. We noted the east-west orientation of the tunnels in this area with a prevailing north wind. Since they were vented only on the south side, the growers had designed the layout appropriately to assure their wind survival. The only improvement might be to erect them on the protected side of a winter windbreak.

In addition to simple venting, the advantage of this design for winter gardening is the ease of harvest. Since low tunnels with the plastic cover anchored by burying it in the soil don't easily allow for daily access, we have never considered them suitable for winter gardening. But with this French caterpillar design the edges lift quickly and lift high enough for the gardener to pull, cut, or pluck the daily harvest and/or to clean up the seed bed, spread more compost, and plant seeds for the next crop in succession. This offers a whole new option in simple winter protection for gardeners from Zone 7 southward. Further north this design would be risky for overwinter use since any wire-framed structure would not hold up long where heavy snow was a constant threat.

A final note is worth mentioning on old versus new techniques. The old-time French winter gardening protective structure on most commercial market gardens used to be the cold frame. The lights were larger and of a different design than the Dutch lights described earlier, but the management was identical. In the extensive market garden area around Nantes, about halfway up the French west coast, where many acres of winter vegetables were once protected by cold frames, the classic glass covers are still in evidence today, but they are no longer in use. Extensive stacks of them, once carefully maintained, have now been

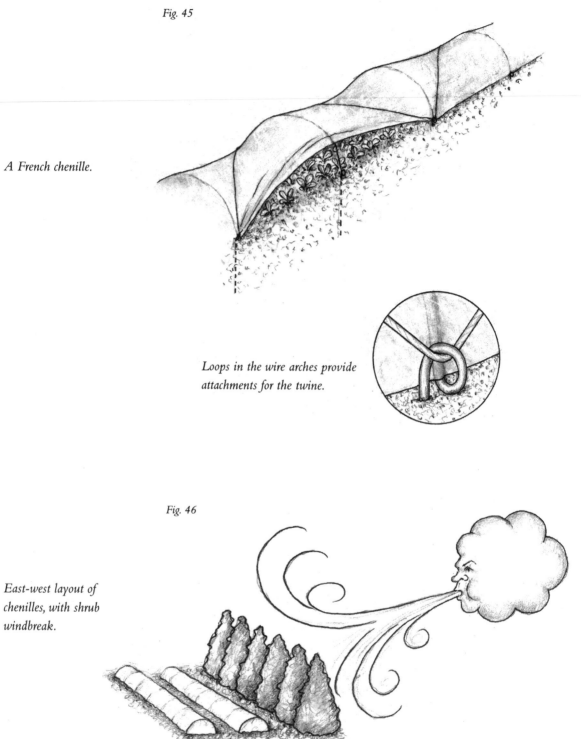

Fig. 45

A French chenille.

Loops in the wire arches provide attachments for the twine.

Fig. 46

East-west layout of chenilles, with shrub windbreak.

90

abandoned to progress. They sit where they were put after their last use, the narrow wooden structural timbers that framed the multiple glass panes rotting slowly in the moist air. Their modern replacements, acres and acres of plastic-covered chenilles, look far more depressingly industrial than the same acreage of glass cold frames could ever have looked. The glass versus plastic controversy for winter gardening is a subject that comes up often. I will discuss the pros and cons in appendix B.

Managing the Cold Frame

Successful cold frame or low tunnel management hinges on two practices: *temperature control* and *watering*. The amount of either that you have to do depends on the time of year.

Temperature control involves venting excess heat. That can be done for you automatically during the winter months by equipping each cold frame with a temperature-activated opening arm (see appendix D). The small amount of winter overheating can easily be vented by using one arm per frame, meaning that only one light opens. These mechanical helpers use a heat-activated pressure cylinder that expands with enough force to lift up to twenty pounds. If you want to use them, you will need to glaze your lights with one of the glass substitutes mentioned earlier. Lights glazed with glass are usually too heavy for the force that the cylinder can exert.

During the spring and fall, when the sun is higher in the sky, more venting will be necessary. Unless you want to purchase an automatic arm for each light on the frame, you will have to do a little hand work at those times of year. We use notched props to hold the lights open. We prop up the sides of the lights rather than the ends, and angle the lights away from the prevailing winds.

This gives the frame a sawtooth pattern and allows more even venting front to back. Early in the spring or late in the fall, you may need only one light open on the lowest notch on the prop. For just a tiny bit of ventilation, you can slightly open the top edge of just one light per frame. Opening more lights or setting the prop at a higher notch increases the venting.

Keep a thermometer in the frame or low tunnel to give you some idea of the temperature. For the most accurate temperature readings, place the thermometer in a small, white, slatted box that sits on the soil in the center of the frame. In this protected enclosure, the thermometer will come closer to measuring ambient air temperature rather than the direct effect of the sun's rays.

On sunny days, venting is an open-and-shut job. On rainy days, it is not necessary. On cloudy days, be sure to check the thermometer, as a lot of the sun's rays can come through clouds. We go out in the morning after the sun has risen sufficiently. Depending on the weather and past experience, we prop the lights open as much as we think will be necessary. We aim for a 70°F temperature inside the frame in spring and 60° to 65°F in fall. We return in late afternoon, when the sun is no longer a major source of heat, and close

Fig. 47

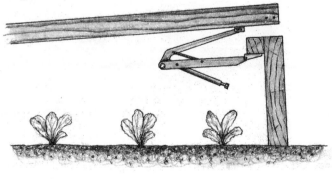

Automatic venting arm.

them again. If we're home and the weather changes dramatically during the day, we take whatever action is appropriate. When we're gone all day, whether sunny or cloudy, we vent more than necessary in case the sun gets stronger.

The amount of venting depends on the season. In winter, you hardly have to vent at all; in fall, you vent progressively less; in spring, you vent progressively more. On average for Zone 5 and north, the line between the fall and winter cold frame seasons is around November 1. The line between the winter and spring seasons falls around February 15. In Zones 6 and 7, the dates will be later in the fall and earlier in the spring. In the real icebox sections of the country, the winter period can begin as early as October 15 and last until March 1. In the coldest parts of New England the frames may hardly need venting for four months, two months on either side of the winter solstice. Whenever you open the frames to harvest during the winter, the plants get all the air exchange they need.

The seasonal transition takes place over a remarkably short time span for much of the country, since the determining factor is the effect of the sun rather than the temperature of the air. As the days shorten, the sun's path is lower in the sky and there is less solar radiation to heat up the frames. Once the sun's path is low enough, there is a period of about three months (six weeks before the winter solstice and six weeks after it) when the gardener's only work is harvesting the bounty. The farther north you go, the longer this period becomes.

We call this season the Persephone months. In Greek mythology, the nongrowing season (the low-sun months of winter) was explained by the myth of Persephone. Persephone, daughter of the

Fig. 48

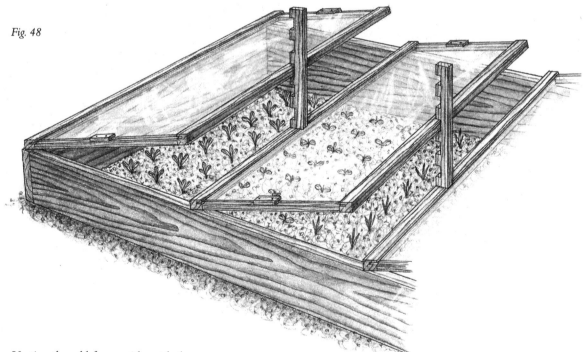

Venting the cold frame with notched props.

earth goddess Demeter, was loved by Hades, who abducted her to the netherworld. Demeter, with the help of Zeus, managed to get her back, but in the bargain, Persephone had to spend a third of the year with Hades. During those months, Demeter went into mourning and nothing grew. The Persephone months are when the cold frame crops reign supreme.

The cold season begins with the first warning of frost in the coldest areas and with the advent of cool nights farther south. At this point, the lights, which have been stored away all summer, are put back on the frames. The frames need to be well vented during the day (use the upper notches on the props) and closed only on nights that threaten a frost. As the season advances and temperatures decline, you will be venting less and closing the frames up slightly earlier in the day. Be conscious of Indian summer, which brings warmer temperatures, and vent accordingly.

The ideal is to keep the crops growing steadily in this protected environment but not to overheat them. With cold frames, it is always better to err on the cool side and vent the frames excessively rather than run them too warm. Very cold conditions are inevitable as winter arrives, and the soft, succulent tissues of plants that have been grown at too high temperatures will not be as hardy. A 65°F daytime temperature in the frame is a good target to aim for early in the fall. Reduce your goal to 60°F later on.

Once winter arrives the system is basically dormant. Your winter food is not dependent on sunny weather for warmth because it is already grown. You don't want to create summer conditions, although it is no problem on bright sunny winter days if the frame temperature goes into the 70s. Cloudy days with frame temperatures in the 30s and 40s are ideal. The cold nights are no problem, since these winter food plants don't

mind freezing. As long as the temperature in the frame is above freezing before you harvest, all will be well.

Winter Cold Frame Crops

As the fall advances, the crops in the frames change. First are the crops for fall consumption. These were planted during the summer and covered with lights once the cool weather began. You will be harvesting many of the same crops from the outdoor garden until they are ready in the frames. Table 5 gives approximate planting dates for Zone 5. Consult Table 16, Planting Dates for an Extended Harvest, to adjust these dates for your area. For further information on specific vegetables, consult the individual vegetable sections in appendix A.

Second, the frames contain crops for winter and early spring consumption. The later plantings of mâche fill in the spaces left by harvested fall crops. Mâche also can be sown under and between the fall crops and will grow in their shadow until they are harvested. Mâche may be the hardiest crop of all. It isn't planted until fall because it germinates best in cool weather. Mâche is the most cold-hardy winter staple for fresh green salads.

Third, the cold frames contain overwintered crops for spring eating. The spinach sowings and the lettuce transplants fill in sections of the frames vacated by crops harvested in the fall.

How much of each crop you grow depends on what you like to eat. These crops can be planted in short rows, so a single frame could feasibly grow all of them. How much total frame space you need depends on how much fresh green food you plan to eat. On average, two cold frames (of the 4-by-8-foot size) for each family member should provide fresh food all winter. The

TABLE 5

Cold Frame Crops
for Fall and Winter Consumption

Crop	Planting Dates	Harvest Dates
Arugula	8/1–8/21	10/1–spring
Endive	7/10–7/20	9/15–11/30
Escarole	7/10–7/20	9/15–11/30
Italian dandelion	8/1–8/15	10/1–spring
Lettuce	7/21–9/7	9/15–11/30
Mizuna	8/1–8/15	9/15–11/30
Parsley	6/1–7/15	10/1–spring
Radish	9/1–10/15	10/1–11/30
Scallion	7/1–7/15	10/1–spring
Spinach	8/1–8/30	10/15–11/30
Swiss chard	7/1–8/1	10/1–spring
Tatsoi	8/1–8/15	9/15–11/30

TABLE 6

Cold Frame Crops for
Winter and Spring Consumption

Crop	Planting Dates	Harvest Dates
Carrot	8/1	12/1–spring
Claytonia	8/1–9/1	11/1–spring
Italian dandelion	8/1–8/15	10/1–spring
Kohlrabi	8/1–8/15	11/1–spring
Mâche	9/15–11/15	12/1–spring
Parsley	6/1–7/15	10/1–spring
Radicchio	6/1–8/1	12/1–spring
Scallion	7/15–8/1	11/1–spring
Sorrel (perennial) transplant	9/1	11/1–spring
Spinach	9/15–10/15	12/1–spring
Sugarloaf chicory	7/1–7/15	11/1–spring

consumption of those crops that don't regrow will open up space for succession plantings of mâche, spinach, arugula, and mizuna.

Most of the crops for winter eating don't do any real growing in the frames during the low sun of midwinter. They grow during the summer and fall, then mark time waiting for spring. That's fine, because the gar-

TABLE 7

OVERWINTERED COLD FRAME CROPS

Crop	Planting Dates	Harvest Dates
Dandelion	7/1–7/15	2/15–5/1
Lettuce	9/15–10/15	3/1–5/1
Onion	8/1	4/1–7/1
Spinach	10/1–10/15	2/15–5/1

dener isn't doing much gardening during those months either. The crops in the third category are hibernating. Once the sun returns for longer periods each day (by mid-February at this latitude), you should begin to see the first new growth following the crops' near dormancy in the cold.

Beginning in mid-January, start sowing short rows of spring crops in any open spots in the frames and low tunnels. These are the succession plantings that will be ready to start picking about the time the winter crops are finished. This group includes arugula, broccoli raab, carrots, claytonia, cress, endive, escarole, lettuce, mâche, mizuna, onions, orach, parsley, peas, purslane, radicchio, radishes, and spinach. In the interests of crop rotation, try to remember what had been growing in that empty spot so as to replace it with a crop from a different family.

Depending on where you live, those tiny spring seedlings and the new growth on the overwintered crops will meet some cold conditions starting in mid-February, when they begin to grow. They will be nipped by frosts and look a little haggard at times before the outdoor temperature begins to rise. Although the sun is out long enough to begin spring in the frames, the outdoor weather is still cold. This is the lag between what might be called solar-winter and thermometer-winter. *Solar-winter* is when the sun is at its lowest, the period on either side of the winter solstice that we christened the Persephone months. It is determined by the tilt of the Earth's axis. It ends by the middle of February. *Thermometer-winter* is the period of the year with the lowest temperatures. It is not synonymous with solar-winter. The coldest temperatures of the year for our garden in Maine usually occur during the first week of February, with a lot of cold still to come.

For us in Zone 5, the four weeks from February 15, when the sun starts serious warming again, to March 15, when the harsh winter cold is over, is the only difficult time in the winter coldframe harvest. Whereas the sun is high enough to start things going, the harsh cold is nipping them back. Even though the cold frame gains extra warmth from the sun during the

TABLE 8

COLD FRAME CROP FAMILIES

Apiaceae	Brassicaceae	Liliaceae
Carrot	Arugula	Leek
Celery	Broccoli raab	Onion, green (scallion)
Chervil	Chinese cabbage	**Polygonaceae**
Parsley	Cress	Sorrel
Parsnip	Kale	**Portulacaceae**
Skirret	Kohlrabi	Claytonia
Asteraceae	Mizuna	Purslane
Endive	Radish	**Valerianaceae**
Escarole	Tatsoi	Mâche
Italian dandelion	**Chenopodiaceae**	
Lettuce	Beet	
Radicchio	Spinach	
Salsify	Swiss Chard	
Scorzonera	**Fabaceae**	
Sugarloaf chicory	Garden (shell or English) pea	
	Snap pea	

day, it will still freeze inside when outside nighttime temperatures drop below 25°F. Mâche isn't bothered (this wonderfully hardy crop could grow on icebergs), but the variety of other winter crops can be limited in exceptionally cold weather. The farther south you live, the shorter this period will be. You can throw a blanket or insulated cover over the frames at night if you wish, or you can take what nature gives you. Spring is on its way, and by the middle of March, all will be well again.

Watering

For four months of the year (November to February), the secret to watering cold frames and low tunnels is to do very little. For the coldest of those months, do none at all. The evaporation of moisture is reduced when the sun is low, and the groundwater table is higher. No water needs to be added. During the transition months, principally March/April/May and September/October (depending upon where you live), you should pay much closer attention to watering because the enhanced warmth inside the frames will increase evaporation and will increase the plants' need for water compared to the need of outdoor plantings. In summer, the frame or tunnel areas are uncovered and will be watered the same as the rest of the garden.

Since we like to water gently, our hose is attached to a watering wand with a very fine rose, which gives a gentle spray. The rose is the plate with small holes at the business end of a wand or watering can. It determines the size of the water droplets. Ideally, a fine rose will ensure that both your watering can and spray wand deliver water as softly as a summer rain. (See appendix D for sources.)

When you need to apply water to the frames, you can do so by hand or turn on a sprinkler if the frames are open. In either case, it is preferable to water in the morning on a sunny day so the leaves can dry off before evening. When watering low tunnels by hand the plastic can be pushed up high enough to give access to the whole area. When watering frames by hand, stand at the lower edge of the frame, open one light, and water the exposed area. Then put down that light, open the next, and proceed along.

If you do not have the experience to judge by garden sense whether you are applying the right amount of water, you can measure and calculate. Use a stopwatch to time how long it takes to fill a gallon jar with your hand sprinkler. Then determine how many square inches are under a light. Knowing that one gallon contains 231 cubic inches you can calculate how long it will take to apply ¼ inch, ½ inch, or however much water you want. On average, 1 inch of water per week is

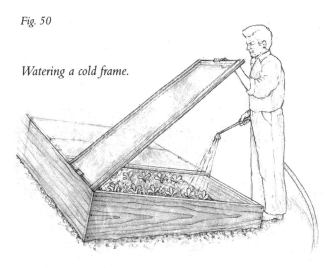

Fig. 50

Watering a cold frame.

recommended, but the quantity of water required will vary with the weather, the season, and the age of the crop.

You might prefer to build an irrigation system for your cold frames. For that you will need a length of PVC pipe fitted with small, 180°-spray emitters normally used in commercial greenhouses (see appendix D). Attach the pipe to the back wall of the frame, extend one end of the pipe through the side wall, and attach a hose con-

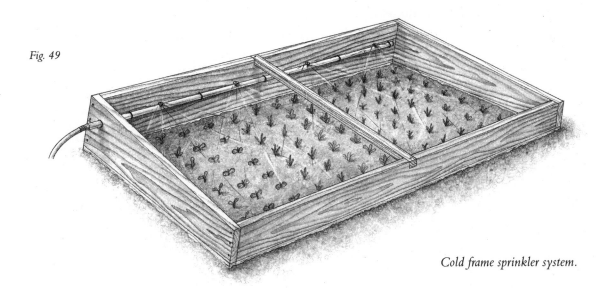

Fig. 49

Cold frame sprinkler system.

nector. Close off the other end. Then you can just click the garden hose into the connector to apply water. If you add a simple timer to your system, the water will shut off automatically. The irrigation system should be drained or removed for winter storage to prevent freezing.

If you improve the soil in the frame and add plenty of compost, you will greatly improve the soil's water-holding capacity and structure. This means that the soil can store more water without becoming waterlogged. On a comparison basis, if the water-holding capacity of a volume of sandy soil is 1 unit, an equal volume of clay soil will hold 4 units, but the same volume of soil organic matter will hold 16 units. This is another way in which compost benefits the garden soil.

Direct Sowing versus Transplanting

We transplant the following crops one or more times during the garden year: beets, broccoli, Brussels sprouts, cabbage, celeriac, celery, kale, leeks, lettuce, onions, parsley, peppers, and tomatoes. You can direct-seed most of these crops, avoid transplanting, and save yourself work, but we find there are benefits to transplanting. Some warm-weather crops, such as tomatoes, peppers, and cucumbers, need the head start to produce well in cool climates. Some crops, such as celeriac, onions, and leeks, are set out as transplants to give them as long as possible to produce greater harvests. Others, such as the cabbage family, make it through the first weeks after germination with fewer problems when growing in the extra fertility of potting soil. We transplant lettuce for overwintering because we can put the seedlings in after earlier crops have been harvested. In that way, transplanting makes small gardens larger, since other crops can continue to grow in the space that the transplant won't need to occupy for three to four weeks after seeding. Finally, transplanting is a great way to stay ahead of the weeds. When seeds are planted in the garden, weeds can germinate along with them. Transplants have the advantage of a three- to four-week head start.

Starting Plants

Your cold frame can serve as a greenhouse for starting seedlings. You can use it for all seedlings that are transplanted except the early-spring sowings of heat-lovers such as tomatoes, peppers, and cucumbers. They should be started in a sunny window in the house. For all the others, the cold frame is an ideal place to start growing. Once you begin raising seedlings in the cold frame, you will find it so simple and successful that you will never go back to flats on windowsills. Here's how to do it:

Spread potting mix about two to three inches deep in whatever part of a frame you wish to use for seedlings. Lay 3-inch boards around the edge as a border, then treat that area as if it were a flat: make furrows, drop in evenly spaced seeds, cover them shallowly, mark them with name and date on a small stake, and water them lightly with a fine sprinkler. The rows can be as close together as they would be in a flat. Space seeds evenly in the seeding row so they won't be crowded. We always try to avoid plant stress at all stages of growing. It takes a little more time, but the results are worth it.

When the seedlings are up, move them to an adjoining section of the frame, which also has a 2-inch covering of potting mix over the soil. Do this as soon as you can handle the seedlings. Within reason, the younger you transplant a seedling, the better. Dig under each one with a small, pointed dowel, lifting and loosening the roots as you extract them from the soil. Always be gentle with seedlings. Hold them by a leaf, not the stem, so you don't crush the vital parts if you squeeze too hard.

Poke holes in the potting soil of the adjoining section with the dowel to make space for the roots, then tuck them in lightly. A good distance for all seedlings is 3 inches apart. When they are large enough to transplant to the garden, use a knife to cut the soil into 3-inch cubes with a seedling in the center of each. It is just like cutting a tray of brownies. If you make sure the soil is moist (sprinkle if necessary before cutting), the blocks will hold together nicely. You can use a bricklayer's or right-angle trowel to slice underneath each cube, lift it out, and set it in a tray for transport to its permanent garden home.

We make our own potting soil. The key ingredient is our own one- to two-year-old best-quality compost. The other ingredients can vary. For example, you might start with a store-bought peat-lite mix (a combination of peat moss and either perlite or vermiculite) and fortify it by adding compost and organic fertilizers. The fertilizers are phosphate rock and greensand (see chapter 3) plus some cottonseed or other meal as a source of nitrogen. (You can purchase cottonseed meal at the local garden supply store.) We mix all three fertilizers together in equal parts to create a special organic fertilizer blend. When making mixes, we measure out the bulk ingredients with an 8-quart bucket and the fertilizer blend with a 1-cup measure. A sample formula goes like this:

POTTING SOIL RECIPE I
4 buckets commercial peat-lite mix
2 cups organic fertilizer blend
3 buckets compost

Mix all together thoroughly.

We usually dump the buckets of ingredients into a wheelbarrow and mix them with a short-handled shovel.

Fig. 51

Cutting the seedlings into 3-inch blocks inside the cold frame.

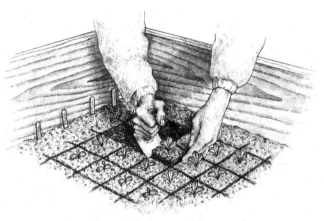

Scooping the seedling with the transplanting tool.

Planting a seedling in the garden.

If you want to make a natural potting soil free of any additives that may be included in the commercial peat-lite mix, you can make it as follows:

POTTING SOIL RECIPE II

3 buckets peat moss
2 cups organic fertilizer blend
1 bucket perlite
3 buckets compost

Mix all together thoroughly.

This formula produces an excellent, dependable mix. It doesn't need to be sterilized because the compost protects against soil-borne diseases.

Sift any peat moss, compost, or soil for these mixes through a ¼-inch screen to remove lumps or stones. When buying peat moss, ask for the best quality available. Some low-grade brands are very dusty and offer little of the air- and water-holding structure that makes peat moss valuable in a mix. If you can't find acceptable peat moss, buy one of the commercial mixes and use the first formula.

Make your potting mix in the fall. All the ingredients will be readily available and not frozen solid, as in late winter. There also appears to be a real benefit to allowing the mix to mellow over the winter. Place the mix in covered garbage cans and store them in the cellar so they won't freeze. Then you are ready to start as early in the spring as you care to plant.

There are many advantages to growing seedlings in a cold frame. No flats are necessary. There is no potting soil mess in the house. The seedlings will be hardy because the cold frame is not artificially heated. Any additional hardening off is easily accomplished by opening the lights slightly wider. Finally, watering is more forgiving, since your seedlings are connected to the earth and they can't dry out as quickly as they can in the limited confines of a flat. Thus, an occasional lapse in watering is not disastrous.

The intermediate transplanting from the seedling row to the 3-by-3-inch spacing makes transplanting seedlings a two-step process. We think it's worth the effort because the intermediate step has been found to stimulate increased root regrowth, resulting in slightly more vigorous transplants. You can do it as a one-step process by simply starting out with the 3-by-3-inch configuration and planting three seeds in each square. After they emerge, you thin to the best one in each square and proceed as before.

With some crops, we use a Dutch idea called multiplants and sow four or more seeds in each square with no intention of thinning them. This allows us to grow transplants in groups rather than as singles. The onion crop will serve as a good example of how to go about it. Sow five seeds together. Plan for four of the seeds to germinate. When the onion seedlings are large enough to go to the garden, cut out the blocks as usual and set them out at a spacing of 10 by 12 inches. If you were growing single plants in rows they would be set 3 inches apart. Four plants in a clump every 12 inches in a row is the same average spacing as one plant every 3 inches. Each onion is allowed just as much total garden space, and the yield is the same. The onions growing together push each other aside gently and at harvest time are lying in a series of small circles rather than single rows. If all the seeds germinate and there are five onions in each clump, that's no problem.

In addition to onions, you can use the multiplant technique for early transplants of beets, broccoli, cabbage, leeks, scallions, and spinach. Not only is this system more efficient because four plants can be transplanted as quickly as one, but it also can be used to control size when desired. A clump of broccoli, for example, will yield three or four smaller central heads rather than one large one. For many families, the smaller unit size is more desirable.

TABLE 9

MULTIPLANT SEEDING

Crop	# of Seeds	Multiplant Spacing	# of Rows per Bed
Beet	4	6"	3
Broccoli	4	24"	1
Cabbage	3	18"	1
Leek	4	12"	3
Onion	5	12"	3
Scallions	10	6"	3
Spinach	4	6"	3

Winter Harvest

In *Love's Labors Lost,* Shakespeare speaks of winter days when "milk comes frozen home in pail." There will be plenty of those days for the four-season harvester. To protect your harvest from freezing, we suggest going to the garden with a covered basket or a pail with a lid. You might even include a few dish towels for extra insulation. We learned this the hard way a couple of times when we absent-mindedly joined our children sledding or chatted with a passing neighbor after harvesting. The cold quickly penetrated, and our greens "came frozen home in basket."

The hardy winter greens tolerate freezing and thawing as long as they are growing, but if they freeze after being severed from their roots, they don't usually recover. Nor do they thaw without wilting if harvested while they are frozen. Only mâche, tatsoi, and scallions can be harvested while frozen and still make a respectable showing. You need to wait until the temperature in the cold frame or low tunnel rises above freezing before you harvest the other crops. Fortunately, the interior temperature will get above freezing on most winter days, whether they are sunny or cloudy. Even on the coldest days, the frame will usually reach harvest temperatures from 11 A.M. to 3 P.M.

During the coldest weather, the freezing temperatures will do considerable damage to the outside leaves of crops such as radicchio, endive, and escarole. In some cases, the radicchio heads will be surrounded by a layer of mushy leaves. Don't let that put you off. If you peel the mush away, a

TABLE 10

Harvest Season of Cold Frame Crops
From September to May in Zone 5

Crop	Sept	Oct	Nov	Dec	Jan	Feb	Mar	Apr	May
Arugula									
Beet									
Carrot									
Celery									
Chard									
Chicory, green									
Cabbage, Chinese									
Claytonia									
Dandelion									
Endive									
Escarole									
Kale									
Kohlrabi									
Leek									
Lettuce									
Mâche									
Mizuna									
Onion, green									
Parsley									
Radicchio									
Radish									
Sorrel									
Spinach									
Tatsoi									

beautiful vegetable is hiding inside. Although the outer leaves of spinach may turn brown, the smaller center leaves remain in great shape through the coldest weather. Harvest spinach leaves by cutting them an inch above the crown, and the plant will regrow when the weather warms again. Whatever the weather, all the hardy winter crops offer something choice to eat.

And how good is the harvest? It can best be described as a season of continuous delight for the table as well as for the soul. Even after all these years of growing a winter garden in cold frames, we still marvel at the miraculous contrast of the cold weather outside and the warm harvest within.

Coping with Snow

Most of the time, we clear the cold frames of snow so the sunlight can enter. We use a heavy-bristle push broom to do the job. You can use a shovel, but after carelessly breaking the glass on a few lights over the years, we've found it safer with a broom. Sometimes we leave the snow on the frame for insulation if the weather report predicts extra-cold temperatures for a few days following a snowfall. The plants don't mind the dark, and with the extra insulation, the frame temperature won't drop as low. When we've been away and not cleared the frames for many weeks, there haven't been any problems. Remember, the plants are not growing, just hibernating. They don't mind some snow.

Cold Frames Redux

As a way to get started, the basic cold frame is the simplest and most dependable aid for the four-season harvest. Table 10 gives an overview of the variety of crops and harvest times that can be expected from cold frame–protected crops in Zone 5.

If you follow the suggestions in this chapter and the discussions about each vegetable in appendix A, we assure you a winter garden bounty at least as good as this chart. For those of you who would like to go a step further and ensure the quality and quantity of an even wider harvest of winter vegetables, I offer our experience with a second layer of crop protection in the next chapter.

Creativity involves breaking out of established patterns in order to look at things in a different way.
—Edward de Bono

CHAPTER 10

THE COVERED GARDEN: GREENHOUSES AND HIGH TUNNELS

The chateau near Avignon, where we spent the night, had passed its days of glory. That probably explained its present renaissance as an inn. But the threadbare elegance, like the drooping petals of a favorite flower, still gave testimony to the grandeur that once existed. Especially when seen, as we saw it, through the veil of low-slanting late afternoon winter sun as we strolled the grounds after arriving, and again in the misty light of early dawn the following morning. We chose this lodging because we had heard of a particularly lovely, old-style glass greenhouse on the property.

Although it was not a large greenhouse, the cathedral-like architectural design, the curved glass cupolas, and the decorative ironwork were unmistakably elegant and old-style. The site, an open grassy area with trees and shrubs behind to break the north and west winter winds, balanced the need for both sunlight and shelter. The mechanical details, such as the trapezoidal venting mechanisms, were like signatures of the practical problem-solving workers who had designed and forged them in an earlier age when greenhouses were the work of local craftsmen. We recorded the best details with our cameras so as not to forget the nuances in case we wished to copy them on a glass greenhouse of our own someday. But, flying in the face of all this promise, the greenhouse was empty. It was disappointing but not unexpected. We had seen it before.

After World War I, as the lifestyles of the original rich and famous became harder to maintain, the sumptuous gardens and glasshouses they had so opulently created were often the first parts of their *demesnes* to fray at the edges. The style and the grandeur in which the old Victorian greenhouses were planned and executed could not begin to be maintained without large staffs of skilled workers who became harder to find at low garden wages once better-paying jobs in factories drew them elsewhere. Furthermore, the glasshouses and wintergardens of the 19th century were designed for great beauty, not practical efficiency, and thus climate control, maintenance, and management costs were enormous.

Whether called an orangery (a greenhouse designed to grow citrus fruit), a conservatory (for the collection and preservation of exotic plants), a wintergarden (usually attached to a residence for ease of access), or a hothouse (for out-of-season cultivation of vegetables), these glass palaces aspired toward recreating the Garden of Eden. By artificially maintaining a perfect climate, they dispensed with the non-Edenic conditions of the European winter and replaced them with paradise. The words of Princess Mathilde de Bonaparte, niece of Napoleon, writing in 1869 about her wintergarden, are filled with that sense of seeking Eden:

There is an inherent wonderful fascination in being able in the middle of winter, to open the window of a salon and feel a balmy spring breeze instead of the raw December or January air. It may be raining outside, or the snow may be falling in soft flakes from a black sky, but one opens the glass doors and finds oneself in an earthly paradise that makes fun of the wintry showers.

By the end of the second decade of the 20th century, the expensive and aristocratic heritage of the old glass palaces spelled their doom. Having been born into such glamour and non-utilitarian excess, no one could envision their transition to a more useful and less pampered future. Thus, when higher heating bills and straitened finances became the new reality, the structures were abandoned. To us, however, this chateau's greenhouse, although only a small example of past grandeur, was a potential paradise still. On our first visit in the evening, we were enveloped by the near tropical atmosphere resulting from merely trapping the winter sunlight during the day, despite the unplanned extra ventilation caused by a number of missing glass panes. On our dawn visit we

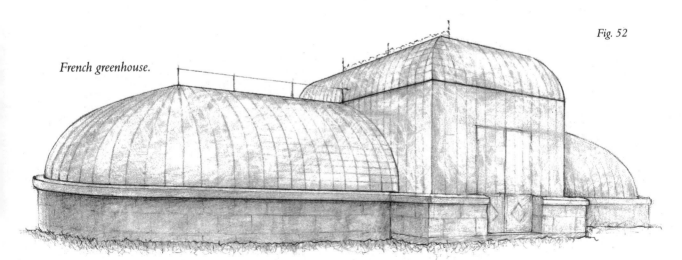

Fig. 52

French greenhouse.

could feel how much of that heat, radiated back by the soil and the stone foundation, was still effective. Some of the more exotic plants which probably graced this greenhouse in the free-spending 19th century might not find that level of "passive" protection adequate, but for many winter salads and herbs it would still be a paradise.

And that brings us to the point. Look what those enormously wealthy Victorians, who could afford anything they wanted, spent their money on! They built greenhouses and then went to even more expense heating and staffing them so they could enjoy what they acknowledged to be the best luxury of all—fresh homegrown fruits, vegetables, and flowers every month of the year. It is the aim of this book to show how easily and inexpensively what were once the pleasures of the few can now be the pleasures of the many. If you have a little sunny space in the backyard, and the desire to grow a garden, you can eat like the Victorian millionaires.

But that winter bounty will not become commonplace until old limitations and old ideas are swept aside by innovative thinking. It's too bad this process did not begin with the classic glasshouses of the 19th century when they needed a new direction. There's no telling where these ideas might have progressed to by now.

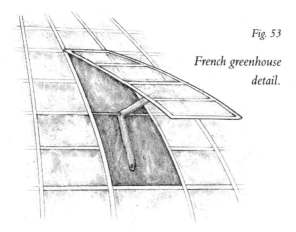

Fig. 53

French greenhouse detail.

The Protected Microclimate

If you already have a greenhouse, there is no need to heat it. The winter sun provides all the input necessary to turn any greenhouse into a practical Garden of Eden for vegetable lovers. If you are a U.S. gardener located in Zone 7 and southward, the protection provided by an unheated greenhouse alone can put gourmet-quality fresh winter vegetables on the table in even the coldest months. Especially since a Zone 7 area such as Greensboro, North Carolina, or Muskogee, Oklahoma, lies on the 36th parallel and enjoys 7 percent more January daylength than the French chateau. Those in the more northerly parts of the U.S., Zone 6 and above, have to face colder, but no less manageable, conditions

Now when you read the word *greenhouse*, don't get nervous and hide your checkbook. Many people associate "greenhouse" only with those expensive additions to country houses or temple-like structures on royal estates mentioned above. Those are, admittedly, beautiful examples of greenhouses. But the word encompasses far less expensive options that work just as well. Any translucent structure into which the gardener can walk is a greenhouse. All you need is a minimal frame and a roof that lets in light.

The simplest greenhouse is basically a translucent tunnel covered with plastic. The popular name is a *high tunnel*. The plastic is supported by a series of curved pipes, like large croquet hoops, spaced at 4-foot intervals. The plastic covering is attached to boards along the bottom on each side. This single layer of plastic over a lightweight frame creates a very inexpensive protected microclimate.

The key to keeping a greenhouse inexpensive is not to heat it. But the reality of the climate in

USDA Zones 3, 4, 5, and 6 during January and February seems so inhospitable that the logical tendency has been to fight the force of cold with the force of heat. Even the "appropriate technology" greenhouse experimenters in the 1960s and 1970s were apparently trapped by those old limitations and old ideas and they continued the combative attitude toward winter cold. Their "energy-saving" alternative to burning fossil fuel was to install thick insulation and massive heat storage. The intent was to trap and hold as much of the sun's daytime heat as possible in order to maintain relatively high temperatures so crops could actually be grown in winter.

In contrast, our winter greenhouse philosophy is downright laid-back. We think a winter-harvest system should be inexpensive to purchase, uncomplicated to build, simple to manage, and completely dependable. Therefore, in addition to having no reliance on outside energy (so we don't have to pay heating bills or feel environmentally guilty), it will have minimal complications (so we won't get fed up and stop using it), and no moving parts (so there is nothing to break down when we are busy elsewhere). However, our combination of cold-hardy plants and just enough climatic protection so those plants can more or less hibernate is so surprisingly non-confrontational, in a predominantly combative world, that few cold-climate gardeners have dreamed it to be possible. But it is similar to the philosophy of the French gardeners we visited along the 44th parallel. They accepted the realities of winter while trying to temper them slightly for the crops they wished to grow.

The winter greenhouses in the Mediterranean parts of France, because they are simple, are also frugal, a quality we as home gardeners especially appreciate. Unlike the greenhouse growers in Holland, where the industrially efficient and technically sophisticated glass greenhouse systems share the 19th-century aristocratic desire to control every nuance of the greenhouse climate, the Mediterranean growers have traditionally depended on funkier homemade greenhouse designs because they lacked either the capital or the desire to invest in costlier solutions. That made it a logical place for northern U.S. gardeners to come for further inspiration.

Years ago, when we began looking for extra climatic protection beyond that provided by the outdoor cold frame, we placed the cold frames inside a high tunnel. If you think of the cold frame as a sweater, then you just have to add a windbreaker over it when the temperature drops below where the sweater alone is adequate. What we saw in France was a simple version of the cold-frame-inside-high-tunnel system we were using. The French, who, as mentioned earlier, had replaced their cold frames with low tunnels (*chenilles*), placed low tunnels inside their high tunnels to achieve the same end.

That made sense because it is certainly simpler and cheaper to use low tunnels rather than cold frames inside the greenhouse. The susceptibility of low tunnels to heavy snow becomes a non-issue once they are protected by the greenhouse. But one inspiration leads to another and we quickly realized that the low tunnels themselves were unnecessarily complicated and restrictive. It made more sense to cover even larger areas and have easier access. We decided the agricultural fabrics sold as "floating row covers" would be a better choice still for the inner layer. Although we assumed they might be less protective against cold than our glass-covered frames, their self-ventilating feature and availability in large sizes were overwhelming advantages.

Further, we did not know if we had yet pushed our crops to the lowest temperatures they

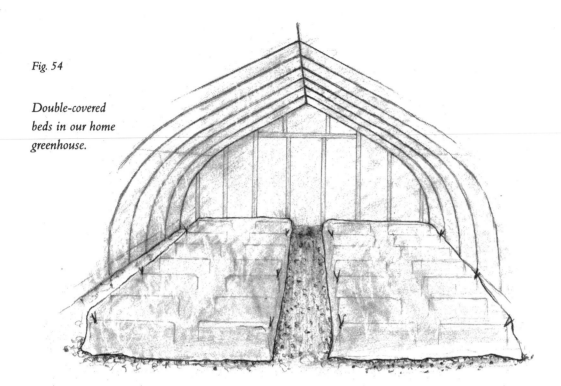

Fig. 54

Double-covered beds in our home greenhouse.

would tolerate in a protected microclimate. Our opinion, after many years of practical experience with winter-harvest systems, is that the protected microclimate we have created is successful principally because it protects against wind (think of wind-chill readings and the desiccating effect of cold, dry winds on winter vegetation), and, secondarily, because it protects against the fluctuating wet-dry, snow-ice conditions of the outside winter. In this microclimate, a few degrees of temperature one way or the other does not appear to be the crucial determinant of survival for most of our crops.

One of the delights of using floating row covers inside a greenhouse is the ease of management. Since there is no wind, there is no need to bury or weigh down the edges. Even large pieces of floating fabric material can be removed and replaced frequently, for harvest or replanting, with no problems. Our interior covers are large

Fig. 55

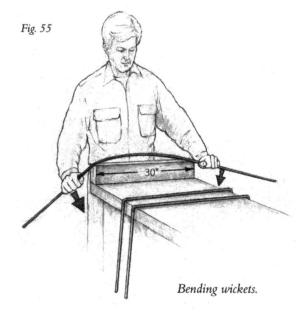

Bending wickets.

enough to each cover one-half of our greenhouse growing area, leaving an uncovered path down the center. They are supported by flat-topped wire wickets which hold the inner cover 12 inches above the soil. We make the wickets from the same 76-inch-long straight lengths of number 9 wire that are used to make hoops for the low tunnels. Instead of bowing them into half circles as we do for the low tunnels, we bend right angle corners so the flat top is 30 inches wide and each leg is 23 inches long.

We space the wickets every four feet along the length of the 30-inch-wide growing beds. That provides sufficient framework to support the inner fabric. When the fabric is in place, we pull it taut and clip it to the end wickets with clothespins. That prevents the fabric from sagging under the weight of condensed moisture. We have noticed occasional frost damage whenever the fabric has drooped down and frozen to the leaves below, as opposed to no damage when it is held up above them.

Evaluating the Twice-Tempered Climate

This two-layer concept takes crop protection a step further than the single layer of the outdoor low tunnel or cold frame. Notice that the word continues to be "protection," not heat input. This is still a low-tech concept. The small outdoor structures like cold frames and low tunnels put a low roof over low plants. The high tunnel puts a taller roof over the low roof and, also, over the gardener, a feature you will appreciate when harvesting on snowy or windy days.

Double layering the winter garden achieves the same effect as the envelope house concept in architecture, which basically puts one building inside another. The inside structure, rather than being exposed to the cold of the outside world, is exposed only to the modified temperature within the first layer of protection—enough of a difference, even in our cold winters, so the double-protected soil rarely freezes. As a rough estimate, each layer of covering is equivalent to moving your plants one and a half USDA zones to the south. Thus, for us in Zone 5, a single layer moderates the temperature to that of Zone 6-plus, and a double layer moderates the climate to that of Zone 8.

When the outdoor temperature drops to 0°F, the temperature in a standard cold frame will drop to 10° to 20°F depending on a number of factors, such as how warm it was the day before, how quickly the temperature dropped, and how long it stays cold. Under the same conditions, the temperature under double coverage would drop to a range of 20° to 35°F. Actual temperature records from our garden demonstrate these differences (see table 11).

TABLE 11

TEMPERATURE GRADIENTS
WITH PROTECTIVE STRUCTURES

Sample nighttime low temperatures (°F)			
Outside	Cold Frame	Tunnel	Double Coverage
–10	6	4	18
0	14	11	25
18	28	24	36
Sample daytime high temperatures, unvented (°F)			
Outside	Cold Frame	Tunnel	Double Coverage
Sunny day			
5	60	42	78
20	75	60	85
Cloudy day			
30	45	45	60

Notice that the single-layer outdoor cold frame is warmer than the single-layer tunnel. That is not surprising; the cold frame is closer to the ground and its glass cover is superior to plastic for retaining soil heat at night.

Layering could go on and on, with third and fourth layers, but just as too many layers of clothing can make you feel awkward, too many layers of glass or plastic inhibit plant well-being by restricting light. Each layer cuts out an additional percentage of light (about 10 to 12 percent minimally and more if the surface is dirty). Two layers are sufficient for the extra

Fig. 56

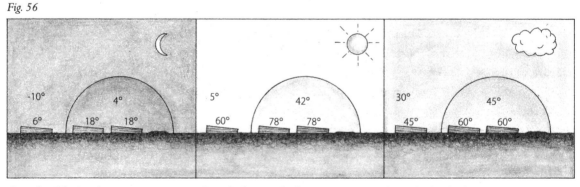

Sample nighttime low temperatures. *Sample daytime high temperatures unvented.* *Sample cloudy day temperatures.*

climate modification we wish to achieve, and they still let in plenty of light for the plants.

There is one last layer to consider. Some sort of insulation could be added at night to provide extra frost protection. Straw mats were used extensively for this purpose by the traditional cold frame market gardeners in years past, and foam blankets are used today. These night-covers do increase nighttime protection, but we don't bother with them for a couple of reasons. The first is effort. This system is successful because there is practically no care involved during the winter. All we do is harvest. Remembering to roll out and remove covers would seem like work after a while. We prefer to keep it simple. The second reason we don't use blankets is reality. The old commercial growers used mats because they did not want any small frost nips to mar the sales potential of their produce. But as noted in chapter 1, this is our garden and commercial rules don't apply. We don't mind peeling away a little frost damage. We accept occasional minor imperfections in return for freedom from placing and removing insulation twice a day.

Constructing the High Tunnel

Low-cost tunnel greenhouses work so well that if the public were more familiar with them, I think every gardening family would have one. They are a very flexible form of crop protection, since they can be erected quickly and covered or uncovered easily. They provide a protected environment that can appear almost at will—protection that did not exist yesterday but is in place today. If you are handy at bending pipe, you can make your own structure. Or you can easily purchase the parts. Inexpensive kits for pipe-frame tunnels are available in 12-, 14-, and 17-foot widths and as long as you want. You also can build a simple greenhouse

structure using 2x4s with gusseted joints or bowed lengths of a number of materials (more on those designs later).

The smallest comfortable size for a food-production greenhouse is about 12 by 12 feet, but we would recommend 12 by 20 feet as more serviceable and 14 by 20 feet as even better. That may seem to be a large size compared to the 6-by-8- or 8-by-10-foot greenhouses offered in many garden catalogs, but it won't seem large once eating fresh produce in winter becomes a habit. You may even be tempted to make it larger. Our tunnel, which attaches to our house so we can walk into it directly from the pantry, is 20 feet wide by 40 feet long. We have room for a patio at one end and our pampered fig trees at the other end, with a 20-foot-square winter garden in the middle.

A plastic greenhouse is the least expensive covered space available (between $1 and $2 per square foot), so if you have more room inside than you need for the winter vegetable garden it won't go begging. You can fill it with winter flowers, a sandbox, a barbecue, the hot tub, or whatever else you can imagine. You soon become aware of the home greenhouse version of Parkinson's Law—the uses expand to fill the space available.

The site for the tunnel should be next to or part of the outdoor garden. It should be a spot where the low winter sun is not blocked by tall trees or buildings. Ideally the site will receive direct winter sunshine at least four hours per day. But don't be dismayed if that is not possible. We know of very successful winter tunnels that receive only two hours of direct sunlight per day during the Persephone months. Since the tunnel site adds year-round growing space, the uncovered garden can be made smaller if there are space constraints in your yard.

If you buy a kit for a high tunnel, the parts will

Fig. 57

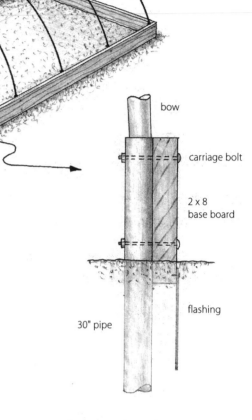

High tunnel construction.

bow

carriage bolt

2 x 8
base board

flashing

30" pipe

consist of curved lengths of pipe, a straight length of pipe, and short pipes with holes drilled in them. To construct a conventional high tunnel you first drive the short pipes, the foundation posts, into the ground every 4 feet in straight lines along either edge of where the tunnel will sit. Wooden baseboards that you purchase from the local lumberyard (2-inch by 10-inch planks work well), are bolted to the outside of these pipes through the predrilled holes, so the bottom edge of the baseboard is a few inches below soil level. That completes the foundation. (We strongly recommend that you do not use treated wood, which is very toxic. Rather, treat conventional wood with one of the non-toxic wood preservatives—see appendix D—or use a rot-resistant wood like cedar.)

The superstructure comes next. The hoops, also called bows, are a smaller diameter pipe than the foundation posts so they can be erected by inserting their bottom end into the top of a foundation post. The hoop pipe rests on the top of the two bolts that hold the baseboard to the foundation post. For structural stability the hoops are

then connected one to the other along the top center with the straight length of metal pipe called a roof purlin. The end hoops can be purchased with curved wooden boards bolted around the perimeter, which give a surface for attaching the plastic and affixing end wall framing.

Whether you make your own tunnel or purchase one, however, you will want to construct your own end walls. When tunnels are erected conventionally, the end walls usually consist of a 2x4 frame covered with plastic with openings for a door and vents.

Putting on the Plastic

The final step is to cover the tunnel. Greenhouse growers usually choose one of the polyethylene plastics made specifically for greenhouses. These products are protected against the degradation caused by sunlight and will last for three years. They are available from greenhouse suppliers (check your Yellow Pages).

Choose a calm day to put on the plastic, as wind will make this job harder than it needs to be. The technique is to roll out the plastic sheet along the ground on one side of the tunnel and pull an edge of it over to the other side. To make that easier, wrap the edge of the plastic around a golf or tennis ball and tie a rope to the base of that knob. You won't harm the plastic, and you can throw the rope over the tunnel and use it to pull the plastic sheet. A soft broom is useful to push the edge past obstructions. A helper standing under the tunnel with a broom can assist the covering process.

Pull the plastic taut and attach it to the planks at the bottom and sides with two strips of wood. Tack one strip down to hold the plastic and the other to lock it in place (see Fig. 59). Shorter lengths of those same strips are used to attach the plastic to the curved boards at the end of the greenhouse.

Even if you tighten the plastic well when you attach it, there may be times when you wish it were tighter. One option is to purchase with your tunnel the two-part plastic-locking rails made specifically for attaching the plastic to baseboards. Since they clamp the plastic in place you can unclamp them to retighten the covering. Alternatively you can run a length of soft rope over the plastic-covered tunnel between every other rib. Tie one end to the baseboard on one side and the

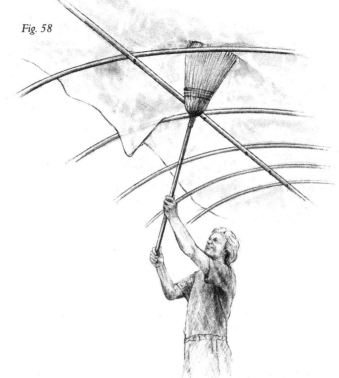

Fig. 58

Using a broom to feed plastic cover over the top of the frame.

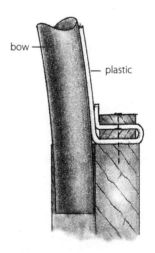

Fig. 59

bow — plastic

Locking the lower edge of plastic to the wooden baseboard.

other end to a short length of stretch cord. Tie that to the baseboard on the other side so the stretch cord keeps the rope under tension. These tensioned ropes will take up any slack that appears in the cover when it expands in warm weather and will not inhibit its contraction when cool weather returns. A tight cover will last longer because it won't be worn by flapping in the wind.

Avoiding Greenhouse Problems

Once you have a greenhouse you need to manage it. That means realizing that covered garden space is different from outdoor garden space. A permanent greenhouse creates artificial conditions that can result in a build-up of pests, diseases, and excess nutrient salt levels in the soil. Old-time greenhouse growers sought to solve that problem by periodically removing the top 18 inches of soil from their greenhouses and replacing it with fresh soil. Another option was to pump steam into the soil to sterilize it. Highly toxic fumigant pesticides have replaced steam nowadays. Heavy applications of irrigation water are needed to flush the excess salts into the subsoil. Fortunately, there is no need for any of these practices if you modify the greenhouse design to help prevent the problems.

The simplest solution to the build-up of pests, diseases, and nutrient salts is to uncover the greenhouse area for part of the time. That way it can share the same advantages as a cold frame, which is frequently uncovered and can be easily moved. The soil benefits from being exposed to the direct effects of the sun, rain, wind, and snow. Those natural forces have a purifying, cleansing, and revitalizing effect thus preventing pest and disease problems and nutrient excesses. There are two ways of working with this concept: the *convertible greenhouse* and the *mobile greenhouse*. We have experience with both. Since the convertible model is the simpler of the two, let's describe it first.

The Convertible Greenhouse

The driver of a convertible car can put the top down when the weather is warm. The gardener with a convertible greenhouse can do the same. This allows the greenhouse area to be covered in winter and uncovered in summer. In climates where temperatures are warm enough and summers are long enough that even tender crops don't need greenhouse help, the convertible greenhouse is the answer.

Since plastic-covered tunnel greenhouses have a minimal frame, they are diaphanous enough to be unobtrusive if uncovered during the warm months of the year. The frame for a convertible greenhouse can be constructed of wood, bowed metal hoops (as described earlier in this chapter), or any other material that works. The end walls, in this case, should be built with an artistic touch. Since the end walls are basically freestanding during the months when the greenhouse is uncovered, you will want to design them as a visual asset to your garden.

Let's build a greenhouse like this as an example. It will be the same 14-by-20-foot size that was suggested earlier. The major new feature will be the use of plastic locking rails both along the baseboards and around the perimeter of the end hoops. For the end hoops there is a wonderful plastic locking rail product called Spring Lock that conforms to the curve of the hoop and is designed for easy insertion and removal of both the top cover and the end wall plastic.

We suggest constructing the end walls as in Figure 60. You can paint them or let them weather naturally, as you prefer. The doors and vents are removable for the summer. They are designed so that without them, the end walls look like attractive garden arches. The greenhouse structure, without its plastic covering, will look a lot like an arbor. During the summer, runner beans or flowering vines can climb the arches, and trellised crops can be grown up the end walls.

Don't get so enthusiastic with your arbor plantings that you create too much shade. The idea is to be able to progressively replace the winter crops with extra early plantings of hot-weather crops in spring, uncover the greenhouse when the outside weather is warm enough, then begin progressively replacing the summer crops at the end of summer with the late summer and fall plantings of the subsequent winter harvest. (See Tables 5, 6, and 7 for planting dates.) When cold weather arrives, the doors and vents are hung, the ends and the top are covered with plastic, and the next season is under way. Whether this greenhouse will be used with an inner layer or will be the only layer of protection for your winter harvest depends on where you live. Gardeners in Zone 7 and south may find that the greenhouse alone provides adequate protection. Conversely, for much less expense, cold frames alone may be all that are needed.

The Mobile Greenhouse

A mobile greenhouse can be moved from one site to another. A few commercial growers in Europe have used mobile greenhouses for much of this past century. They allowed the growers to get maximum return from their financial investment in a greenhouse. The houses sat on railroad wheels

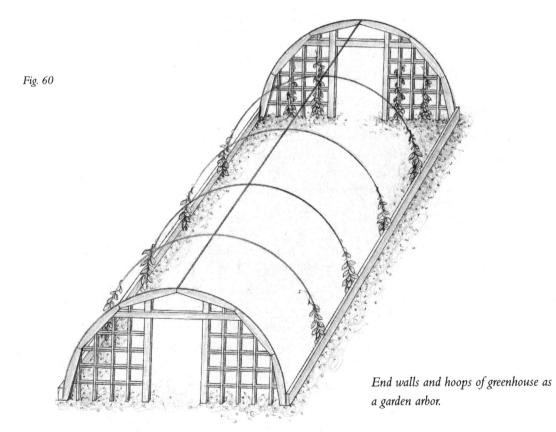

Fig. 60

End walls and hoops of greenhouse as a garden arbor.

and rolled on iron rails. The rails extended two, sometimes three or more times the length of the house. A sample cropping sequence might go something like this: An early crop of lettuce is started in the greenhouse on Site 1. When the spring climate is warm enough so the lettuce can finish its growth out-of-doors, the ends are raised and the house is wheeled to Site 2. Early tomato transplants, which need protection at that time of year, are set out in the greenhouse on Site 2. When summer comes and the tomatoes are safe out-of-doors, the house is rolled to Site 3 to provide tropical conditions during the summer for transplants of exotic melons or greenhouse cucumbers.

At the end of the summer, the sequence is reversed. Following the melon and cucumber harvest, the house is returned to Site 2 to protect the tomatoes against fall frosts. Later on, it is moved to Site 1 to cover a late celery crop that was planted after the early lettuce was harvested. Following celery, Site 1 is planted to early lettuce again and the year begins anew.

The classic mobile glass greenhouse was quite a piece of work. Although heavy and expensive, it was elegantly and ingeniously constructed. We copied the inspiration, not the expense. Instead of iron wheels and rails, we have wooden skids sliding on wooden rails or metal skids sliding on the ground. Our mobile tunnels are much simpler and much more manageable than the glass galleons of yore.

Building the Backyard Mobile Tunnel

The mobile tunnel is the perfect year-round growing structure for the colder parts of the country. In spring, it gives warm-weather crops such as tomatoes, peppers, and cucumbers a four-week head start. In summer, with the vents and doors wide open, it provides them with slightly more tropical conditions for enhanced flavor and ripeness, an important aid in our cool, moist coastal summers. In fall, it extends the summer-crop harvest for a month or more. In winter, it covers the inner layer of protection for winter vegetables.

I'm sure you've seen pictures of gardens with raised beds framed by planks. They look more or less the way your cold frames would look if you put soil in them. Well, envision a bed that is 14 feet wide—the width of your greenhouse. A row of planks stands above the soil along each edge. The planks are bolted to posts driven into the ground every 4 feet. Those are the rails. The base of this greenhouse, where the hoops attach, is made of planks, as in Figure 61. The 2-by-4-foot skid on the outside edge of the baseboard slides along the top of the rail. You can wax the surface to reduce friction.

The forces on the greenhouse hoops tend to push them out at the bottom. Thus, the baseboards run inside the rails, and the natural pressure holds them in tight. The hoops are fastened to the baseboards with bolts and metal plates. A purlin connects the hoops along the top center. That is the same structure for the hoop house described earlier. You can easily adapt any home-built greenhouse to this system by incorporating the baseboards into the lower structure when you build it.

When you simplify a technology as we have done, think it through thoroughly to prevent problems before they occur. If we can move this greenhouse, so can the wind. It is almost an axiom that if the wind can blow something about, sooner or later it will. The vision of an object the size of a small house wafting skyward on a stiff breeze is unnerving. Thus, although the mobile greenhouse is simple, it is not casual. When the house is in place, we take precautions

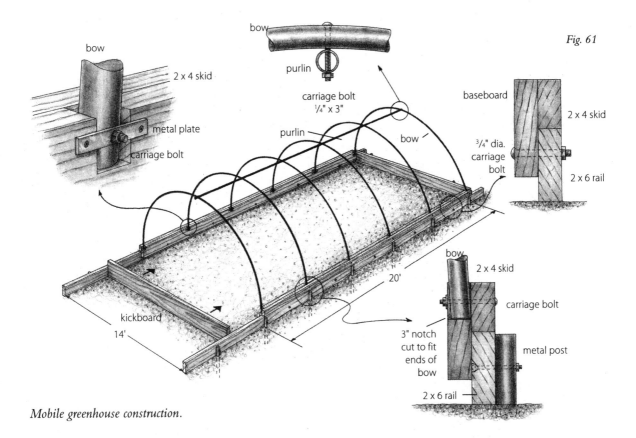

Fig. 61

bow

bow

2 x 4 skid

metal plate

carriage bolt

purlin

carriage bolt
¼" x 3"

baseboard

2 x 4 skid

purlin

bow

¾" dia.
carriage
bolt

2 x 6 rail

bow

20'

kickboard

14'

bow

2 x 4 skid

carriage bolt

3" notch
cut to fit
ends of
bow

metal post

2 x 6 rail

Mobile greenhouse construction.

to make sure it will stay there. There are ¾-inch-diameter bolts through both the baseboard and the rail every 4 feet.

Building the Ends

For a mobile tunnel, you have to build the ends differently. You need to be able to lift or remove the bottom of each end so as to clear any crops or structures over which the tunnel will be moving. If you purchase a tunnel, order wooden-framed end bows as an option. As the first step in constructing the ends, bolt a 2x4 crossbar horizontally to the wooden frame of the end bow. On most small tunnels, that crossbar should be about 5 to 5½ feet above ground level. Try to to leave at least 16 inches between the top of the crossbar

and the top of the tunnel arch. Then build two doors (see Fig. 62). The lower door is hinged to swing below the horizontal 2x4. You can lift it up to open it. A small, conventionally opening door with hinges on the side can be incorporated as part of the structure of a large end door to make frequent entry easier. You will have to duck your head when entering in either case.

A small upper door, which is hinged at the top, serves as a vent. Equip this door with an automatic temperature-activated opening arm so warm air will be vented from the tunnel when the inside temperature rises above the thermostat setting. When more venting is needed, the lower doors are either propped open or, as in summer, taken off altogether. We use loose pin hinges so both doors can be removed easily as required.

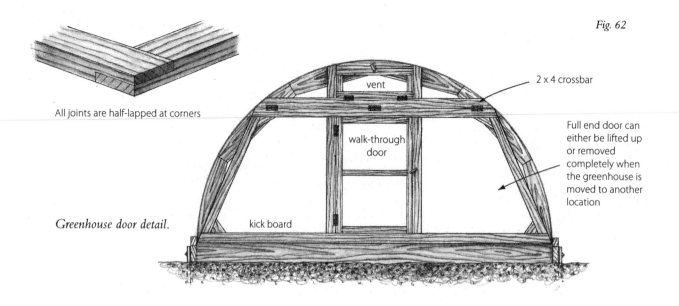

Fig. 62

All joints are half-lapped at corners

2 x 4 crossbar

vent

walk-through door

Full end door can either be lifted up or removed completely when the greenhouse is moved to another location

Greenhouse door detail.

kick board

Door Details

Build the doors carefully to fit the framed end spaces. Construct them out of 2x4s, with lapped corners and joints. Use plywood gussets or metal braces at all points of stress. Cover the doors with a single layer of plastic attached on the outward-facing side.

The bottom doors hang to within 10 inches of the ground. A 2x12-inch plank extends across the bottom of the opening and is bolted to the bow frames on either side. This plank serves as a kick board (see Fig. 61) and as the sill for the door to close against at the bottom. By keeping the door 10 inches above the ground, you can make sure that it will clear any build-up of snow when opened in winter. This plank is removed along with the door before the tunnel is moved to a new location.

The Mobile Greenhouse in Action

Let's talk about the management of this magic cover. The rails run east to west, so one of the curved sides of the tunnel faces south for maximum light input. Build the rails twice as long as the tunnel. That means there are two potential sites, A and B. How do you manage this operation to make full use of the covered space? Let's begin in a hypothetical fall.

At the moment, the tunnel is on Site A, where it has been all summer. Growing under the tunnel are tomatoes, cucumbers, melons, peppers, and celery. The doors and the vents have been removed for the summer. When the cooler evening temperatures of autumn appear, you replace the doors and begin closing them at night. The tender crops are thus protected against the early fall frosts.

Site B looks like an outdoor garden—which, at the moment, it is. There are four parallel 30-inch-wide beds. They are separated by 12-inch paths. As the fall progresses the beds are being planted to lettuce, spinach, arugula, parsley, scallions, Swiss chard, carrots, mâche, claytonia, radicchio, and so on.

Sometime between October 15 and 30 in Zone 5, it is time to say goodbye to warm-season production. By then, the crops that summered under the tunnel have had their day. Harvest anything that is ripe or will ripen and add the spent plants to the compost heap. Then remove the end door and the kick board, invite some friends to help push, and slide the tunnel to Site B.

Since Site A is going to be uncovered for the next year it makes sense to grow a green manure on it. In our climate most legume green manures have to be sown by early September to get established before winter. We sow on September 1 by sprinkling clover seeds under and around the summer crops and working them shallowly into the soil with a small rake. This is a practice known as undersowing. If we water thoroughly the seeds will germinate successfully in the shade of the standing crops, and when we remove the summer crops six weeks later our clover field is already off and running. If for some reason we have to wait till mid-October when it is too late to sow, we will cover the soil with rough compost to protect it over the winter and plan to sow a spring green manure of field peas and oats as early as possible the following year. Although it would be uneconomical to grow a green manure in the expensive confines of a greenhouse, it makes perfect sense to grow one on the uncovered site. Thus, clovers,

grasses, and many other crops known to benefit soil health and improve its fertility can become part of the protected crop rotation.

For the winter crops on Site B, the single layer of plastic that has just arrived is the first step in their winter protection. The second step will be the addition of the inner layer supported by wire wickets a few weeks later.

Mobile Greenhouse Potential

How far can you go with this mobile greenhouse idea? We have always imagined pampering our palates by extending the system to include three favorite foods—asparagus, strawberries, and raspberries. The system to do that might go something like this.

Extend the potential covered area five times the length of the greenhouse. Now there are five sites—I, II, III, IV, and V. We would grow the following crops on those sites:

  I. Asparagus
  II. Strawberries
 III. Summer crops
 IV. Fall raspberries
  V. Winter crops

Sites III and V are used for basically the same sequence as was described for Sites A and B in the previous section. Sites I, II, and IV are used for growing our favorite foods.

Let's start on March 21, when the tunnel is moved to Site I. Normally in this climate, the first asparagus doesn't appear until mid-May. With the aid of the earlier soil warmth under the tunnel, that can be sped up by three weeks. Thus, by late April, the tunnel could be moved to Site II. (Granted, we may lose a few spears to May frosts, but that's a small price to pay.)

TABLE 12

CROP PLAN FOR MOBILE GREENHOUSE

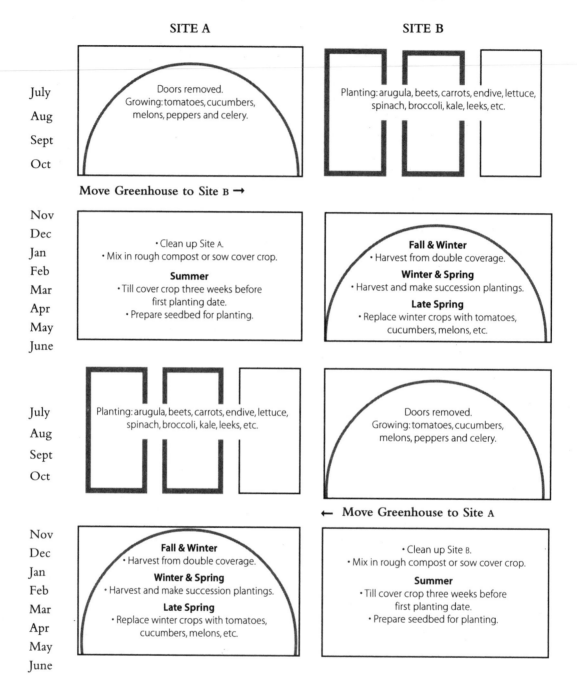

SITE A   **SITE B**

July / Aug / Sept / Oct

SITE A: Doors removed. Growing: tomatoes, cucumbers, melons, peppers and celery.

SITE B: Planting: arugula, beets, carrots, endive, lettuce, spinach, broccoli, kale, leeks, etc.

Move Greenhouse to Site B →

Nov / Dec / Jan / Feb / Mar / Apr / May / June

SITE A:
• Clean up Site A.
• Mix in rough compost or sow cover crop.
Summer
• Till cover crop three weeks before first planting date.
• Prepare seedbed for planting.

SITE B:
Fall & Winter
• Harvest from double coverage.
Winter & Spring
• Harvest and make succession plantings.
Late Spring
• Replace winter crops with tomatoes, cucumbers, melons, etc.

July / Aug / Sept / Oct

SITE A: Planting: arugula, beets, carrots, endive, lettuce, spinach, broccoli, kale, leeks, etc.

SITE B: Doors removed. Growing: tomatoes, cucumbers, melons, peppers and celery.

← Move Greenhouse to Site A

Nov / Dec / Jan / Feb / Mar / Apr / May / June

SITE A:
Fall & Winter
• Harvest from double coverage.
Winter & Spring
• Harvest and make succession plantings.
Late Spring
• Replace winter crops with tomatoes, cucumbers, melons, etc.

SITE B:
• Clean up Site B.
• Mix in rough compost or sow cover crop.
Summer
• Till cover crop three weeks before first planting date.
• Prepare seedbed for planting.

Without any protection, the earliest strawberries don't mature here until late June. With the aid of the tunnel to warm things up, we are looking at a two-week head start at least.

The next move in this imaginary sequence comes at the end of May when the tunnel would be moved off the strawberries and onto Site III, where it would spend the summer. Site III is growing warm-season crops as on Site A in the previous sequence.

Everbearing raspberries are growing on Site IV. We would move the tunnel off the summer crops on September 21, slightly earlier than under the sequence for Sites A and B. We would do it to protect the raspberries against fall frosts. That would give on average another six weeks of rasp-berries, not to mention a much higher quality of fruit because of the improved growing conditions under the tunnel. When the raspberries are finished in early November, we would cut the canes to the ground and add a mulch of compost covered with chipped brush trimmings. The raspberries would then be ready for the following year.

In the final move of the year, the tunnel would go to Site V, where it would spend the winter covering winter vegetables as on Site B in the previous discussion. The following March 21, when the fabric-covered crops could just make it on their own under a single layer, the tunnel would return to the asparagus to start the sequence all over again. Gardeners in warmer climates will want to adjust the dates mentioned

Fig. 63

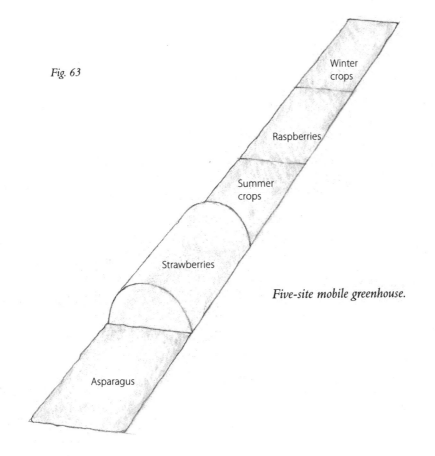

Five-site mobile greenhouse.

here to accommodate the times and temperatures in their area.

This is only one sequence. The sites could be growing spring flowers (earlier daffodils and tulips) or fall flowers (mums and calendulas until mid-December). You might move a greenhouse to protect a bed of globe artichokes or a group of fig trees in a climate where they would otherwise not survive the winter. Once you turn your imagination loose with this simple harvest extender/climate moderator, the potential is as wide as your gardening interests.

In addition to our tunnel, we still keep a few cold frames in the outdoor garden, since that gives us wider climatic options, from the most protected (double coverage in the tunnel), to the next most protected (the cold frames), to the least protected (the open garden). For example, as the weather gets colder, the fall salad harvest will move from the open garden, to the cold frames, and finally to the tunnel. In the spring, a wintered-over crop or a succession planting of peas, for example, will mature first in the tunnel, next in the cold frames, and finally in the open garden. Our spring planting dates are chosen to reflect the Zone 8 climate under double coverage, the Zone 6 climate in the cold frame, and our normal Zone 5 climate in the outdoor garden. Varying the amount of protection is another factor to be used in extending the harvest of a specific crop.

Harvesting the Winter Garden

Summer vegetable gardeners often harvest early to get the crops picked in the cool of the morning, and they protect against sunburn and mosquitoes. Winter harvesters must wait until the greenhouse temperature warms above 32°F before they can begin to pick and they protect against frosty fingers and chilly feet. On the cold-est, cloudiest days we can only count on a limited harvest window from 10:00 A.M. until 3:00 P.M. Before 10:00 everything is still frozen and after 3:00 it starts to freeze up again. If particularly cold weather is predicted we pick the day before. On sunny days the harvest window extends into the evening and the greenhouse temperature is downright pleasant.

We've learned from experience to replace the inner covers as soon as we finish harvesting. Once the temperature drops below 32°F, the light row-cover material quickly freezes to itself and is impossible to lay back over the supporting wickets without tearing. Some alternative inner cover materials (see appendix D) are stronger and less of a problem in that regard but, nevertheless, it is still the best practice to re-cover promptly.

Pests

We have often joked that our worst pests in the winter harvest are delighted dinner guests who want extra helpings of salad. It may not be quite that perfect, but pests in the form of insects and diseases have never been a real consideration. It would appear that our convertible and/or mobile greenhouse technique is as effective as we had hoped. The major pest that has developed is not a bug or a microbe but a mammal. We are engaged in a battle of wits with the meadow vole.

Meadow voles (*Microtus pennsylvanicus*) look like chubby, extra-furry mice. They live out-of-doors. They are serious pests for fruit tree growers because they girdle the bark of young trees. They are bothersome to us because they are vegetarians and seem to like our crops as much as we do. They need to eat their weight in plant food every day because their metabolism is so high. They can breed at thirty-five to forty days old, they can breed year-round, and they can have up to five litters a year with three to six young each time. They burrow under the soil and thus into the greenhouse. They live in underground burrows and they like to line their nests with chewed-up shreds of row-cover material. Not surprisingly, they consider our greenhouse an idyllic place to spend the winter.

At present we rely on snap traps for control and we keep trapping year-round in the vicinity of the greenhouse. The usual rat and mouse baits give varying results with these fruit and vegetable eaters, likely because there is just too much delicious greenery available. In addition to the peanut butter and slices of raw fruit, we have found one other bait that will often produce good results. We bait some of our traps with wild strawberry-flavored Bubble Yum. Whatever devious ingenuity went into concocting that flavor to tempt little children, it is equally effective at tempting voles in mid-winter when fruit has been scarce in the vole diet. At other times of year we depend mainly on placing the traps to intercept their lines of travel. That means, for example, at the entrances to their burrows, across the surface runs they use to go from one burrow to another, and up against walls because they like to scurry along edges. These traps seem to catch them as much because of accurate placement as because of any scent of bait, so it is worth experimenting with placement and moving the traps to new positions if nothing is being caught.

Our first response to any problem is prevention rather than cure. That would seem to be the obvious course of action in this case. We recommend that you attach aluminum flashing to the bottom of the baseboard (see fig. 64) so it extends 8 inches into the soil. Pay particular attention to corners and end walls. However, even after we have taken all precautions, the forces created by winter freezing and thawing can open new holes.

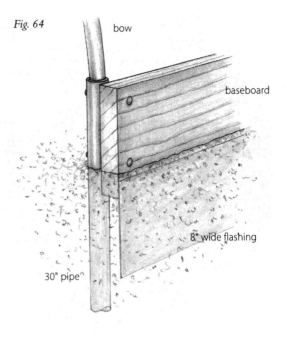

Fig. 64

bow

baseboard

8" wide flashing

30" pipe

In short, we have not always been successful at keeping voles out. We keep looking for a better solution than trapping, but for the moment it provides the best control we have found.

Mediterranean Tunnels

During our trip to France we were especially interested in two aspects of European tunnel construction—how the plastic is attached to the structure and how hot air is vented from the tunnels. Those two concerns are often cited by many home gardeners whom we have queried about their experience with different greenhouse designs. Although tunnels are simple in concept, just a single sheet of plastic supported by hoops, the process of effectively turning concept into practice involves many twists and turns, possibly explaining why such amazingly productive garden aids have remained a relative rarity in American backyards. We knew the French gardens would offer some new ideas and solutions to help move concept nearer to reality for legions of aspiring winter gardeners.

Different cultures often solve the same problem in different ways. Perhaps various cultural backgrounds generate their own unique thought patterns thus envisioning solutions from novel perspectives. Or it might be that the sizes and shapes of materials available in Europe had dictated a different approach to tunnel design than those available in the U.S. Whatever the reason, we saw two ideas that offered positive steps toward a better tunnel design for winter gardening.

Take the attachment of the plastic, for example. Most U.S. tunnel designs use a baseboard at ground level and hold the plastic to the board with wooden nailing strips or with matched metal rails that snap together. All the European tunnels we saw secured the plastic at the base of the structure by simply burying it. A shallow furrow was made along each side of the tunnel and after the plastic cover was placed over the structure its edges were tucked into the furrow and covered with soil. The deeper the furrow, the more secure the plastic. If the gardener wished to remove the cover in summer, the edges could easily be unburied leaving no nail holes or crimp lines to complicate replacing it in the fall.

We found a similarly novel approach to attaching the plastic to the last hoop at each end of the tunnel. Whereas on U.S. designs boards have been bolted to the end hoops of the tunnel so the plastic can be attached to them as to the baseboards, on European tunnels the plastic is attached directly around the end hoops with simple clamps. Some were specially designed stainless steel spring clamps that fit snugly around the circumference of the pipe hoops, but on the majority of houses the gardeners had made their own clamps from 3-inch lengths of black plastic water pipe with a slit down one side. These homemade clamps were soaked in hot water for a few minutes to soften them so they could be opened up and slipped over to secure the plastic around the end hoop. Sections of old inner tube about 4 inches square were placed over the plastic before sliding on the clamp, both to protect the plastic from abrasion and to increase the holding friction between hoop, plastic cover, and clamp.

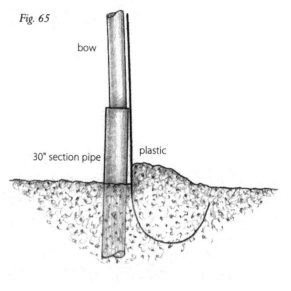

Fig. 65

bow

30" section pipe

plastic

Methods for securing plastic.

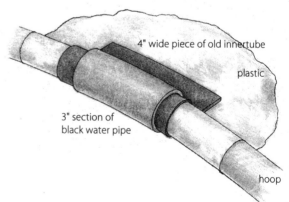

Fig. 66

4" wide piece of old innertube

plastic

3" section of black water pipe

hoop

We also saw simple solutions to the problem of ventilation. Passive ventilation in most U.S. tunnel designs is accomplished with roll-up sides. The bottom edge of the plastic on the south side of the tunnel is attached to a pipe with a handle at one end. The pipe is tied down when the tunnel is closed but can be untied and, by turning the handle, the plastic covering can be rolled up as high as the design permits. The concept is reasonably simple, but in our experience it doesn't ventilate as well as might be hoped since the hot air, being lighter than the cool air, ideally wants to rise and exit out the top. Additionally, for winter gardening, this technique could be awkward since snow or ice could hinder the attaching or detaching of the pipe roller.

Instead of roll-up sides, many of the French tunnels were constructed with vents across the entire top part of each end wall. Vents in the upper part of the end wall are common in some U.S. designs, but they are usually small rectangular openings. These vents, in contrast, comprised the whole half-round, upper part of the end wall. The French call them *demi-lune* (half-moon) vents. They were hinged on their straight bottom edge to a bar running side to side across the tunnel and opened at the top. Some were operated manually,

but others were fitted with heat-activated spring-loaded arms that opened and closed them automatically at a set temperature. The area below the half-moon vent was one large door, like on our mobile tunnel design, hinged at its top to the same cross bar so that it could be opened and propped up for extra ventilation if needed.

Although these demi-lune vents would not provide adequate ventilation during the summer, they were just the perfect size to handle the minimal ventilation needs in the winter months. The large doors beneath them could be fully removed for summer ventilation. Removing the ends will provide adequate summer ventilation of a tunnel as long as the length of the tunnel is no more than three times its width.

The above were all simple and efficient ideas for low-cost and low-tech small greenhouses suitable for winter gardening. We tucked them away into our thick mental file of solutions to greenhouse design problems. Each new idea is yet another step on the path to the perfect winter greenhouse. It doesn't exist yet, but we know the requirements. It must be simple to construct, easy to manage, environmentally sound, and pleasing to the eye. Some day soon the horticultural equivalent of Henry Ford (for affordable price), W. Edwards Demming (for efficient organization), John Muir (for environmental awareness), and Frank Lloyd Wright (for eye-pleasing lines) will create a revolutionary greenhouse design so perfect it becomes a fixture in every garden. Until then we will continue to pioneer on with our incremental improvements.

The Starter Greenhouse

Given everything we have learned, what is the simplest and least expensive greenhouse for beginners? What design will allow the greatest

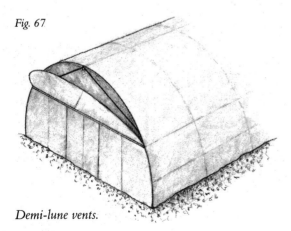

Fig. 67

Demi-lune vents.

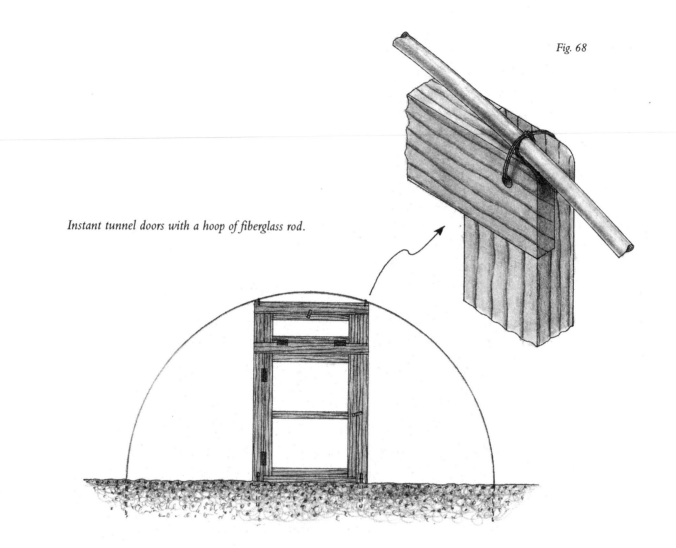

Fig. 68

Instant tunnel doors with a hoop of fiberglass rod.

number of gardeners to begin the winter harvest adventure? The answer is probably an instant greenhouse, one without a permanent structure. Temporary tunnel frames (easy up, easy down) can be and have been made from any number of materials, such as rebar (metal reinforcing rod), rigid PVC pipe, fiberglass rods, or even saplings. The trick is finding a material that is easily available, comes in long enough lengths, is bendable into large hoops, and is strong enough to stand up to pressure from wind and snow.

The most dependable instant greenhouse design we have found combines two of these possibilities. It uses hoops made of lengths of rebar slid inside lengths of plastic pipe. Rebar is almost strong enough and comes in 20-foot lengths, which are long enough, but it has a rough surface that can abrade the plastic cover. Plastic pipe is not strong enough by itself, but has a smooth exterior. By placing the 20-foot-long rebar inside an 18 foot length of plastic pipe you get a bendable yet strong rod just the right size for making a home greenhouse.

These rebar/plastic rods will make a tunnel that is 12 feet wide, 6 feet high in the center, and as long as you wish. Lay out two parallel lines 12 feet apart. Make marks every 4 feet (every 2 feet in heavy snow country) along the lines. Insert the end of a rod into the soil (about 12 inches deep) at the first mark, bend the rod over, and insert the other end at the corresponding mark 12 feet away. That makes a half circle hoop with a 6 foot radius. Continue the process until all the hoops have been erected. A 20-foot-long tunnel with hoops at 4-foot intervals will require 6 rebar/plastic rods. Take one more rebar length and tie it to the apex of all the hoops as a ridge purlin. One of the best tying materials is strips of rubber cut from old inner tubes.

You can cover this tunnel with 20-foot-wide, 6-mil builder's plastic from the lumberyard. This is the least expensive plastic available. Since it does not contain ultraviolet (UV) inhibitors to protect it against the sun, you will have to replace it every year. Instead of attaching the plastic to boards along the ground, this model uses even more basic technology. Dig a little trench along the bottom edge on each side and bury the edges of the plastic with soil. Pack the soil with your feet, and the plastic will be held securely in place. Once the ground freezes, it will not budge.

The end walls for this instant tunnel are made to fit inside the curve of the bow. They are lightweight and prefabricated, so they can be put up, taken down, and stored as easily as the rods. They consist of a wooden frame containing a door with a space above it for the automatic vent. The upper corners of the frame are wired to the end bow where they meet. The bottom corners are attached to stakes driven into the ground. The plastic cover for the tunnel is pulled around the end bows and fastened to the wooden frame. It is buried along the bottom edge the same as on the sides.

Coping with Snow

Heavy snow accumulation on a tunnel greenhouse can do more than just block sunlight; it can collapse the structure. I don't mean normal snowfalls, unless the snow is very wet, but the heavy blizzards that come along occasionally. If a big storm is predicted, or if you plan to be away for a while, you should take precautions. Place a 2x4 or similar structural upright under the center of every other hoop to provide extra support against heavy loads. Remove these supports when the danger has passed, as they make it awkward to move around in the greenhouse.

Shovel away any snow that slides off the roof. If it's too deep, it not only will block sunlight but also can press in on the side walls of the house and bend the frame. In most years and in most climates, snow will not be a major problem. But you should be aware that on rare occasions it can carry a lot of weight.

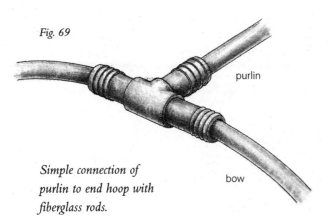

Fig. 69

Simple connection of purlin to end hoop with fiberglass rods.

purlin

bow

TABLE 13

HARVEST SEASON OF TUNNEL-COVERED COLD FRAME CROPS FROM SEPTEMBER TO MAY IN ZONE 5

Crop	Sept	Oct	Nov	Dec	Jan	Feb	Mar	Apr	May
Arugula	░	░	░	░	░	░	░	░	░
Beet	▓	▓	▓						▓
Broccoli	░	░	░	░					
Brussels sprouts	▓	▓	▓	▓	▓				
Carrot	░	░	░	░	░	░	░		
Celery	▓	▓	▓						
Chard	░	░	░	░	░	░	░	░	░
Chicory, green	▓	▓	▓	▓	▓	▓	▓	▓	▓
Claytonia	░	░	░	░	░	░	░	░	░
Dandelion	▓	▓	▓	▓	▓	▓	▓	▓	▓
Endive	░	░	░	░	░	░	░	░	░
Escarole	▓	▓	▓	▓	▓	▓	▓		
Kale	░	░	░	░	░	░	░	░	░
Kohlrabi	░	░	░	░	░	░	░		
Leek	░	░	░	░	░	░	░	░	
Lettuce	▓	▓	▓				▓	▓	▓
Mâche	░	░	░	░	░	░	░	░	
Mizuna	▓	▓	▓	▓	▓	▓	▓	▓	▓
Onion, green	░	░	░	░	░	░	░	░	░
Parsley	▓	▓	▓	▓	▓	▓	▓	▓	▓
Radicchio	░	░	░	░	░				
Radish	▓	▓	▓				▓	▓	▓
Sorrel	░	░	░	░	░	░	░	░	░
Spinach	▓	▓	▓	▓	▓	▓	▓	▓	▓
Tatsoi	░	░	░	░	░	░	░		
Turnip	▓	▓	▓	▓	▓				▓

The Complete Winter Garden

With the double layer of protection—greenhouse over inner layer—you can harvest a wider range of crops for a longer period of time than under a single layer. Table 13 gives you some idea of the variety and season of availability of the major winter crops. Table 16 gives planting guidelines for all sections of the United States. These are not all the possible winter crops, but they are the ones with which we have experience. They provide a fabulous winter feast as is, but they will have more company in the future.

Envisioning the Future

A fascinating aspect of new ideas is the way in which they catch on and why. During the late afternoon of the eighth day of our French journey, ignoring the main highways and making our way along a web of small country lanes as usual, we came upon the village of Les Bastides des Jourdans. It was a delightful example of a new idea taking hold like the spreading ripples of a pebble in a pool.

Logically, we had been looking for and commenting on gardens the whole time we had been driving in France. We paid particular attention to those that appeared to be active winter gardens, as opposed to those whose crops were only hardy leftovers of a summer effort. We had seen some fine examples here and there, but Les Bastides was a step above. We saw numerous well-maintained winter gardens. They contained not only outdoor crops such as leeks, cabbage, carrots, kale, chard, and Brussels sprouts but also small plastic-covered greenhouse structures and glass-covered cold frames filled with salad crops.

The obvious town-wide garden passion was so striking that we slowed the car to a crawl and then stopped and got out so we could walk around. Along the narrow main street were a half-dozen productive gardens with others distinguishable in the background. There was no one around to ask and we were too shy to knock on the doors of strangers, so we pondered between ourselves about the genesis of this unique hotbed (to make a bad pun) of winter garden fervor. We both reached the same conclusion—the power of example. One of these gardeners, producing every year a splendid winter bounty, likely inspired another and then more joined in.

A traveler driving the rural road past our place in Maine would notice a similar situation. Greenhouses, cold frames, and winter gardens abound. Along a one-mile stretch of our road there are seven households with greenhouses, coldframes, or both, in addition to the numerous commercial winter greenhouses on our farm. Our neighbors have been exposed to the wonderful fresh winter vegetables and salads that we serve at our table or bring as our contribution to potluck dinners. They have done what most anyone who loves to eat does when encountering good food: they try to get more of it. And since it is so easy to grow your own, why not?

Whereas the neighbors along the road were inspired by our success, our own inspiration came from even earlier practitioners who were also neighbors. Scott and Helen Nearing, authors of *Living the Good Life,* the back-to-the-land classic, had a simple lean-to glass greenhouse against a south-facing section of the stone wall that encircled their garden. During late summer and fall Scott would transplant it full with seedlings of Swiss chard, lettuce, collards, escarole, and endive. He would sow spinach and radishes. Large bunches of leeks would be heeled-in along a side wall. The earliest plantings were used for fresh vegetable harvest until December, when the Nearings traditionally left for their winter lecture tour. The later plantings, protected by the greenhouse, wintered over successfully and were ready to eat when Scott and Helen returned in early March.

Although we were inspired by the Nearings' winter greenhouse, it is interesting that none of us who were neighbors at the time ever built one of our own. That inaction is testimony to the difficult acceptance faced by wonderful ideas when they add an unfamiliar step, in this case a greenhouse, to a familiar process, like gardening. Not being aware at the time that the new step could be simplified, we looked at the challenge and expense of building a glass greenhouse against a stone wall and found it daunting. It was only in later years, as we tinkered with the idea and found ever simpler, less expensive, and more productive ways to do it, that it became a part of our lives, and through example, part of our neighbors' lives as well.

For whatever reason, be it the eminent simplicity of the system, a missionary passion on the part of the initiator, or the irresistible freshness of the produce, the winter garden enthusiast in the village of Les Bastides appeared to have collected an equally enthusiastic set of imitators. Simplicity may be the key because, peeking over the walls, we saw that the small greenhouses had homemade curved supports covered by a sheet of plastic with edges buried in the soil. This is the simplest example of a protective winter greenhouse. If it takes missionary preaching, well, when it comes to food the French must be the most receptive audience anywhere. And for freshness there would appear to be no contest. We had seen so often on the trip how that most important food quality is highly treasured in France. Tipping an imaginary hat to our fellow winter gardening proselytizer, whomever he or she might be, and hoping our own proselytizing might spread ripples all across the U.S., we returned to the car as the January sun quickly diminished, and headed off to find a hotel.

CHAPTER 11

THE UNDERGROUND GARDEN: ROOT CROPS, ROOT CELLARS, AND INDOOR HARVESTING

W e are not often stumped by a vegetable crop, but the name *Campanula raiponce* on the neat sign next to one group of plants had us scratching our heads momentarily. We were visiting the Prieuré de Salagon near the small village of Fourcalquier, France. The buildings and grounds are maintained as an ethnological and ethnobotanical center for the Haute Provence region. We were particularly interested in the Salagon gardens because the time represented is the 15th century. The gardens are true to that pre-Columbian age and contain only the plants known and cultivated at that time. We wanted to see what a 44th-parallel gardener on a misty day in late January five hundred years ago might have been able to harvest for supper.

The Latin name *Campanula rapunculus* gave us the clue. The heroine of Grimms' fairy tale "Rapunzel" had the same name as the plants that were stolen from the magician's garden in the story. The name is "rampion" in English. We remembered that it was listed in Jean Luc's catalog. A white, spindle-shaped edible root, rampion has leaves similar to those of mâche. It belongs to the Campanulaceae or Bellflower family. Rampion is the only plant in the family to be widely cultivated as a food plant, though it has been forgotten long enough to be a rare sight in the vegetable garden today. Evelyn in *Acetaria* (1699) calls it the "esculent campanula" and says its tender roots are eaten like radishes, "but much more nourishing." Vilmorin in *The Vegetable Garden* (1885) claims the seeds are the smallest of all kitchen garden seeds and should be mixed with a little fine soil or sand

Fig. 70

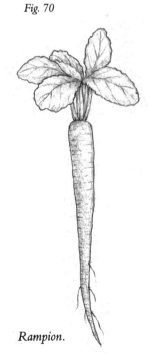

Rampion.

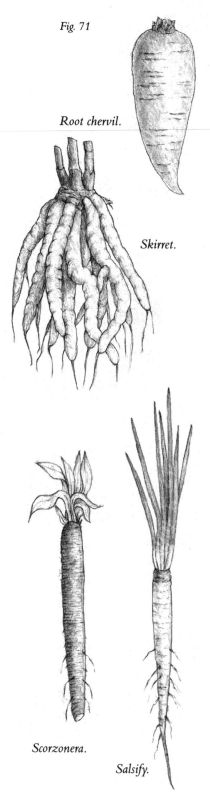

Fig. 71

Root chervil.

Skirret.

Scorzonera.

Salsify.

to make them easier to plant. He also states that roots from a June sowing are ready to be harvested by October or November and "will continue to yield a supply through the winter."

It is easy to forget root crops as important winter garden foods. They hide their glory in the cool, damp protection of the earth. Their summer leaves, still marking the spot but usually no longer erect and striking, have fallen back to make space for next year's growth. In the priority scheme of these biennials, the root is grown as a storage organ the first season to ensure the early nourishment of the seed stalk and its accompanying reproductive processes of flowering, pollination, and seed dispersal during the second season. Over the years, we humans have selected for roots that are larger, tenderer, of better color, or that store longer in order to enhance the pleasure of consuming that stored nourishment ourselves.

In addition to rampion, there are other root-eating pleasures of the past, forgotten by today's gardeners. One such is skirret *(Sium sisarum),* which according to Vilmorin "may be left in the ground all winter, and only taken up as they are wanted." Skirret forms a bunch of roots in a bundle something like dahlia bulbs "but much longer and more slender." They have a woody core, best removed before cooking. Another ancient crop is turnip-rooted chervil *(Chaerophyllum bulbosum).* We didn't find any in this medieval garden, but it must have been known at the time since it is a native of Southern Europe. However, its traditional method of culture, planting in fall for late summer harvest, may mean it had all been harvested, or had so little top growth left we didn't notice it. One enthusiast quoted by John Organ in *Rare Vegetables* considered its "deliciousness to the epicure . . . fully supplying the place of the potatoes."

The long roots of salsify *(Tragopogon porrifolius)* and its dark skinned relative scorzonera *(Scorzonera hispanica)* were also more popular in ages past. They are the renowned vegetable oysters whose flavor and texture are said to resemble that of the delicious bivalve when they are properly prepared. Both are winter hardy and, in addition to their edible roots, will also produce a salad crop if the leaves are cut back in late fall and the tops of the roots covered with six inches of soil. As winter abates, the new leaf growth pushes up through the earth in the same manner as the chicons of Belgian endive. John Organ says, "quite a few people consider this the best way of using salsify."

Parsnips have remained in semi-popular use. In our Maine winter they cannot be harvested from the outdoor garden until the frozen ground thaws in spring. But that is actually a bonus because the flavor is sweeter due to the stress of winter cold causing some of their starch to turn to sugar. We have taken advantage of that effect of cold temperature on root sweetness to turn normal carrots into "candy" carrots. We plant in early August and leave the baby carrots in the ground all winter under the protection of a cold frame or tunnel. The cold temperature transformation of our carrots from popular food to near addiction status is attested to by our friends and customers, whose demand has turned that lowly root into our most acclaimed winter crop.

Many of the popular root vegetables are not stored in the soil during our cold winters. For them we borrow an ancient technology which we consider the third simple miracle in this year-round food system: the root cellar—a hole in the ground to store root crops. The root cellar is a basic technology that works in harmony with the natural world, just like compost and cold frames. Whereas compost provides the energy to grow the food and the winter protection from frames and tunnels provides a snug home for cold-season greenery, the root cellar is your winter home for the rest of the garden's bounty.

We think of our root cellar as a secret underground garden into which we spirit away many of our crops when winter threatens. The crops don't grow in this garden. They just sit there respiring quietly and looking beautiful. For root crops, the most delightful place to spend the winter is not some sunny tropical isle but a cold, damp, dark cavern. If that's what they like, that's what we try to provide. It couldn't be easier.

A root cellar requires no fancy equipment or energy source because it takes advantage of the cold, damp conditions that exist naturally underground. It will keep working through the deepest winter snows and the longest electric power outage. It is easy to overlook the miracles of the root cellar because it is so simple and so unpretentious. From Zone 6 and northwards, where winter temperatures dip too low to leave most root crops in the soil or in outdoor pits or buried barrels, the root cellar ensures low-cost cold storage.

The true root crops grow their edible parts underground. Root crops have always been staple foods of the winter season. Included in this category are the potato, carrot, beet, radish, parsnip, and rutabaga, as well as the lesser known celeriac, parsley root, chicories, and the even rarer roots we found in the Salagon garden. For storage purposes, cabbage and kohlrabi are considered root crops because they store well in the same underground conditions. Certain varieties of Chinese cabbage and unrelated crops such as leeks and fall celery also store well for considerable periods.

Creating a Root Cellar

No one wants second best. A slimy cabbage from a dingy corner of the basement will never compete with the crisp specimens on the vegetable shelf of the supermarket. Wilted, dried-out carrots look unappealing next to the crunchy, plastic-wrapped beauties in the refrigerator. When home storage is unsuccessful, a case can be made for artificial refrigeration. But the cabbage need not be slimy nor the carrots wilted. A properly constructed root cellar does not take a backseat to any other method of food storage. It is no great feat to manage a simple underground root cellar so that the produce will be equal or superior in quality to anything stored in an artificially refrigerated unit, even after long periods of storage.

A successful root cellar should be properly located, structurally sound, weather tight, convenient to fill and empty, easy to check on and clean, and secure against rodents. Proper location means underground at a sufficient depth so frost won't penetrate. The cellar should be structurally sound so it won't collapse on you. It needs to be weather tight so cold winds can't blow in and freeze the produce. You need to have easy access to fill it, to use the produce, and to clean it at the end of the winter. And it should be rodent-proof so all the food you have stored away won't be nibbled by rats and mice.

Provision must be made for drainage as with any other cellar, and the cellar should be insulated so that it can maintain a low temperature for as long as possible and provide properly humid storage conditions. Finally, microclimates within the cellar (colder near the floor, warmer near the ceiling) should allow you to meet different temperature and moisture requirements for different crops. The cellar will be most successful if it incorporates your underground food storage needs into one efficient, compact unit. It's surprising how easily a hole in the ground meets all those conditions.

Any house with a basement already has a potential root cellar. You just need to open a vent so cold air can flow in on fall nights, and sprinkle water on the floor for moisture. The temperature control in the root cellar is almost automatic because cold air, which is heavier than warm air, will flow down, displacing the warmer air, which rises and exits. This lowers the temperature in the cellar incrementally as fall progresses and the nights get cooler. By the time outdoor conditions are cold enough to require moving root crops to the cellar (around October 21 to November 7 here in Maine), conditions in the underground garden are just right—cool and moist. With minimal attention, they will stay that way until late the next spring.

No wood or other material that might suffer from being wet should be used in root cellar construction. The ideal root cellar is made of concrete or stone with rigid insulation around the outside. Any permanent wood in a root cellar

soon becomes damp and moldy. Wood will not only rot but also will serve as a home for bacteria and spoilage organisms and is subject to the gnawing entry of rodents. The stone or concrete cellar is impregnable. It won't rot or decompose, and the thick walls hold the cool of the earth.

The easiest way to make a root cellar is to wall off one corner of the basement as a separate room. The best material is concrete block. There is no problem even if the rest of the basement is heated. You simply need to insulate one temperature zone from the other. Leave enough space between the top of the walls and the joists of the floor above so you can install a cement-board ceiling with rigid insulation above it. Also attach rigid insulation to the heated side of the cellar walls you build. The insulation can be protected with a concrete-like covering such as Block Bond. Install an insulated metal door for access, and the structure is complete.

There are several simpler options, especially for storing small quantities of vegetables. If your house has an old-fashioned cellar with a dirt floor and there is enough drainage below floor level, you can dig a pit in the floor 18 to 24 inches deep, line it with concrete blocks, and add an insulated cover. You will want to open the cover every few days to encourage air exchange in the pit. The pit won't be as easy to use as a room you can walk into, but like any hole in the ground, it should keep root crops cool and moist. In warmer climates, you can use similar pits or buried barrels for storage either outdoors or in an unheated shed.

One of the simplest techniques we ever used, before we had a root cellar, was to dig pits in one section of the winter greenhouse. In that case we used metal garbage cans and buried them to their edge in the soil under the inner layer. To make sure they stayed cool we insulated their lids. We filled those cans with all the traditional root crops

Fig. 72

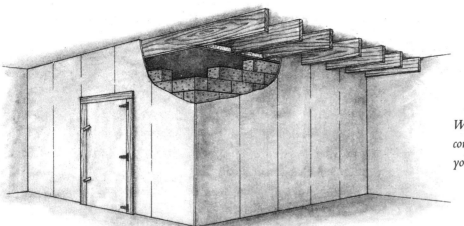

Wall off and insulate a corner of the basement for your root cellar.

Root cellar option—a buried box works well in cellars with dirt floors.

A buried barrel as a simple root cellar.

after their late fall harvest. Our whole winter food supply that year was in one central spot and when we went out to harvest fresh spinach and scallions for dinner we would bring back stored potatoes and cabbage at the same time.

Controlling the Temperature

An underground cellar takes advantage of the cool temperatures of the earth. The venting system takes advantage of the cold fall nights to drop the temperature in the root cellar more quickly than it would normally drop. There should be at least one window in the corner of the basement chosen for the root cellar. If there is no window, you will need to provide some opening for air access to the outside. The idea is to establish a good storage temperature before the season requires you to harvest your root crops and put them in the cellar. There is a time lag, since the cellar won't get to the ideal low temperature until late in the fall, but things always work out. Keep the vents mostly closed during the winter. If you let too much cold midwinter air into the cellar, the temperature could drop too low and freeze your crops, although most root crops will not be damaged by freezing unless the temperature goes below 28°F.

The air vent for a home cellar should be at least 12 inches wide by 6 to 8 inches high for adequate airflow. The minimum size would be 6 by 6 inches. It should be screened with ¼-inch hardware cloth. The opening will allow cool air to enter the root cellar and warm air to exit. That natural air movement is what will cool down the cellar in the fall and allow you to regulate its temperature when necessary. The easiest way to manage that airflow is as follows.

Divide the air vent in half horizontally. On the inside of the cellar, use sections of galvanized metal duct to cover the lower half of the window or vent and extend to the floor. This allows the heavy cold air to enter. On the outside of the cellar, install duct to cover the upper half of the window or vent and extend up along the side of the house a few feet. This will act like a chimney so the lighter warm air can exit. That sets up the natural airflow. In autumn, when outside night temperatures begin to drop, both vents are left open. Once cellar temperatures reach the mid-30s, the vents are closed partially or completely to keep the temperature inside the cellar from going below freezing. The ideal temperature for root crop storage is 32° to 36°F. That's the goal, but storage will be adequate even in less than ideal conditions.

To help you keep track of temperature, mount a thermometer in the

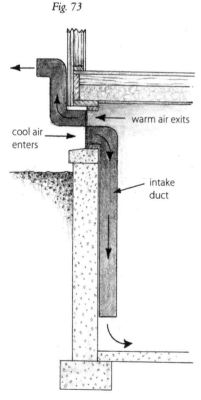

Fig. 73

cool air enters

warm air exits

intake duct

Cellar air vent.

cellar. Put it near the ground, where the temperature will be the coldest. To take full advantage of temperature levels in a cellar, you can preferentially stack some crops on the floor and others higher up. Beets and kohlrabi like it the coldest. Carrots, rutabagas, radishes, and celeriac prefer the mid-30s. Potatoes do best at 40°F. Concrete blocks can be used as supports to raise containers above floor level. Storage temperatures for each crop are given in appendix A.

After midwinter, close the vents completely to keep the cellar cold as long into the spring as possible. At this time of year, the lag of cellar temperature behind outdoor temperature is just what you want. Of course, the cellar will eventually warm up in summer, but by then everything is fresh from the garden again. Summer is the time to clean out the cellar. Remaining vegetables go to the compost heap. Hose down the walls and ceiling, using a stiff-bristle brush to remove any mold. You can apply a coat of whitewash if you wish. A carefully cleaned and managed cellar will store food impeccably.

Controlling the Humidity

In most cases when crops keep poorly and shrivel in cellar storage, the air is too dry. One practice is to store carrots, beets, and others in damp sand or peat to keep them from shriveling. That is a lot of extra work. We prefer to correct the cause rather than treat the symptom. You do that by keeping the humidity high in the storage area.

Roots can be stored directly in boxes or bags with no covering when the cellar atmosphere is humid. Keep the humidity as high as possible (90 to 95 percent) by keeping the floor and walls moist. Whenever you go to the cellar, take along a bucket of water to splash the walls and floor. Then you can fill the bucket with food to carry to the kitchen. You may want to mount a humidity meter on the wall along with the thermometer, but the crops themselves are an excellent gauge. If they stay crisp, all is well. If you have to store roots under less than ideal humidity conditions, then packing them in damp sand or peat will help them stay crisp.

Keeping the Root Cellar Dark

Any part of the cellar window that is not used for vents should be blocked off completely to insulate and darken the cellar. The best storage takes place in complete darkness. This is most important for potatoes. When potato tubers are exposed to light, their skins turn green and a chemical called solanin is formed. Solanin also is found in potato leaves and is the reason they will give you a bellyache if you eat them. To prevent potatoes from greening in storage, keep them in the dark. The occasional light from opening the door and getting food from the cellar is not a problem. If you have a light bulb in the cellar (which is a good idea so you can see what you are doing), put it on a timer switch. That way it will turn off automatically if anyone forgets and leaves it on.

Storage Containers

Pictures of root cellars usually show wooden bins of root crops and wooden shelves laden with canning jars. Our cellar is different. Since we have fresh food year-round in the garden, there's no need for canning jars. And, as mentioned, we avoid wood in cellar construction. Root crops are contained in bushel-sized plastic boxes that stack one on the other, instead of wooden bins. The woven plastic bags in which grain is sold by feed stores are another option. Five-gallon plastic pails used for bulk peanut butter or yogurt, often avail-

Fig. 74

Root cellar storage containers.

able secondhand from health-food stores and food co-ops, also work well. You should drill a few ½-inch holes in the bottom and sides to provide some ventilation. Fill them with root crops and stack them on the floor. If you wish to use wooden crates, pay attention to their care. Remove them from the cellar as soon as they are empty. Wash them out, dry them in the sun, and store them dry until next year. They will last much longer and work better that way. The plastic containers also should be cleaned after use. The woven plastic grain bags can be turned inside out and laundered in a washing machine.

Other Stored Crops

For some vegetables, the cold and damp of the root cellar are unsuitable for storage. The onion family and winter squashes keep much better under cool, dry conditions. Both these crops should be allowed to cure in warm, dry temperatures for two weeks after harvest. Spread them out in single layers on drying racks in the sun or in the attic. After curing, a mesh bag is the best storage container for onions, and wooden shelves are best for the squashes.

Reasonably ideal winter conditions for storage of these crops can be found in a number of places around the home. Squashes like it warmer (50° to 55°F) than onions (32° to 35°F), so if there are options, let that be your guide. Sometimes the corner of a heated basement farthest from the furnace will suffice. You may have an unheated room in the house or an enclosed porch that doesn't freeze. In many cases, after the weather cools, the attic can provide close to ideal conditions. People often store onions and squashes in boxes under the bed in a cool bedroom. Once we stored them under a couch by an exterior wall in the living room, opposite the wood stove. Ingenuity and imagination will help you come up with one solution or another. You will know when you have found the right spot by how long the stored foods keep. Under good conditions, the squashes will last until April and the onions through May.

Check on the condition of your cool, dry vegetables every time you get some for cooking. If the onions start to sprout, you can use the sprouts as you would green onions. If a squash develops mold spots, cut them out and use the rest of the squash within a few days. The more care you took in growing and curing these crops, the better they will hold up in storage.

Really Dry Storage

We use one other storage method—drying. Practically all vegetables can be dried for winter storage, but given the choice, we prefer to eat them fresh from the garden or the cellar. We have, however, developed one near-addiction in this category—dried, vine-ripened tomatoes.

It was when we first dried tomatoes that we finally freed ourselves of any lingering desire to can vegetables. Tomatoes hung on as the last canning crop because they were indispensible for many of our favorite recipes. They still are indispensible. But the dried product does it all. What a marvelous food! Dried tomatoes store easily in glass jars and can be used in almost any dish that calls for tomatoes.

If you live in a hot, dry climate, the drying of foods will pose no problem. For those in less favored areas who enjoy a construction project, there are many designs for homemade solar dryers (see appendix D). For our dried tomatoes, we have chosen ease and efficiency. A small electric air-convection drier with an automatic temperature control (see appendix D) does the job. It is clean and dependable, and the results are professional. Cut small tomatoes in half and cut the larger ones into ⅜-inch slices, then set them on the drying trays. They are ready in about 12 to 24 hours.

We also dry herbs, but don't need the drier for them. We hang them in bunches from the beams on the kitchen ceiling. They are out of direct sunlight, and the conditions are dry and airy. Their aromas make the kitchen atmosphere that much more delightful. When they feel dry and crinkly, take the herbs down, separate the leaves from the stems, and store the leaves in opaque glass jars so light won't fade them. The stems go to the compost heap.

The Indoor Garden

The underground garden serves a further culinary function beyond storage of roots to eat during the winter. It is also the source of roots to sprout during the winter. Stored root crops can be coaxed into producing sprouted leaves by moving the roots from the cellar to a warmer environment. This technique is known as *forcing*. The word forcing makes the process sound harsher than it is. We prefer to think of it as gentle encouragement.

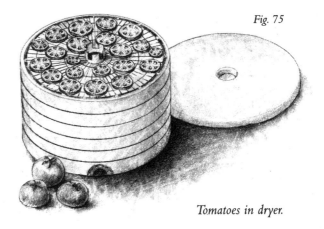

Fig. 75

Tomatoes in dryer.

Stored root crops are biennials. Biennials grow a storage organ (the root) during the first year. They use the food stored in the root to help produce seeds the second year. The leaves that the root grows prior to sending up the seed stalk can be harvested for winter eating. You enable the root to grow those leaves by providing springlike conditions. The expensive Belgian endive, also called witloof or white leaf, that you find in the grocery store is grown that way. You can produce it and many other delicacies at home in the winter.

Growing Belgian Endive

The Belgian endive you eat (the French call it a *chicon)* is the sprout from a stored endive root. The root was grown in the garden the summer before. Commercial endive growers use special climate-controlled chambers for producing chicons. You can do just as well with homegrown conditions. Most important is to find a spot in the house that comes close to the 50° to 55°F temperature for the perfect crop. After that, the rest is easy. Cover the sprouting roots with an upside-down black plastic bucket to maintain high humidity and keep them in darkness. In our house, a favorite spot is under the kitchen sink.

The temperature emulates spring conditions.

In cooler temperatures, the sprout grows more slowly; if the temperature is too warm, it grows too quickly, with some loss of quality. The high humidity keeps the leaves from wilting. The darkness blanches the leaves (keeps them white). Endive is bitter if grown in sunlight. The leaves sprouted in darkness don't contain the bitter quality.

We manage our endive production as follows. When the roots are harvested from the garden in October, cut off the leaves to within an inch or so of the top of the root. Don't cut it too close, or you will cut off the central bud that grows the largest sprout. Also cut off the bottom of the roots so they are all 6 to 7 inches long. Then place them, a dozen or more depending on size, upright in a 10-quart plastic bucket. You can fill around them with sand up to the tops of the roots to support them, or stuff a few more in so they hold each other upright. Then store the buckets in the root cellar.

Starting in late November or early December, when thoughts turn to winter eating, bring up

Fig. 76

Endive sprouting in buckets of sand.

one bucket every ten days to initiate the forcing process. (The endive season can last through April, so multiplying · five months times three buckets per month (one every ten days) would require storing fifteen buckets. When you bring up a bucket, add water up to the shoulder of the roots, place the bucket under the kitchen sink, and cover it with a large, black 5-gallon bucket. Every few days, check to make sure the sand is moist and add water if necessary (better too wet than too dry). Within three weeks, you will be eating delicious Belgian endive. The parade of new buckets maintains the supply all winter.

Harvest is simple. You cut the chicon off where it meets the root. When all the chicons are harvested, remove the 10-quart bucket, put the roots on the compost heap and the sand (if you used it) on the icy driveway, and store the bucket till next year. If the chicons begin to grow too large, you can harvest all of them at once and store them in the refrigerator. It's possible to get a second (and third) harvest of smaller chicons from the outer buds on the root, but we prefer to move on to the prime chicons from the next 10-quart bucket.

If temperatures are too warm or if you grow a variety of Belgian endive that was bred for growing *under* a covering of sand rather than just planted in sand, the leaves on the chicons may open out at the top rather than remaining neatly closed. That is only a problem for the commercial grower, who wants to sell a perfectly shaped product. The less-than-perfect chicon will taste just as good chopped in your salad or baked in a cheese sauce. This should not be a problem, though, since the modern varieties of Belgian endive all are bred for uncovered production.

You can use this same forcing process for other members of the chicory family or for close relatives, such as the dandelion. The sprouts may not be classic in shape, but they will taste good.

LYNN KARLIN

KAREN BUSSOLINI

The young seedlings of spring, the bounty of summer, curing onions in the fall, and the hardy crops of winter. Four seasons of great meals from the home garden. (Photographs are by Barbara Damrosch except where noted.)

This 20-foot by 40-foot gothic arch hoophouse is attached to the pantry of our house. There is a 10-foot-wide brick patio at the house end, a 20-foot-square growing area at the center, and a graveled work area where we winter-over two fig trees at the other end. This photo was taken in early October. In early November a layer of floating row cover fabric is added to provide protection for the low-growing crops. The fig trees are wrapped individually.

Below: Swiss chard is a hardy and beautiful home-garden crop that will feed you in all four seasons.

Bottom: Moving an experimental sled-style greenhouse with a little help from our friends.

Far left: An edible California weed, also known as "miner's lettuce," claytonia will provide a dependable salad harvest through the coldest winter when grown under two layers of protection.

Left: A visit to the underground garden of stored crops in the root cellar.

Below: My harvest outfit indicates that this isn't summer, but these hardy salad crops think that it's perpetually spring, with the added protection of a layer of floating row cover fabric.

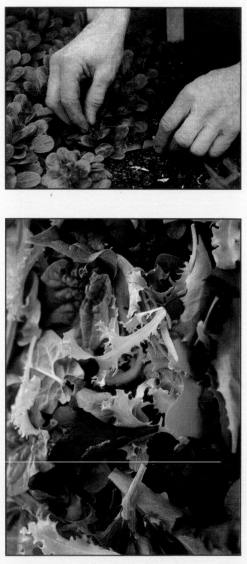

Left, top and bottom: Brush the snow off the cold frames, slide back the glass, and a fresh harvest awaits within.

Above, top: Mâche, the absolute hardiest of all the winter crops, is a tender and delicious salad ingredient. Serve the small plants whole with cold baked beets and a classic vinaigrette.

Above: A bowl of mixed salad like this in mid-winter should convince anyone that the four-season harvest is a reality.

Above, top: Short rows of fresh young salad ingredients, like this minutina, are a delight to the eye and the palate.

Above: 'Bull's Blood' beet.

Right (inset): Trellised crops such as these early peas can join low-growing salad ingredients in a spring cold frame if the glass angle is raised to accommodate them.

Above: Flats of spring seedlings share greenhouse space during May with a few remaining crops of the winter harvest.

Right, top: The broadfork is fun to use and is a terrifically effective soil aerator that doesn't disturb the natural soil layers.

Right: This cultivator—made from a piece of #9 wire hammered flat, sharpened, then bent around and inserted into an old file handle—is an example of a simple, homemade garden tool.

For those in cooler climates or those who just want an earlier tomato harvest, setting out plants in a plastic-covered tunnel assures a bounteous crop, and the longest possible season. Long-season greenhouse tomato crops need to be pruned and trained to overhead supports.

Once you realize how productive this can be, you might want to try forcing some of the less familiar subjects. In addition to those forced in darkness, a number of food crops can be grown in the light. This is a case of sacrificing the root to get it to grow leaves.

Forcing Winter Greenery

We bring celeriac, beets, and parsley root up from the cellar and plant them in large pots of damp sand in a sunny window. You can also do this with turnips, onions, and carrots. There is no need for darkness because, in this case, you want the new growth to be green. Water the pots every few days to keep the sand damp. A normal room temperature of 60° to 65°F is ideal. The vigor of the roots themselves determines the quantity and quality of your production. You will learn to adjust your harvesting techniques and growth expectations accordingly. The celeriac grows small, flavorful celery stalks; the beets grow beet greens; and the parsley roots produce a pretty good parsley. The turnips grow turnip greens, the onion tops can be used like green onions, and the ferny carrot tops make a nice nibble. Even the smallest shoots of sprouted greens are a flavorful garnish for a midwinter dish.

To add bulk to a salad, you may want to try another winter growing idea from the underground garden. When you harvest cabbages in the fall, remove the loose outer leaves and pull the cabbages—head, stem, and roots—from the soil. Store them upright on the cellar floor, leaning against the wall with a little sand over their roots. They store very well that way. When you bring a cabbage up to the kitchen, cut the head off for eating, then plant the leftover roots and stem in an upright position in one of the damp sand pots in the window. Add water to keep the sand moist.

Fig. 77

Sprouting cabbages.

Within a few days, sprouts will begin to grow from the leaf nodes all along the stem. You will soon have a bushy mound of fresh green cabbage shoots, which are the foundation for many a fine winter salad, soup, or casserole.

Historical Vegetables

After exploring the Salagon gardens, we spent a few hours with some of the gracious and helpful staff discussing pre-Columbian vegetables. It made us aware that the old Europeans were not missing anything as far as the winter garden was concerned. All of the popular New World crops, which would not have been known to a 15th-century European gardener, are either warm-weather crops or not tolerant to frost. None of them—tomatoes, peppers, green beans, squash, pumpkins, corn, potatoes—have ever appeared on the fresh winter crop lists of our home garden.

We also visited the priory's research library. Our command of French faltered somewhat at the gates of the old technical books and was bested entirely by the truly ancient volumes, but we dutifully wrote down author, title, and date of ones like *Écologie et Biogéographie des Plantes*

TABLE 14
AVAILABILITY OF ROOT CELLAR CROPS

	Cellar Storage		Cool, Dry Storage		Forced in Warmth (for leaf production)		

Crop	Oct	Nov	Dec	Jan	Feb	Mar	Apr	May
Beet								
Belgian endive								
Cabbage								
Cabbage, Chinese								
Carrot								
Celeriac								
Garlic								
Kohlrabi								
Onion, bulb								
Parsley root								
Potato								
Radish								
Rutabaga								
Squash, winter								

Cultivées chez les Carolingiens au IX'ème Siècle [Ecology and Bio-Geography of the Plants Cultivated by the Carolingians in the 9th Century] in hopes of acquiring greater proficiency for future research efforts. We were able to purchase more modern books in the museum shop and eagerly acquired copies of *Les Légumes Oubliés* [The Forgotten Vegetables] by Elizabeth Scotto and a reprint of the 1892 volume *Le Potager d'un Curieux*, by A. Pailleux and D. Bois, the book that had so inspired Jean-Luc Danneyrolles.

The 15th century enveloped us one last time as we left the priory. The farm's sheep were being driven to their night pasture by a shepherd and his dog. The shepherd carried the traditional shepherd's crook and wore an old-time farmer's smock. The low clouds had settled into mist and the late afternoon light sat like a halo on the scene. We stopped as the flock blocked the road ahead of us, crossing from one field to another. We both got out of the car. Freed from that traditional encumbrance of the 20th century, it was easy to imagine having stepped down from an ox cart or a pony-drawn dray, heading home after a day in the fields. Not too far from the truth. After our day in our "field" we were headed off to the home of a French farmer, where we had booked lodging for the night.

The success of an agricultural system depends on its ability to mimic the natural ecology.

—G. F. Wilson and R. Lal

CHAPTER 12

THE NATURAL GARDEN: PLANTS AND PESTS

Our garden exists as a part of the natural world, and we pay attention to the patterns of that world. Thus, we don't speak in terms of "secrets to gardening success." There are no secrets. The facts are written boldly on every piece of field and forest right in front of your eyes. The plants that thrive in that spot are those whose needs are best met by the conditions where they grow. Those conditions include light levels, temperature, humidity, and all the possible combinations of air, water, organic matter, and rock particles that make up the soil that anchors their roots. Our role as vegetable gardeners is to create ideal conditions for vegetable crops.

The interconnection between soil nutrients, soil structure, soil organisms, sun, heat, cold, moisture, and the health and vigor of plants in the garden may appear complex until you see that it follows logical principles. Those factors create the environment for plant growth and all organisms thrive best in a congenial environment. This is wholeness rather than complexity; this is the elemental order of Nature. Nature's systems only seem complicated if we miss their elegance. We have a simple rule: If what we are doing in the garden seems complicated, it is probably wrong.

This approach to gardening celebrates our partnership with Nature, but we are definitely the junior partners. The more time we spend in the garden, the more reading and studying we do about gardening, the more impressed we become—awed, actually—by Nature's design. There are enough miracles in the garden to fill hundreds of books. There are more fascinating creatures and more interconnected activities in the world under our feet than one could ever imagine. These activities all function because the natural world is a world of fluid and dynamic balances. It is a world of life, growth, death, decay, and rebirth where all the parts of that cycle have their indispensable roles. It is a world where not only the woodchuck but also the maple leaf, the wilted daisy, and the mandrake root vanish to leave behind a poem. It is a world where there are answers to pests (insects and diseases) that don't involve poisons.

As the reader may have inferred from my fascination with the life processes of compost and fertile soil, I have little use for the fragmentation of natural processes caused by the shortcut of agricultural chemicals. Whether intended as drugs to induce artificial fertility or as weapons to turn live creatures into dead ones, chemicals attempt to influence single parts of a rich and interconnected system. Chemicals miss the elegance. They were conceived in an age of hubris by minds that ignored the marvelous balances of the natural system. They have persevered in an age of awareness through the aggressive marketing of large industrial concerns. The peddlers of chemical fertilizers appreciate the sales potential of products that need to be applied frequently and create user dependence by their mode of action.

Pesticides are similarly misconceived. They are a crude bludgeon. The use of poisons to attack pests ascribes a malevolence to the natural world that is belied by even a quick look at the intricate system of balances that nature maintains. Learning to tip those balances gently in favor of the plants we wish to grow is the simple answer to pest and disease problems. Most organic gardeners are familiar with this philosophy and seek to apply its principles in their gardens. However, this thinking applies over a broad range.

We can define that range as extending from the "reactive" at one end to the "preventive" at the other end. At the reactive end, the gardener focuses on those natural practices that tend to disadvantage the insects, such as trapping, releasing lady bugs and other predators, timing of plantings to avoid hatching periods, and, at the most extreme, "natural" pesticides. This general approach is called "integrated pest management." At the preventive end of the spectrum, the gardener concentrates on those practices that strengthen the natural immunity of the plant, such as creating optimum growing conditions, adding micronutrient fertilizers or plant-enhancing foliar sprays when called for, and other cultural practices aimed at creating ideal growing conditions and thus lessening plant stress. We could call this integrated *plant* management or "environmental crop management" (ECM), defined as the manipulation of cultural practices to reduce pest susceptibility. Although we favor the latter approach (more on that shortly), we are very aware of the wide latitude the natural world offers to those who carefully observe its systems and try to work within them. To learn more about the integrated pest management end of the spectrum we paid a visit to an exceptional French greenhouse grower.

Protecting Plants: The Reactive Approach

The civilized world would be a step closer to perfection if a copy of this small and productive farm existed in everyone's home town. It would be a world of happy eaters. Not only does this French farm grow and sell high-quality organic food, but the freshness and quality are assured because the customers know the growers as neighbors. The owner, Monsieur Audier, and three generations of his family are devoted to their business. Through the store on their farm they sell their own produce in addition to grains, beans, dairy, wine, and similar staples from other organic growers. A large greenhouse is attached to the store and their outdoor fields are directly adjacent. This gets our vote as a model of local food production and marketing for the 21st century.

There were crops in the outdoor fields but we concentrated on exploring the greenhouse. It was a beautiful structure covered with glass and built in a style called gutter-connected, which means the roof resembles a series of peaks and valleys. The entrance opened right off the rear of the store to encourage customers to wander back and see where and how their fresh winter food was grown. What they see is mighty impressive since the greenhouse covers two acres.

To someone unfamiliar with greenhouses, two acres will seem huge, but in the commercial greenhouse industry this is a medium-size operation. The playing surface of a football field is slightly larger than an acre, so picturing two football fields side by side will give a close approximation of the scale. There is certainly enough room to grow every plant one could imagine. With complete disregard for conventional thinking, M. Audier was doing exactly that.

Most conventional greenhouses specialize in one crop. Endless rows of either tomatoes or cucumbers or peppers or eggplants stretch to a glass-walled horizon. But rather than monocultural, this greenhouse was polycultural. Most greenhouse experts would not believe their eyes. Even to our eyes, which are familiar with our own polycultural efforts, there was a wider variety of plants than we imagined could cohabit successfully in a commercial vegetable greenhouse.

Traditionally, different greenhouse crops are grown under temperature and humidity regimes specifically tailored to their preferences. Certain combinations of plants may be grown in the same house where their needs are similar. But here we saw a disregard for all the standard greenhouse rules. Rows of small white-tipped French breakfast radishes, a cool-temperature crop, were growing alongside rows of trellised beefsteak tomatoes. Heat-loving summer squash, the small, dark green French *courgette* type, were thriving right next to closely spaced beds of young mâche.

But it was the lemon trees more than anything else, yes, ten-foot-tall lemon trees loaded with fruit, and the rows of the ripening strawberries growing alongside them, that really caught our attention. The whole complement of plants growing together that bright January day in M. Audier's greenhouse included arugula, beans, beets, carrots, chard, Chinese cabbage, dandelion greens, eggplant, lemon trees, lettuce, mâche, parsley and other common herbs, peppers, radish, strawberries, summer squash, tomatoes, and turnips, all in many varieties and many stages of maturity. What

Fig. 78

Tachinid parasitoid.

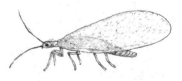

Lacewing.

a wonderful model for the home greenhouse gardener who wants to have a little of everything.

We expressed our awe to M. Audier, and eagerly began to question him about how he makes this all happen. The greenhouse is heated, since many of these plants will not thrive in an unheated winter greenhouse even in the Provençal climate. M. Audier told us he had found through trial and error that a nighttime temperature of 12°C (54°F) seemed to be the happy medium for all the inhabitants of his successful polyculture. It is a temperature high enough so the heat-loving plants are adequately maintained through the night hours, but not so high as to disadvantage the cool-season crops which are normally grown at a lower nighttime temperature.

By all the inhabitants, M. Audier meant not only the plants but also the insects. In this realm, his already impressive operation ratcheted up another notch of awe. He was more fearless about insects than any greenhouse grower we have ever encountered. Not that we are fearful. We consider our attitude rather enlightened, albeit unconventional, on the subject of garden insects. But we have always considered greenhouses to present a slightly different situation. Inextricably tied with the healthy plant's resistance to pests is the healthy environment in which it grows and all the balances maintained by the natural systems of that environment. The greenhouse interrupts those balances to a degree by imposing a glass or plastic shield between the plants and the natural world outdoors. Although this shield adds a positive factor by protecting against cold temperatures, it also keeps out rain, wind, snow, ice, and all the known and unknown influences of those weather forces on the natural balance in an unenclosed outdoor situation.

Our solution to restoring naturalness has been either to move or uncover a greenhouse so it could be more like a seasonal cold frame. But a two-acre glass greenhouse is probably best left where it sits. Thus, large-scale organic greenhouses have traditionally used other techniques than moving to achieve a plant-pest balance. The principal focus has been on the importation and dispersal of beneficial insects. A large insectary industry has sprung up to sell beneficial insects and pest-destroying parasites to greenhouse growers. But this system is devised for the pest problems of the standard greenhouse monocrops. Most commercial beneficial insect suppliers would hardly know where to begin setting up a program for M. Audier's polycultural paradise.

M. Audier himself had no such problems. He was, as we noted, totally fearless in this regard and had set out to create the natural conditions he wanted to see. Thus, a small section in the middle of his greenhouse was set aside as an insectary. "Insects are my passion," he told us. All his reading, studying, and practical experience had convinced him that nature could be encouraged to create a balance in any environment. However, since a balance has two sides, he was aware of the need to make sure both sides were equally represented. Thus, in this special section of the greenhouse where he reared countless beneficial insects, he was also growing strains of a wide range of those vegetable varieties known to be particularly susceptible to pest problems under greenhouse conditions. He reared the beneficials on foods they liked, such as the decomposing skins of a local variety of pumpkin, which were covered with countless small black specks. The pest-susceptible vegetable varieties, which, as we could see, had pests on them, were growing in neat rows right alongside.

The whole idea, M. Audier affirmed with unassailable logic, was to have plenty of pest insects around for the beneficials to prey on or parasitize, so the beneficials would multiply. Then they would be available to spread naturally, or be distributed, to the rest of the greenhouse. We had never seen these ideas carried out as thoroughly as they were here. But then we had never seen a greenhouse as magical as this one with all its plant and insect "inhabitants," its nature-as-ally philosophy, the contagious enthusiasm of M. Audier, and his faith in the benevolent design of the natural world.

The Preventive Approach

We share M. Audier's faith in the benevolent design of the natural world. But our approach to solving the problem has been from the other end, from the preventive end of the spectrum. The garden has taught us clearly over the years that pests should not be seen as enemies of plants but rather as indicators—signals—of plant stress. Insects and diseases are visible symptoms that all is not well with the plant, just as a headache is a symptom that all is not well with me. Instead of treating the symptom, I prefer to correct the cause. The cause of the plant stress is some malfunction in the growing conditions for the plants. Plants under stress are susceptible to pest problems.

Let's state that point again because it is basic to our philosophy of gardening. There is a direct relationship between the growing conditions of plants and the susceptibility of those plants to pests. Problems in the garden are our fault through unsuccessful gardening practices, rather than Nature's fault through malicious intent. The way we approach pest problems in the garden is to correct the cause rather than treat the symptom. The cause of pest problems is inadequate growing conditions. Not only does correcting the cause solve the problem, but it keeps the problem from recurring so it does not have to be

treated again tomorrow and the day after and the day after that. These conclusions are based on thirty years of observation and experience in vegetable growing.

We are not alone. There is extensive scientific evidence that negative changes in the internal composition of plants can result from imbalanced fertilization and inadequate growing conditions. Those changes affect the resistance of plants to insects and diseases. When the growing conditions are improved by adding compost, aerating the soil, watering, letting in the sun, and so forth, the symptoms (pests) disappear—just as my headache will go away when its cause (emotional stress, polluted air, allergy-producing food) is removed. If you take a painkiller for a headache, you risk other complications as a consequence. Similarly, if you use pesticides to kill a pest, you risk upsetting other balances in the garden system that may exacerbate pest problems in the future. If, however, you improve the growing conditions that benefit plants, you can tip the balance in the plants' favor without disrupting the system. It is similar to adopting a healthy lifestyle to keep your immune system functioning effectively in order to preserve your own health.

How do you learn to correct causes of pest problems in your garden? A good way to start is by imagining yourself as the roots of a plant. Would you like to live in that soil? Is it too compact or too fluffy? Too wet or too dry? Are there enough of both the major and minor nutrients? Will the soil provide all the lesser-known and only slightly understood benefits of a well-decomposed compost? All gardeners instinctively recognize the rich, dark, fertile look of a soil that has been well cared for. That is what the roots of vegetables will thrive in. That is what you want to create. (The soil fertility information and techniques in chapters 3 and 4 tell you how.)

Why is it that insects multiply on stressed plants and not on unstressed ones? The best explanation we have found goes something like this: Most insects remain at a low population level in relation to the potential amount of food around them because there is inadequate nitrogen in that food for insect nutrition. When plants are stressed by poor growing conditions, one consequence is that they become a richer source of nitrogen. In other words, stressed plants become an insect snack bar.

How does this process work? The scientific evidence indicates that the effect of stress on a plant—whether from lack of nutrients, excess or deficiency of water, soil compaction, temperature, or other soil or environmental factors—is to inhibit the synthesis of protein by the plant. When protein synthesis is inhibited, the plant accumulates increasing levels of free amino acids (also called free nitrogen) in its aerial parts, especially the phloem. Under nonstressful conditions, those amino acids would have been used by the plant to form protein. As mentioned, insects thrive on plants high in free nitrogen and are thus attracted to and feed upon those plants. When protein synthesis proceeds normally, the nitrogen is locked up in completed protein. The insects are not attracted to unstressed plants because they cannot feed successfully on them.

Farley Mowat, the wildlife biologist, describes a similar example of the balance between predator and prey in his story of wolves and caribou in *Never Cry Wolf* (Bantam, 1984). Mowat was expecting to see wolves slaughter caribou indiscriminately. He was puzzled when he saw wolves only scaring the caribou and watching them run. The wolves seemed to be testing the caribou. Mowat's companion Ootek told him this was precisely what was happening. Wolves cannot catch a healthy caribou. They can catch only the weak, the sick, and the unfit. By testing the caribou to see them run, the wolves hope to spot any that are below par. Ootek explained that there was a balance between the wolves and the caribou. After hard winters, when the caribou are stressed and weakened, the wolves can catch more of them, and the wolves thrive. When the winter is mild and adequate food supplies favor the caribou's well-being, the wolves are at a disadvantage. Ootek understood instinctively that the predator-prey relationship was part of the elegant balance of natural systems.

The same situation exists in a well-composted garden. Healthy, unstressed plants are not bothered by insects. Despite the amount of scientific evidence that backs up this theory, the idea meets great resistance. It seems too good to be true. In a wonderful passage in the book *Organic Farming* (Faber, 1957) by Hugh Corley, an English organic farmer, Corley pauses at this same stage in his discussion of the idea to say, "Now I quite sympathize

Fig. 79

Lady beetle larva.

Trichogramma wasp on host egg.

with the skeptical reader who up till now has thought me a fairly moderate crank and not as mad as some organic enthusiasts—and who now says, 'Well, really, there are limits to what I can believe!'" (p. 172).

In many attempts to explain this concept to gardening audiences, I have seen that look of skeptical disbelief often enough. I call it the Brooklyn Bridge look. "And if I believe that, you'll tell me next that you have a bridge in Brooklyn to sell me." Why is this idea so difficult to accept? Is it just because it is unfamiliar?

There seem to be deeper reasons. Human beings may have difficulty understanding a benevolent nature with elegantly simple systems because we have made nature in our own image. As members of the human species, we find ourselves surrounded by conflict, confusion, violence, and war. We interpret nature to fit our pattern. We see natural processes as if they were projections of our actions. Thus, we see malevolence in the relationship of one organism to another and in nature's relationship to us. We don't notice the beneficial balances between predator and prey that are maintained throughout the natural world. We miss the obvious garden logic of tipping that balance in our favor by creating optimum growing conditions for our plants. Instead we see the temporary agents of that balance (insects and diseases) as threatening forces to be battled and defeated. We need to look again.

It can be a refreshing mental exercise to look at something familiar from a different perspective; to reappraise nature as a system that is not malevolent but benevolent; to see "pests" as helpful signals or indicators, not enemies; to see the relationship between predator and prey as natural management rather than violence; to understand that when we work against the system by killing pests and doping up sick soil we are contributing to the problem. We need to reevaluate our place in the garden. The gardener's aim is not to protect sick plants but to enable healthy ones. You enable plants to attain their natural insusceptibility by removing plant stress. You remove plant stress by working to optimize all those factors involved in plant well-being that have been emphasized in this book.

Our movable greenhouse technique and M. Audier's homegrown insectary are both attempts to use knowledge and understanding so as not to blunder about and create chaos in the natural order. Their differences only serve to emphasize the wide latitude that exists within the natural world for garden techniques that achieve mankind's needs without breaking Nature's laws.

Our visit with M. Audier confirmed two of our fondest beliefs. First, that there are no insurmountable barriers to successful organic food growing on either the home or commercial scale, if attention is focused on working *with* rather than *against* the natural world. Second, that most of the advances in gardening (and probably in other fields as well) come so often from the minds and hands of real people—gifted practitioners with a capacity for wonder at Nature's miracles and an ability for diplomacy among her inhabitants.

Louis Bromfield, widely recognized as a gifted practitioner during his years of agricultural experimentation at Malabar Farm, expressed the same sentiment with regard to the "contributions and advances" in agriculture which

> have come not out of the laboratory but from the smart farmer . . . who lives with his soils and his animals, observes them and employs his imagination and powers of deduction. . . . Nature has provided the means of producing healthy and resistant plants, animals and people and if these means

and patterns can be discovered and put into use, the need for 'artificial' and curative as opposed to preventive methods is greatly reduced. . . . The simplest answer is that we at Malabar, along with countless other intelligent farmers throughout the U.S., have frequently been doing what some teachers and scientists should have been doing for some time past. Frequently we have been doing things which "cannot be done."

(From My Experience, Harper and Row, 1955)

M. Audier, in his passion for doing the undoable, echoes the spirit of his countryman, Napoleon I, who replied in a letter to one of his associates, "You write to me that it's impossible; bah, the word is not French."

The Balanced Garden

We do not spray our garden, even with "natural" pesticides, and we have very few pest problems, none of an extent that would make us want to spray even if we were so inclined. We can refer you to organic gardeners and farmers all over the world who have the same experience. Occasionally, when we think we have done everything right, the system goes against us. It shows we haven't yet achieved adequate growing conditions for that particular crop. The majority of problems usually solve themselves after the first three years in a well-composted garden. Sometimes a crop is hard to adapt to a specific soil or climate. In most of those cases, if you just observe, you will find the eventual damage so slight as to be no bother. The more difficult cases can often be solved by changing varieties. Once or twice we have given up on a crop until we figured out what was amiss between that crop and our conditions. There are some low-impact cures and palliatives for those difficult moments (for example, a vacuum cleaner is very effective against flea beetles, cucumber beetles, potato beetles, and Japanese beetles), and they will be given on a crop-by-crop basis in appendix A. Some of them involve cultural practices; others use physical barriers. There are also a few "natural" pesticides to use only as temporary crutches in time of dire need. We much prefer correcting the cause of the problem. That preference reflects a philosophy that is important not only in the garden but also in the broader world beyond.

We live in a world that has practiced violence for generations—violence to other creatures, violence to the planet, violence to ourselves. Yet in our garden, where we have nurtured a healthy soil-plant community, we see a model of a highly successful, non-violent system where we participate in gentle biological diplomacy rather than war. The garden has more to teach us than just how to grow food.

L'Envoi

ON OUR LAST DAY IN FRANCE WE DROVE EASTWARD ACROSS THE BASSES Alpes toward the Italian border. The road led us up over a couple of 4,000-foot passes into serious snow country. There was a ski area at each crest with lifts running and we stopped to watch the skiers and throw some unhorticultural snowballs. For one short stretch we drove through a mini-blizzard. All in all a very New England–like scene.

While in snow country we saw no gardens with any plants in them, not even leeks. This was significant because we had often wondered whether the French love of fresh food had created a tradition of winter gardening in only the warmer areas or whether it extended to all parts of the country. Apparently it did not. Each time we descended in altitude below where the snow line of an average winter might lie we would see home gardens with leeks in them again.

That is not to say there were no small towns and houses and gardens above the snow line, because there were. This was settled country. However, the gardens were empty of all produce. Where the snow was thin we could see that most gardens had been carefully forked over in preparation for spring. But there were no *chenilles*, cold frames, or small greenhouses. In other words, the world we saw was like most of the world we knew at home.

I mentioned earlier what a powerful inhibiting effect the New England winter must have on the will to garden. The same seemed to be true here. Is it just the below-freezing temperatures? The average January temperature in these mountains is obviously below 30°F, compared with 41°F in Avignon. Or is it the cold look of that soft white blanket of snow? If so, then snow is more a psychological barrier than it is a physical barrier since one of the joys of the winter harvest, because the contrast is so striking, is to sweep the snow off of a cold frame and be greeted by the vibrant colors of the sheltered vegetables inside. Or is it just the seeming impossibility of harvesting garden fresh vegetables under these conditions when you have always assumed that it couldn't be done?

For the rest of the day we discussed these issues, as we had so often on the trip, and pondered the same old question. How to encourage gardeners to look beyond the cold exterior of winter to the potential bounty underneath? We came to the conclusion that the increasing interest in fresh vegetables for good health may be a very powerful motivator. More and more people are realizing how their own actions can positively affect their health. Logically, a backyard full of fresh vegetables is a good place to start. If the idea of "vegetables for good health" is going to be the key to a new home garden renaissance, then the Italian author of a book about vegetables written four hundred years ago can be considered the prophetic announcer of the new age.

Giacomo Castelvetro, who died in 1616, wrote a short book two years before his death. He called it a *Brieve racconto* of "all the vegetables and all the herbs and all the fruits which either raw or cooked are eaten in Italy." The book emphasizes how intuitive and longstanding the connection is between vegetable consumption and health. He was living in England at the time and, believing that the English did not eat nearly enough vegetables for good health, was motivated to write about "the herbs, fruits, and plants we eat in my civilized homeland . . . so that the English no longer need be deprived through lack of information of the delights of growing and eating them."

Unlike many vegetable books, Castelvetro's *Brief Account* has a true four-season outlook. He discusses the crops of the fall, the winter, and the spring seasons in addition to the traditional summer fare. His winter crop suggestions—chicory, endive, watercress, hardy crucifers, scallions, carrots, turnips—are all of them star performers in the winter-harvest today. He wrote eloquently about cool weather salads because "the mixed salad is the best and most wonderful of all . . . a pleasure to the eye, a treat for the palate, and above all, a really important contribution to our health."

> Take young leaves of mint, those of garden cress, basil, lemon balm, the tips of salad burnet, tarragon, the flowers and tenderest leaves of borage, the flowers of swine cress, the young shoots of fennel, leaves of rocket, of sorrel, rosemary flowers, some sweet violets, and the tenderest leaves or the hearts of lettuce.

He goes on to explain in great detail how the salad leaves must be carefully washed, carefully dried, and artfully presented. He heaps scorn on what some "uncouth nations do," in terms of salad preparation and then he sets the English straight.

> You English are even worse; after washing the salad heaven knows how, you put the vinegar in the dish first, and enough of that for a footbath for Morgante, and serve it up, unstirred, with neither oil nor salt, which you are supposed to add at table. By this time some of the leaves are so saturated with vinegar that they cannot take the oil, while the rest are quite naked and fit only for chicken food. So to make a good salad the proper way, you should put the oil in first of all, stir it into the salad, add the vinegar and stir again. And if you do not enjoy this, then complain to me.

Since the techniques, the ingredients, and the background information about Castelvetro's seasonal menus are similar to our experience, it is striking, in light of today's assumptions that fresh seasonal eating is something new, to realize that his paean to the joys and the importance of fresh seasonal vegetables was written in 1614. That fact is both hopeful and discouraging. Discouraging because Giacomo Castelvetro, despite the wisdom of his message, has been nearly forgotten, his words languishing on dusty shelves over centuries during which the dietary contribution of vegetables continued to be ignored. Yet hopeful because it demonstrates so clearly that fresh garden vegetables were as highly valued by the experiential wisdom of ages past as they are by the growing body of scientific studies from modern medical researchers.

Those wishing to heed the counsel of Giacomo Castelvetro will find the four-season harvest techniques a great help. For example, Barbara and I enjoyed a fresh winter salad for lunch on January 15, just before departing for Europe and, twenty-two days later, upon our return, we ate a celebratory home-garden meal for dinner. Our simple backyard system had taken care of itself quite nicely in our absence, and all the crops under the inner layer of our attached hoophouse glowed with well-being. The ducks, who spent the time in the care of a neighbor, had just begun to lay, and thus there were fresh eggs for a spinach quiche to accompany the mixed salad. Upon sitting down to that welcome-home dinner, we raised an appreciative toast to the winter gardens of both the old and the new worlds.

The Cast of Characters

ARTICHOKE, GLOBE *Cynara scolymus*

Planting Distance: 1 row per 30-inch-wide bed; plants 24 inches apart.

Crop Rotation: Related to chicories, dandelion, salsify, and lettuce.

Growing Tips: Rich soil, lots of organic matter, and plenty of moisture. Mulch heavily for best results.

Storage Tips: Can be stored in the refrigerator for two weeks.

Variety Tips: For annual culture—'Imperial Star'

Yes, you can grow globe artichokes in cold climates where they won't survive the winter. We've succeeded in the chilly mountains of Vermont and on the cool coast of Maine. Other gardeners have succeeded all around the country. The trick is to turn the artichoke from a biennial into an annual. All that's required is a little horticultural sleight of hand.

If you plant an artichoke seed, it will usually grow only leaves the first year. The following year, it will send up a stalk from which grow the artichokes—actually edible flower buds. If the winter is too severe (as winters in most of the northern half of the U.S. are), the first-year vegetative plants won't survive to become second-year producing plants. The sleight of hand involves fooling the plants to think they are two years old in the first year.

To achieve that, you need to grow the young artichoke plants first in warm and then cool temperatures. (The following system works for many artichoke varieties, not only the ones that have been bred to behave more like annuals. You can plant newer varieties such as 'Imperial Star' later as long as they will get an adequate cold period.) Start the seeds indoors in a warm, sunny window six weeks before the earliest date on which you could safely move them to a cold frame. Move them to a cold frame when you are sure the temperature inside the frame will no longer go below 25°F. In New England, February 15 is a dependable sowing date and April 1 is the date for moving the plants to the frame. Once they are in the frame, leave the frame open as much as possible. The cooler they are for the next six weeks, the better.

The change of growing temperatures from warm to cool is what fools the plants. The first six weeks of warm growing conditions was sufficient time for

Globe artichoke.

the plants to complete their first "summer" season. The subsequent six weeks of cool temperatures make them think they have experienced their first winter. Thus, although they are only twelve weeks old when transplanted to the garden, they think they are beginning their second year. The second year is when artichoke plants begin to produce the flower buds that we eat as artichokes.

The care they receive after transplanting to the garden will determine the number and size of the artichokes. Under the best conditions, you can get eight to nine artichokes of medium to medium-large size per plant. The best conditions are plenty of organic matter (mix in compost, manure, or peat moss generously) and plenty of moisture (mulch with straw and irrigate regularly).

Space the plants 24 inches apart in a single row down the center of the 30-inch-wide bed. That is much closer spacing than for perennial artichokes, but these plants won't get as large. Harvest by cutting the stem beneath the bud with a sharp knife. Don't wait too long. Once the leaf bracts on the bud begin to open, the flesh gets tougher and more fibrous. Almost any variety of seed-sown artichoke will work to some degree under this system, but there is one exceptional variety that is better adapt-

ed than any other—'Imperial Star', available from a number of sources. 'Grande Beurre', from Thompson & Morgan, is a second choice. In New England, the production season is August and September—two months of the best, freshest, and most flavorful artichokes you will ever eat.

ARUGULA   See Salad Greens

ASPARAGUS   *Asparagus officinalis*

Planting Distance: 1 row per 30-inch-wide bed; plants 24 inches apart.

Crop Rotation: None needed; perennial.

Growing Tips: Asparagus will thrive on all the compost and manure you can spare.

Storage Tips: Can be stored in the refrigerator for one week.

Variety Tips: For dependability— 'Jersey Knight'

Asparagus is the classic spring food to anticipate, to enjoy, and to anticipate again. It seems almost magical when asparagus spears begin poking out of the soil just after winter has lost its grip. Either nibbled raw or served in one of a dozen different ways, asparagus is a favorite gourmet vegetable.

The asparagus plant is a well-designed system. The roots are a food storehouse and resemble a thick-legged octopus living underneath the ground. The food stored in the roots is what allows the asparagus plant to keep sending up new stems (spears) in the spring despite the fact that the gardener keeps cutting every one of them off. That's why there has to be an end to the harvest season after a month or two. The plant needs to spend the rest of the growing season storing up more food from photosynthesis by its ferny leaves to be able to put up with the same exhausting process again next year.

Logically, the more you can enhance food storage, the more vigorous the production. But asparagus tends to be forgotten as the season progresses. Its virtue, the dependability of coming back every year at a time when fresh vegetables are treasured, is often its downfall. Lavish attention is paid to asparagus in the picking and eating season, and then it becomes just a ferny background. At that point, weeds and inadequate fertility will hamper next year's crop. Asparagus doesn't need to be pampered, but it does need to be weeded, watered, and fed.

The asparagus bed should be weeded at least two times. The first weeding is early in the spring. That is necessary because the worst weed in asparagus is asparagus itself. Asparagus plants produce seeds in that ferny growth (except for the new sterile male hybrids). Asparagus seeds sprout into volunteer plants that will crowd the bed and lower the production of quality spears. They are easily controlled. Volunteer asparagus germinates near the soil's surface. Your producing asparagus plants will have their crowns well below the surface. A vigorous, shallow hoeing of the bed in early spring will discourage the interlopers.

The second weeding period comes at the end of the harvest. Make a point of cultivating every so often for the next few weeks to prevent weeds from getting established. Once the stalks get tall and ferny and cast shade, you should have little problem except with perennial weeds. Perennial weeds such as witch grass can be the death of a perennial crop such as asparagus. Be vigilant and watch for invasion from the edge of the patch. Dig up witch grass plants and their roots when you see them. Prevention is the key.

Feeding the asparagus bed is best done in the fall. If you want to be lavish with organic matter, this is the crop to pamper. It is hard to overfeed asparagus. We have used compost, manure, and fresh seaweed, all with good results. The fall feeding prepares the bed for vigorous spring growth. Before feeding, cut and remove the asparagus fern. Wait until it has turned brown but before too many of the red berries containing the seeds have fallen. Spread the manure or compost over the surface of the bed and cover it with a few inches of straw for winter protection. Remove the straw in the spring. The early spring hoeing will incorporate the compost or manure residue into the surface soil.

The final ingredient in asparagus care is water. Whenever the rest of the garden needs to be irrigated, the asparagus also will benefit from the extra water. The fern will grow taller and be more vigorous. That vigor will be reflected in next year's harvest.

Asparagus is a perennial and the ferns are tall. Gardeners often establish the bed in an out-of-the-way location where it will not cast shade. That may be why it's often ignored in the off-season. It's wiser to put the bed wherever the sun shines and the soil is fertile. That way you can tuck a few lettuce or spinach plants in its shade during the hotter months of the year.

Harvesting asparagus.

You can establish an asparagus bed by purchasing crowns or growing your own plants. We prefer the latter. These strong little seedlings fit nicely in a standard 4-inch pot. If you have a greenhouse, you can start them six months before the last spring frost and get production a year earlier, but two months ahead is fine. Set out the plants in the bottom of an 8-inch-deep hole made with a post-hole digger. Space them 24 inches apart down the center of a standard bed. Fill the hole with enough soil to cover partway up the plant stem. As they grow taller, continue to add soil until it is level with the bed. Plan to harvest your first asparagus spears two years after setting out the seedlings. At harvest, cut the spears just below soil level, being careful not to injure spears yet to emerge. A very sharp, fishtail-shaped asparagus knife is the tool of choice.

BEAN *Phaseolus* spp.

Planting Distance: Rows 16 to 18 inches apart across bed; seeds 3 inches apart; thin to 6 inches apart.

Crop Rotation: Beans are a legume and are related to other legumes such as peas and clovers.

Growing Tips: Sow seeds singly with the eye down for best germination.

Storage Tips: Can be stored in the refrigerator for a few days, but are much better freshly picked.

Variety Tips: Bush bean—'E-Z Pick'
Pole bean—'Fortex'
Most versatile—'Garden of Eden'

Beans offer more variety than any other crop. If you include the dry beans, there is sufficient range of color, pattern, size, shape, and flavor to provide a lifetime of gastronomic fascination. There are seed-saving enthusiasts with collections of hundreds of distinct varieties of dry beans. Among the green beans, you can choose varieties selected for length, diameter, color, flavor, and tenderness. The delights of many of the green beans are available only to the home gardener.

A customer at my market stand years ago began a conversation by remarking on the exceptional quality of our green beans. I agreed that they were good, but this gentleman was positively effusive, and with good reason. He was the president of a company that processed gourmet canned and frozen vegetables. He said the crop that most dissatisfied him was green beans. The varieties suitable for machine picking and processing were not the exceptional culinary varieties. They just didn't have the same fresh snap and flavor. He said that he dreamed of the day his company could process beans as good as ours.

He knew his beans. Fresh eating beans are thin and tender and don't all mature at once. They are not pickable by machine. Processing beans need to be tougher and more fibrous to survive picking and processing. Will the two ever meet? Someday, maybe, but we grow only the best eaters, and we enjoy them fresh for as long a season as possible. Although we prefer the thin French *filet* types, other gardeners favor a thicker, fleshier bean. Fortunately, there is a wide selection of fresh eating varieties for all tastes.

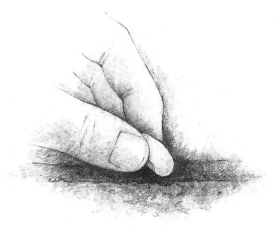

Plant bean seeds with eyes looking down.

Green beans need to be picked every day or so for the best quality. They are a perfect crop for the small succession plantings of the four-season garden. If you plant too many beans, you have to pick more than you want or feel guilty because you haven't kept up with them. Not so with small, succession plantings. When there are too many beans, you just yank out the older plantings and add them to the compost heap, then replant to some other crop. The new beans will continue producing until their replacement comes along. Of course, if you grow a variety that develops good-size seeds, you can leave the old plants and harvest them later as shell beans.

Plant beans in short rows across the beds. Since green bush beans should be thinned to at least 6 inches apart, there may be only five or six plants in a 30-inch row. That's ideal. A few short rows like that in each succession planting will keep the bean harvest well managed. Put the rows 16 to 18 inches apart. You may want to modify that spacing depending on the variety of bush bean you prefer. If the plants do get too crowded, cut off and compost every other one.

You can plant pole beans in the trellised beds along with other climbing crops. Put four seeds in each hill with 16 inches of space between hills. The vines grow up a single length of untreated 4-ply garden twine tied to the trellis at the top and buried in the soil at the bottom. When they are finished producing, cut the twine and compost the vines, twine and all.

If we were to plant only one bean it would be the 'Garden of Eden' pole bean from Johnny's Selected Seeds. This family heirloom has the versatility of the perfect home garden vegetable. The pods are edible and delicious both raw and cooked from when they first appear up through coarse old age. When they get really old they make great shell beans for succotash with the late sweet corn. If you find

your schedule too busy to keep up with picking in the summer garden, this is the bean for you.

BEET   *Beta vulgaris*

Planting Distance: 2 or 3 rows per 30-inch-wide bed; seeds 1 inch apart; thin to 2 to 4 inches apart.

Crop Rotation: Related to Swiss chard, spinach, and orach. Beets do well following a leguminous green manure.

Growing Tips: Beets benefit from fertilization with seaweed products.

Storage Tips: Store in root cellar at 32°F. Beets keep better than any other root crop.

Variety Tips: Early—'Merlin'
All-around use— 'Forono', 'Detroit Dark Red', 'Red Ace'
Winter storage—'Winter Keeper', 'Long Season'
Winter salads—'Bull's Blood'

Beets are one of our favorite vegetables. We often feel like proselytizers for *Beta vulgaris*—red root rooters. Beets are far more delicious and adaptable than their public image might indicate. I remember been told by visiting children in days past that they "don't eat beets." They have never eaten mine, I would reply. And sure enough, once they tried just one bite of tiny, tender, freshly harvested baby beets and greens steamed lightly and served with a pat of butter, nine out of ten would ask for more.

Given their long season of availability, culinary flexibility, and ease of cultivation, beets have a lot to offer. The season begins with the first tiny thinnings for spring salads. Next come beet greens for cooking, baby beets, mature beets for fall storage, and, finally, sprouted beet tops for tasty greens in the winter. Beet roots can be cooked as a vegetable, pickled as an appetizer, used as the base for marvelous soups, or served cold in salads. In the garden, they are a dependable grower. They germinate quickly and once established are very vigorous plants.

Beets are a sensitive crop, and there is a big difference between good beets and exceptional beets. The extra care required to grow exceptional beets is repaid in the quality of roots and tops. The beet is one plant (the cabbage and onion families are others) that defines the health of garden soil. Beet leaves have a vigorous and vibrant glow when conditions in the garden approach the ideal.

Beets grow best in a nearly neutral soil. If they don't thrive it is often attributable to soil acidity. The gardener should plan to add enough lime to attain a pH of 6.5 to 6.8, a level at which most garden vegetables will do well. Beets also grow best in a soil with adequate organic matter. A generous application of compost will be well rewarded.

Beets are sensitive to deficiencies of trace elements. When beets are not sweet and tender, a lack of boron or other trace element may be the cause.

Beets may benefit from added boron in soil.

Boron can be supplied by sprinkling borax *very lightly* over the soil. Trace elements can be most easily added to the soil with greensand or a dried seaweed product. A garden with plenty of organic matter from a compost of mixed ingredients usually has an adequate supply of trace elements and should present you with no difficulties in growing tasty beets.

Professional beet growers choose separate varieties for greens, baby beets, and storage. In the home garden, one all-around variety such as 'Red Ace' will serve well for the whole season. Beets may be sown from January to August. Sow the earliest seeds in your protected garden. You can grow them there or transplant them to the garden. Direct sowings in the garden can be made until early August for a late-fall harvest of tender baby beets. The beet seeds you plant are actually small pods containing two to three seeds. They grow best if thinned to avoid overcrowding. Let them grow to 1½ inches tall, then use the thinnings in salads. Thin carefully so as not to disturb the roots of the plants nearby. Thin beets for greens to 2 inches apart, for summer use to 3 inches, and for winter storage to 4 inches. Rows for regular-sized beets should be 12 inches apart. If you want larger beets, plant rows 16 inches apart.

For a most colorful and delicious ingredient in winter salads we grow 'Bull's Blood' beet. It is an heirloom variety that has been selected for its bright scarlet leaves rather than its root. Sown during the first two weeks of September and eventually protected under the inner layer, this beautiful and tasty leaf will be harvestable all winter. The colder the weather the more strikingly colored the leaves. This is the best bet for a standout red color in your winter salad mix if you don't want to grow radicchio.

BROCCOLI   See Cabbage Family

BRUSSELS SPROUTS   See Cabbage Family

CABBAGE FAMILY   *Brassica* spp.

Planting Distance:

Broccoli—1 row per 30-inch-wide bed; plants 16 inches apart.

Brussels sprouts—1 row per 30-inch-wide bed; plants 18 inches apart.

Cabbage—1 row per 30-inch-wide bed; plants 16 inches apart.

Cauliflower—2 rows per 30-inch-wide bed; plants 16 inches apart.

Crop Rotation: Related to mustard, rutabagas, kale, turnips, collards, kohlrabi, and radishes. They do well after a leguminous green manure.

Growing Tips: Till autumn leaves into the soil in fall.

Storage Tips: Cool and moist. Broccoli lasts one week, cauliflower two weeks, Brussels sprouts three weeks, and cabbage six to eight months.

Variety Tips:

Broccoli— 'Arcadia', 'Packman', 'Windsor'
Brussels sprouts— 'Oliver', 'Diablo'
Earliest cabbage— 'Gonzales'
Red cabbage— 'Ruby Perfection'
Savoy cabbage—'Famosa'
Cauliflower—'Fremont'

Broccoli—A healthy broccoli plant is almost a perpetual vegetable. Once you cut the main head, it is followed by an endless stream of smaller subheads. These small shoots are the perfect size for any dish. When you read seed catalogs, look specifically for varieties that have "good side-shoot production." As long as you keep harvesting them, the plant will keep producing, right up until heavy winter freezes.

Brussels Sprouts—This delicious winter vegetable has an image problem. Many centuries of being one of the last green plants in the garden have made it seem a plebeian winter survival food. Well, it certainly is designed for hardiness. The stem is a storage and feeding unit for rows of miniature cabbages. The large leaves, which droop progressively as the weather cools, provide very effective winter insulation. But it also has gourmet potential. Think of all the uses for miniature cabbages.

The onset of cold weather and freezing temperatures enhances the flavor of Brussels sprouts. Once the fierce cold of December arrives here in Zone 5, however, the sprouts begin to decrease in quality. At that point, you can cut the whole stem, remove the leaves, and store the stem with sprouts attached in the root cellar for up to three weeks. If you have grown plants where they will be covered by your mobile greenhouse, it will provide enough protection to extend the harvest at least another month and a half.

Cabbage—Cabbage is a year-round food. It is fresh from the garden in summer and fall and fresh from the cellar in winter and spring. Well-grown cabbages in the cellar keep so successfully that we usually eat the last root cellar cabbage just prior to maturity of the first spring planting.

We favor red and savoy cabbage so much that we often don't grow the standard, round, smooth-leaved green cabbage. Red cabbage is a vigorous plant, it stores well, and it is the basis for sensational sauerkraut and cooked dishes. Savoy cabbage, with its crinkly green leaves, is by far the most flavorful of the green cabbages either cooked or raw.

Cauliflower—Cauliflower is the most troublesome and least productive of the cabbage family crops. The cauliflower has only a single head, is available for only a short period, and requires tying and blanching to keep it white. The self-blanching varieties, whose leaves fold over the head to exclude most light, don't always do the job adequately. Cauliflower needs a certain amount of cool weather to initiate head formation, but early cauliflower transplants are liable to bolt and produce only small button heads when temperatures are too cool in their youth.

These remarks are not meant to disparage cauliflower. It is great food. But the difficulties of growing it are real. Many home gardeners find this crop easy to ignore because so many other vegetables offer a lot more eating for a lot less work. If you want to grow cauliflower, it is most successful as a fall crop. The cool fall temperatures keep the heads in a harvestable condition for a much longer period. You will want to start the plants about two and a half months before the first fall frost. Choose a self-blanching variety to save yourself some work. The purple and green cauliflower varieties don't require blanching and are easier to grow, but they are so similar to broccoli that we usually grow the latter instead.

We start all the cabbage family members in potting soil in the cold frame and set them out as transplants. They get off to an excellent start in the highly fertile potting soil, and this early growth carries through to their future growth. Vigorous seedlings are the foundation of vigorous plants.

Cabbage family plants grow exceptionally well and have fewer pest problems (especially from cabbage root maggot, *Hylemya brassicae*) when soil nitrogen supplies are optimal. There are two simple ways to supply extra nitrogen to the soil in a form that the cabbage family will thrive on. First, you can add autumn leaves to the soil. Either till under a few inches of autumn leaves in the fall or spread decomposed leaf mold and work it in shallowly. Add lime at the rate of 1 pound for every 20 square feet. The decomposition of the leaves liberates ideal quantities of nitrogen by the following spring.

Self-blanching cauliflower.

A second option to give your cabbage family transplants a nitrogen shot is to plant a leguminous green manure the summer before the bed will be used for the cabbage family. Turn that growth under two to three weeks before setting out the plants. The nitrogen stored by the legumes is available to your cabbage family transplants when this green manure is incorporated into the soil.

If you still have root maggot problems despite these soil-improvement techniques, hunt out red or purple cultivars such as red cabbage, purple cauliflower, and red Brussels sprouts. There seems to be some quality in the genetics of these variants that makes them much more resistant to this pest.

The other common cabbage family pest is the imported cabbage worm, *Pieris rapae,* which is the larva of the white cabbage butterfly. Although considered a common pest, these green worms are not a problem when plants are growing well. Pest access to the brassicas can be prevented by covering the plants with a lightweight floating row cover. Or in case of need, you can use a bacterial pathogen, *Bacillus thuringiensis,* which is specific to lepidopterous larvae. It is sold under a variety of brand names (Dipel, Thuricide, and Biotrol, among others) and offers excellent control of the worm.

CARROT—*Daucus carota*

Planting Distance:

Cold frame crop—Rows 4 inches apart; seeds 1 inch apart; thin to 2 inches apart for earliest spring crop.

Main crop—3 rows per 30-inch-wide bed; seeds ½ inch apart; thin to 1 inch apart.

Crop Rotation: Related to parsley, celery, celeriac, and parsnips.

Growing Tips: Carrots grow well in soil where autumn leaves are incorporated. Carrots benefit from the minerals in greensand.

Storage Tips: Store in root cellar at 32°F. Can be overwintered in soil with protection such as cold frame or heavy mulch.

Variety Tips: Early—'Mokum', 'Nelson'
Main crop—'Scarlet Nantes', 'Bolero'
Overwinter— 'Napoli'

The carrot encompasses a wider range of quality and flavor characteristics than any other vegetable. Most home gardeners can grow a decent carrot, but a *decent* carrot only scratches the surface. The peaks of flavor attainable with the right variety, adequate and balanced minerals, and carefully composted soil are positively awesome.

Our children used to come home from school with their friends and head out to the garden, the cold frame, or the tunnel, depending on the time of year, to pull and eat carrots. They weren't told to do this; they did it because the taste of the carrots was so exceptional that it had more appeal than any goodies from the cupboard or refrigerator. We have seen a similar reaction from customers, both young and old, to our commercial carrots. Most people comment that high-quality carrots seem to be another vegetable entirely from the pale, petroleum-tasting, bitter pseudo-carrots sold in the supermarket.

And no wonder. Many studies have shown that carrots absorb and concentrate pesticide and heavy metal residues when grown in a soil containing those pollutants. Their flavor also is adversely affected by the petroleum oils used as herbicides in chemical carrot growing. Furthermore, large-scale growers favor varieties with strong tops so they can withstand the tug of the harvesting machine. The juiciest and most flavorful of the marvelous French varieties can be harvested only by hand and are found only from specialist growers or in your own backyard.

Carrots respond well to the soil fertility tenets of this book: a well-decomposed, mostly vegetable compost; rock powders; and enough lime to keep the pH around 6.5. Carrots also respond well in a soil where a lot of deciduous leaves (up to 4 inches) have been incorporated with the tiller the previous fall. Oak leaves seem to be the best in this regard, but you can use whatever is available.

Soil temperature affects both the growth and flavor of many root crops. Carrots suffer when soil temperatures are too warm. Mulching in warm

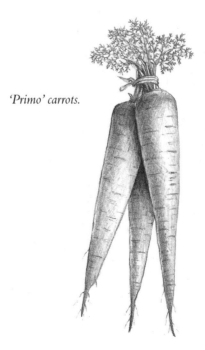

'Primo' carrots.

weather will improve growing conditions, but carrots are at their peak during the cooler months of the year. You can take advantage of that situation for a whole winter of delightful carrot munching by planting carrots in an area to be covered by a cold frame or tunnel. Plant on the latest date possible in your area. Here in Zone 5, that is about August 1. Starting in late October, give the carrots one or two layers of covering to keep them growing and protect them from hard freezes. Sometime between mid-November and mid-December, sprinkle enough compost over the bed (an inch or so) to bury them, tops and all. Then, if they are in a cold frame, fill the frame with straw and replace the glass cover. In a tunnel, add the inner layer.

That planting of small, tender carrots will be available for harvest throughout the winter. They will be fresher, crisper, and sweeter than any carrots you ever tasted. The cold storage in the soil changes some of the starch to sugar, and the result is carrot nirvana. Our children called them "candy carrots."

Spreading the compost over the bed prepares the soil for planting early crops the following spring. Remove the straw as you harvest each section of carrots and replant to early hardy crops. If you use straw in a cold frame, cover the carrots with a sheet of plastic or fine mesh netting before you put in the straw. That way any detritus from the straw will be contained and it won't require extra effort to separate it from the soil before replanting.

When planting cold frame carrots or any carrots to be harvested small, you can put the rows as close as 4 inches apart with the carrots an inch apart in the row. For the earliest harvest, thin the carrots to a wider spacing—2 inches apart. They grow more rapidly with extra space immediately around them. In the garden, plant main crop carrots in rows 10 inches apart, then thin to 1 inch apart in the row. At harvest, use a fork to loosen the soil, pull the carrots, cut the tops to within an inch of the crown, set them

in the storage container, and place the container in the root cellar. They will remain in excellent condition through May. Carrot seeds planted in an empty spot in the cold frame or tunnel in January or February will usually be up in four to five weeks and yield early new carrots in May to start the cycle all over again.

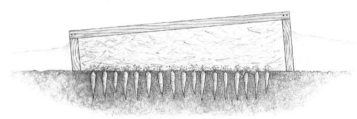

Carrots covered with a cold frame and straw mulch can be harvested all winter.

CAULIFLOWER   See Cabbage Family

CELERY & CELERIAC   *Apium graveolens*

Planting Distance: 3 rows per 30-inch-wide bed; plants 10 inches apart.

Crop Rotation: Related to carrots, parsley, parsnips.

Growing Tips: The richest of soils and plenty of water.

Storage Tips: Celery can keep for two months at cool temperatures. Celeriac will store all winter in the root cellar at 32°F.

Variety Tips: Celery—'Tango'
Celeriac—'Brilliant'

Your children can learn a lot about plant breeding and selection if you show them the difference between these two vegetables. Whereas celery has been selected for the crispness and flavor of the stalks, the selection of celeriac (also known as knob-rooted or turnip-rooted celery) has emphasized the dense, white, rootlike matter at the base of the plant. The result of these efforts is that good celery has crisp stalks and not much base, and good celeriac has a round knob of base material and stalks that are pithy when large. Their roles are not interchangeable, but they serve admirably at what they do best.

Celery is not difficult to grow if you pay attention to three cultural practices. The first is soil moisture. Watering will solve more celery problems than any other practice. Celery thrives on a moist (not sodden) soil and will repay any special treatment you give it in that regard. An easy home garden practice is to mulch around the newly set out celery plants with flat rocks (flagstones or slate tiles are excellent, as they are easy to place and remove). The stones retain both moisture and warmth.

The second key to exceptional celery is organic matter. Celery grows best in a rich soil, and that means plenty of compost or well-rotted manure. It is hard to find a soil too rich for celery. Years ago I knew an enthusiast who would collect waste eggs from a hatchery; smash them up, shells and all; dilute them with water; and pour the mixture down the rows between the celery plants. That was a rich diet, but that was also *some* celery.

Third, and in many ways the *sine qua non,* is seedling temperature. If you start celery indoors and transplant it to the garden when the weather is still cool, many of the plants will bolt—that is, go to seed. When four- to eight-week-old celery plants are moved from warm indoor temperatures to spend the next ten days or so at an average temperature below 50°F, the celery assumes it has had a summer (the warm temperatures) and winter (the cool temperatures) and is now in its second year. With globe artichokes, this same pattern, done intentionally, produces the edible part. When it happens with celery, however, the result is celery seed rather than celery stalks. You can avoid this temperature-induced

bolting by waiting until average outdoor temperatures are dependably over 50°F before setting out the plants. For the earliest crop, this means transplanting them to the protection of a tunnel or cold frame.

Everything said so far about celery also applies to celeriac, only less so. Celeriac is much more forgiving. When conditions are less than perfect, celeriac will still grow admirably in the home garden. It will excel, however, and produce positively sensational roots, when given the best celerylike growing conditions.

Sow both crops indoors in small flats. Celery and celeriac are slow to germinate and benefit from being kept warm and moist during the process. For lack of anything fancier, you can place the flats in a plastic bag to keep them moist and set them on top of the refrigerator to keep them warm. Check them every day and move them to a sunny spot when the seedlings emerge. Transplant the small seedlings to a wider spacing once you can distinguish enough to choose the best plants. Set them out in the bed in three rows 10 inches apart with the plants spaced at 10 inches in the row.

We make our earliest celery seeding around March 1, then transplant the seedlings to a cold frame or tunnel. We start the fall crop about June 1, then transplant the seedlings to the edge bed of the mobile tunnel, where they will be protected well into the fall. We sow celeriac in April and set the plants out in June. If necessary, both celery and celeriac can remain an extra week or so in the flat as long as the potting mix is well fortified with compost, or a liquid feed such as compost tea, fish emulsion, or seaweed is used.

You can harvest celery by removing the outer stalks or cutting the whole plant. If you want celery early in the season, you can harvest small plants. Remember, this is your garden and conventional size standards don't apply. The stalks may not be large, but the flavor is just as good. Even after celery has been frozen in the fall, the inner stalks remain usable for many weeks. Protect fall celery in the tunnel or cold frame with a couple of extra layers of plastic on cold nights.

Harvest celeriac in the fall along with the other root crops. Brea k off the stalks, shake extra soil from the roots, and put the roots in your storage area. Celeriac will keep until late the following spring. Use it to flavor soups, stews, and stir-fries. Grated raw, it complements many salads. It is especially tasty baked whole in a covered dish and served with hollandaise sauce.

Resprouting a celeriac root for winter greens.

CHARD   See Swiss Chard

CHERVIL   See Salad Greens

CHICORY FAMILY   *Cichorium* spp.

Planting Distance:
Endive—3 rows per 30-inch-wide bed; plants 10 inches apart.
Escarole—3 rows per 30-inch-wide bed; plants 12 inches apart.
Belgian endive—2 rows per 30-inch-wide bed; plants 4-6 inches apart.

Sugarloaf—Rows 10 inches apart; plants 10 inches apart.
Italian dandelion—Rows 8 inches apart; plants 8 inches apart.
Radicchio–3 rows per 30-inch-wide bed; plants 10 inches apart.
Varieties for cutting—Rows 4 inches apart; plants 1 inch apart.

Crop Rotation: Related to salsify, dandelion, lettuce, and globe artichokes. Generally considered a beneficial preceding crop for others.

Growing Tips: These are vigorous plants that will thrive in any fertile soil.

Storage Tips: Store Belgian endive roots in buckets of sand as described in chapter 11.

Variety Tips: Endive—'Rhodos'
Escarole—'Natacha'
Belgian endive—'Totem'
Sugarloaf—'Poncho'
Italian dandelion—'Clio'
Radicchio—'Indigo'
Cutting—'Bianca Riccia'

The chicory family encompasses an array of unique vegetables that are indispensable for the year-round harvest. Chicories are a shining example of the seasonal food resources this book celebrates. The Europeans have dined well from winter gardens for centuries. They had no California to ship them summer produce during the winter months, so they learned to be imaginative with winter crops. Chicories became a staple because of their versatility. For example, endive and escarole add texture and tang to a salad and are much hardier than lettuce; Belgian endive, or witloof as it is often called, may be served raw or cooked; the sugarloaf types of green winter chicories are used for braising and salads; Italian dandelion is planted in summer for winter and early-spring eating; the beautiful radicchio adds color and bite to cool-season salads; and the cutting varieties are a great addition to mesclun mixes.

Endive & Escarole—These are both slightly bitter greens that will add snap to a bland salad. Traditionally, these crops are blanched for a week before harvest by tying up the leaves or covering the head to make the leaves milder tasting. By limiting their season to the cooler months, you can dispense with blanching, as they are not disagreeably bitter when grown in cold weather. We plant in late July to early August for a fall and winter harvest and as early in the spring as possible for a summer harvest. Escarole is the hardier of the two, but the hearts of both remain edible right through most of the winter in the protected garden.

Escarole varieties grow larger than lettuce and need to be planted at a 12-inch spacing. The *très fine* endives have smaller heads and can be grown at lettuce spacing (10 by 10 inches) or even closer (8 by 8 inches).

Belgian Endive (Witloof)—The plants you grow in the garden are the first of two steps in growing the edible parts of this plant. The second step is when you force the roots to get the chicons. The roots must be of good size to grow the best chicons. A diameter of 1½ to 2 inches at the shoulder is optimal, but don't be discouraged if they are not all perfect. Even small roots will grow surprisingly vigorous chicons. Be sure to plant enough. We have rarely met anyone who didn't find these crisp, crunchy white winter leaves to their liking. A full description of growing and storage methods can be found in chapter 11.

Sugarloaf—I became curious about this tall, romaine lettuce-shaped chicory plant years ago in Europe after seeing fields of them in autumn. The cool fall weather and the natural blanching of the inner leaves by their enclosure in the outer ones removes much of the traditional chicory bitterness. Sugarloaf is a delicious green crop that survives extremely cold conditions. Even when the outside appears frozen, brown, and mushy, there is still a tender and delicious heart inside. You can stuff the outer leaves with filling, then steam or braise them. Use the inner leaves in salads by cutting the tightly wrapped hearts on an angle into thin, decorative strips.

Italian Dandelion—The leaves are more tender and ready earlier in the spring than the French dandelion varieties, which are *Taraxacum* rather than *Cichorium*. Italian dandelion also grows upright, so harvesting the leaves on a cut-and-come-again basis is easier. Cut the leaves back above the crown, and they will resprout. Under the double coverage of both inner and outer layers, the leaves are available throughout the winter. Use them in cooked dishes just like conventional dandelion or raw in a delicious Italian salad.

Radicchio—Radicchio is the classic Italian red chicory. The color of this vegetable is as delightful to the eye as the slightly bitter bite is to the palate. The small, round, dense heads of the 'Chioggia' or 'Verona' types are two to five inches in diameter. The 'Treviso' types are pointed like Belgian endive. It used to be that you needed to cut back the green leaves of the summer growth in early fall to encourage the red heads to form. Those old heirloom varieties were temperamental and inconsistent headers. You can still grow them for the horticultural challenge, as well as for their exceptional quality, but modern plant breeding has made radicchio easier to grow. The newer varieties such as 'Chioggia Red Preco' and 'Treviso Red Preco' do not require cutting back to initiate head formation. They are more dependable and uniform, like lettuce. Their development has greatly

Endive.

Dandelion.

Radicchio.

extended the season for radicchio. Whichever type you grow, the leaves will quickly become a staple in your salad bowl.

The garden chicories are closely related to the wild chicories, which have cobalt-blue flowers and grow in fields or along the road and bloom in midsummer. The cultivated varieties, like their vigorous weedy relatives, are no trouble to grow. They sprout quickly from seed and thrive in any fertile soil. The subtlety of their garden culture is in the timing. The gardener's main concern is timing the sowing to produce the desired result for each family member.

The first to be planted are the earliest cutting chicories for inclusion in salad mixes. They will be harvested young on a cut-and-come-again basis. Along with them, sow a spring radicchio variety and endive for early summer use. About the third week in May, we sow seeds for the roots that will be forced as Belgian endive next winter. Belgian endive is a long-season crop that won't be harvested until October. Early in June, we plant the heirloom radicchios, such as 'Verona' and 'Treviso', and by early to mid-July, we start sowing Italian dandelion and the new-style radicchios that don't need to be cut back. By mid-July, we are seeding the endive and escarole varieties for fall and winter eating.

Once the planting is done, the next subtlety is cutting back the heirloom radicchios so that they will have nice heads by late fall. Radicchio is very hardy, and the heads will survive for winter-long harvest in the protected garden if they are up to size before the weather gets too cold. We cut off the green summer leaves during the first half of September. The new growth that follows is the red radicchio. If we cut the leaves back too late, they grow very slowly in winter and are excessively bitter. This is more of an enjoyable art form than a clearly defined process, so you will have to keep experimenting with dates based on your knowledge of the variety and your assessment of the fall weather to come.

Because there is so much variety and potential with chicories, they are an adventurous crop. Over the years, I have been served chicories in Europe that went beyond what I was familiar with at the time. Surely there are many more to come as the full spectrum of this seemingly inexhaustible family is explored. Try them. Trying out new varieties, new techniques, and new seeds is how you learn. As a four-season gardener, you will be motivated to find additional winter crops. New chicory family cultivars are an adventure waiting to happen. Start them on their way.

CHINESE CABBAGE See Oriental
Vegetables

CLAYTONIA See Salad Greens

CORN *Zea mays*

Planting Distance: 1 row per 30-inch-wide bed; hills of two to three plants 1½ to 2 feet apart.

Crop Rotation: Corn grows almost anywhere with plenty of compost.

Growing Tips: Start a few corn seeds in pots and transplant for the earliest crop.

Storage Tips: Don't store. Fresh corn cannot be equaled. However, sweet corn can be blanched, cut off the ear, and dried for a winter treat.

Variety Tips: 'Early Sunglow', 'Seneca Horizon', 'Double Standard', 'Golden Bantam', 'Seneca Chief', 'Sweet Sue', 'Silver Queen', 'Country Gentleman'

As you will notice from the varieties of corn listed, we prefer those that are either open pollinated or the original hybrids. We avoid the "sugary enhanced" or "super-sweet" types. They were bred for the corn-selling requirements of supermarkets, not for the home garden. They may be sweet, but it is a sweetness akin to eating sweet plastic. There is more to corn than that. The old varieties may not be as uniform or as perfect looking, but they have an honest corn flavor and are naturally sweet because we grow them in composted soil and eat them right from the garden.

Anyone who has ever found their sweet corn ravaged by hungry raccoons realizes how much these masked marauders like raw corn. You can protect your corn with a simple, lightweight electric fence. You also may find, as we have, that the coons are on to something. Raw corn as a snack or as a meal right in the garden is a wonderful way to enjoy this crop. Just pick a ripe ear, peel back the husks, and eat along the ear as you normally would. We also love cooked corn, but we're becoming more enamored of the raccoon style of eating the more we practice it.

Plant corn in hills down the center of a 30-inch-wide bed. Plant four seeds per hill and thin to three seedlings. Place the hills 1½ (early) to 2 (late) feet apart, which gives an equivalent spacing of 6 to 8 inches per plant. To have corn for as long a season as possible, purchase small packets of a half-dozen varieties with progressive maturity dates and plant a few hills of each. The extra-early varieties are often not great eating, so you might want to get the earliest corn by starting a few hills of an early corn in

Plant corn in hills.

4-inch pots and transplanting them once the danger of frost has passed. Set them out shortly after they germinate (no more than 10 days old) so they don't become pot-bound. Since corn doesn't transplant easily, you need to tap the plants and root ball gently out of the pot and set them in the soil with minimal root disturbance.

If you grow corn in one of the trellised beds of the garden you can cover the early plants with a plastic A-frame greenhouse (see chapter 6). You can also interplant extra-early varieties in the spring among salad crops in a cold frame and let the corn take over once the salad crops are harvested. The lights have to be raised and eventually removed as the plants begin to push against them. To extend the season at the other end, plant a few hills of a very late variety every spring. When weather conditions permit, you get a delightful late-season treat. When fall frosts come too early, you get extra material for the compost heap. Even after being frosted, however, mature corn is protected in the husks and is often edible for up to two weeks.

Corn is a vigorous feeder and will thrive on all the compost or manure you can provide. It can be fertilized with rougher compost than most other crops. First-stage compost can be put on the corn bed the fall before and will finish decomposing in the soil. Like any other vigorously growing crop, corn will do best if you can provide extra moisture by irrigating in dry periods. Whatever effort you make is worth it for this crop.

CRESS See Salad Greens

CUCUMBER *Cucumis sativus*

Planting Distance:
Trellis—Plants 18 inches apart.
Ground—Plants 30 inches apart.

Crop Rotation: Related to squash and melons. Generally considered a good preceding crop.

Growing Tips: Try fertilizing the soil with dried seaweed to make the plants more pest resistant if you are bothered by cucumber beetles.

Storage Tips: Can be stored in the refrigerator for one week.

Variety Tips: Trellised—'Sweet Success', 'Orient Express', 'Lemon'
Low-growing—'Diva'

The home garden is paradise for the cucumber lover. You can choose to grow your favorites—whether long or round, tiny or curved—and you can choose to grow them right. There seems to be a special quality to cucumbers cultivated the old-fashioned way with lots of organic matter.

In the prechemical days, professional market gardeners appreciated the exceptionally fertile soil needed for superior cucumbers. I remember an afternoon years ago spent with one of France's most experienced organic growers. When he spoke about soil preparation for cucumbers, his eyes lit up like those of a chef describing the ingredients for a classic dish. He would dig a trench in the greenhouse about 12 inches deep and the width of a straw bale. He would then lay straw bales end to end in the trench, cover them with guano and blood meal, and water the supplements in with a hose. The moisture plus the nitrogen in the guano and blood meal started the bales composting. Within a month, they were sufficiently broken down that he could cover them with soil and well-decomposed sheep manure (he specified sheep manure for cucumbers) and set out the cucumber transplants on top. The bales would continue composting slowly, thus providing a gentle bottom heat for the cucumbers, as well as plenty of organic matter. In addition to watering, he applied a compost tea once a week. The plants were trained to the roof of the greenhouse and then back down. Any cucumber lover would have genuflected.

You don't have to copy that French system to have great cucumbers. The story is a metaphor of old gardening wisdom. It celebrates the care and competence with which perceptive growers long ago learned to create biological systems in harmony with the needs of their crops. Their obvious success in creating unparalleled quality and flavor belies the modern myth that soil life can be replaced with lifeless chemicals.

We provide cucumbers with all the fertility we can spare by adding extra compost and dried seaweed to the soil. The extra trace minerals in the seaweed seem to enhance pest resistance. We grow cucumbers on the trellis structures described in chapter 6 by training them up a string. With trellising varieties such as 'Orient Express' or 'Sweet Success', you prune the plants to one stem by removing all the shoots that form in the leaf node between the main stem and the leaf branch. After the plants are two feet high and well established, allow one fruit

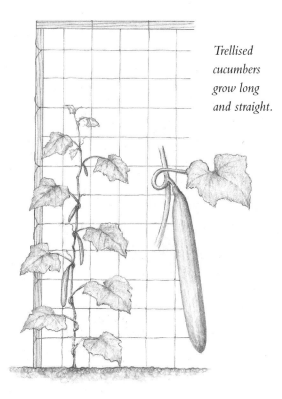

Trellised cucumbers grow long and straight.

to form at each node but continue to remove the other shoots. Wind the stem around the string for support as it goes up. If you don't want to prune, you can hang pea netting from the trellis and encourage all the stems and branches to weave their way upward. The netting will support the fruits. Trellised cucumbers grow long and straight, and they are easy to see and pick.

We start the cucumbers two weeks ahead of the safe outdoor planting date in 4-inch pots in a sunny window and transplant them down the center of the bed at an 18-inch spacing. If the early summer weather is at all unfavorable, turn the trellis into a temporary A-frame greenhouse as described in chapter 6.

We extend the season both early and late by growing cucumbers under the tunnel greenhouse in its summer location. The late crop shares space with tomatoes, melons, beans, and New Zealand spinach. The earliest crop is a non-trellising variety that we start indoors and transplant as early as possible. With a tender crop like cucumbers, it's wise to start a second planting a week after the first in case unseasonably cold weather sets back your first try. Pick them daily for best quality.

DANDELION   *Taraxacum officinale*

Planting Distance: 3 rows per 30-inch-wide bed; seeds 1 inch apart; thin to 6 inches apart.

Crop Rotation: Related to chicories, salsify, lettuce, and globe artichokes. Generally considered a beneficial preceding crop.

Growing Tips: Provide moist, rich soil.

Storage Tips: Will store in the refrigerator for one week.

Variety Tips: 'Fullheart Improved'

The dandelion is a cool-weather crop and at its best in the spring. Legions of dandelion lovers go out

Dandelion.

every April to collect wild dandelion greens. The French have selected cultivated varieties to grow in the garden. Cultivated varieties have large, vigorous leaves and hearts that are easy to clean. With a little protection, they can be harvested over a very long season. Sow small plantings in the protected garden, outdoor cold frames, and the open garden so you can harvest progressively from each area in turn.

We have always enjoyed the flavor of this plant, but it would not be amiss to grow it just because it is good for you. The botanical name *Taraxacum* means "remedy for disorders" in the original Greek. The dandelion has high levels of all sorts of desirable nutrients. Herbalists can write tomes on its virtues. The Europeans, who seem to appreciate the edible qualities of weeds, have developed a special strain, 'Mauser's Trieb', that can be grown, stored, and sprouted like Belgian endive. That way gardeners can enjoy blanched dandelion from buckets under the kitchen sink whenever they feel inclined.

ENDIVE   See Chicory Family

ESCAROLE   See Chicory Family

GARLIC   *Allium sativum*

Planting Distance: 5 rows per 30-inch-wide bed; plants 6 inches apart.

Crop Rotation: Related to leeks, onions, shallots, and chives. Don't plant where cabbage family grew the year before. Generally considered a beneficial preceding crop.

Growing Tips: Plant in mid-October for next year's harvest.

Storage Tips: Store well-cured bulbs in a cool, dry place.

Variety Tips: Try a number of varieties until you find the one that grows best in your garden. Different garlic strains have specific soil and climate preferences.

Fortunately, garlic is as easy to grow as it is indispensable in the kitchen. The most important cultural advice is to find a variety adapted to your conditions. Test-plant as many garlic strains as you can and choose the one that thrives in your soil. After that, just select the largest bulbs each year to be saved for replanting.

We plant only fall garlic. We wait until mid-October, then break the selected bulbs into cloves and plant them at 6-inch spacings. Poke the blunt end into the ground so the pointed tip is just at soil level. The idea is for the clove to be able to establish good root growth but no top growth in late fall, the same as with fall-planted flower bulbs. Plant garlic where no member of the cabbage family grew the year before. Crop rotation trials have found that the growth and yield of onion family members can be inhibited by as much as 60 percent following a cabbage family crop.

In late fall, cover the bed with straw to protect the soil over the winter. Remove the straw in spring and top dress the bed with compost. Be sure to keep the garlic plot well weeded. Determining garlic maturity for harvest depends upon the type of garlic you grow, softneck or hardneck. All the nuances of harvest timing are meticulously described in *Growing Great Garlic* by Ron Engeland (Filaree Produc-

Garlic.

tions, 1991; distributed by Chelsea Green). You should consult that book for the definitive word.

We harvest by loosening the soil with a fork and pulling up the bulbs. Garlic must be cured after harvest to prevent decay in storage. The ideal curing conditions are in a garden shed out of the direct sun and with good air movement. Those conditions can be achieved by placing the garlic on a homemade drying rack. You can make the simplest rack by setting a window screen across two sawhorses. Set the rack on a porch if you don't have a garden shed. Garlic can be considered cured when the neck is tight and the outer skin dry. You can either weave the dry tops into a braid (softneck) or store the heads without tops in a net bag.

If you end up with more garlic than you need, or if you have a number of small or substandard heads, you can make a meal from them next spring. Plant them out a couple of inches apart in an unused part of the fall garden and harvest them early next year as tender green garlic (like green onions). Trim off the roots, sauté them slowly in butter, and serve them on toast with the sauce of your choice.

HERBS

You'll certainly want to grow some herbs to complement your vegetables. You don't have to become an herb specialist, but every garden needs at least basil, dill, French tarragon, savory, sage, and thyme for fresh use and drying. Start the annuals from seeds and divide and replant the perennials as necessary. We also grow rosemary outdoors in summer, but in this climate, it needs to spend the winter in a sunny window. We grow peppermint and German chamomile for tea and carefully tend a lemon verbena plant for the classic vervain tea. The latter also must spend the cold months indoors.

Our simple technique for drying herbs is to pick them at their best and dry them out of the sun in a warm, airy place. We tie them in small bunches and hang them from the beams in the kitchen. That's not only functional, but also beautiful and aromatic. They are dry when crisp and easily crumbled.

Perennial herbs can be transplanted into the cold frame for fresh production beyond the outdoor season. Some good bets are sage, oregano, thyme, and chives. For the coldest weathers pot up a few plants and winter them inside in a sunny window.

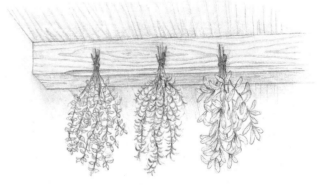

Drying herbs.

KALE *Brassica oleracea*

Planting Distance: 2 rows per 30-inch-wide bed; plants 16 inches apart.

Crop Rotation: Related to mustard, rutabagas, collards, broccoli, cauliflower, cabbage, Brussels sprouts, kohlrabi, and radishes.

Growing Tips: Leaf mold is a wonderful soil amendment for kale.

Storage Tips: Can be harvested fresh all winter in most climates even without protection.

Variety Tips: Hardiest—'Vates', 'Winterbor'
Prettiest—'Red Russian'
Tastiest—'Toscano'

Any lover of the winter season has to be fond of this cold-weather vegetable. Not only does it taste good on its own, in a casserole, or chopped into mashed potatoes with a couple of fried eggs on top, but it is also loaded with vitamins and minerals. Even if you don't use cold frames and greenhouses, you can harvest kale well beyond the growing season. If you pick it from under a snow cover in December, it will still be at its best. Many years ago, I took fresh kale along for supper on a November camping trip in the White Mountains of New Hampshire. I had more than I needed, so I tucked it in the rafters of the

Kale under snow.

shelter the next morning. Two months later when I returned to the same shelter on a winter trip, the kale was still there and still edible. We threw it in the pot that night.

The hardiness of kale varieties depends to some degree on their style of growth. The taller types are not as hardy as those with the growing heart closer to the ground. 'Winterbor' is the hardiest of the tall varieties. 'Vates' is a very hardy lower-growing variety. The lower-growing varieties are ideal for overwintering in a cold frame, since the new leaf growth starts close to the ground and can be picked before it touches the glass.

Kale responds to the same soil conditions as the other members of the cabbage family. Either autumn leaves, leaf mold, or a preceding leguminous green manure will result in excellent growth. Start kale in July to have vigorous plants for cool-season eating.

KOHLRABI *Brassica caulorapa*

Planting Distance: Rows 8 inches apart across bed; plants 8 inches apart.

Crop Rotation: Related to mustard, rutabagas, kale, and the rest of the cabbage family.

Growing Tips: Plant only as a fall crop for best quality.

Storage Tips: Winter-storage varieties will keep for months in the cellar.

Variety Tips: White—'Winner'
Purple—'Kolibri'
Storage—'Kossack'

Kohlrabi is a perfect case of the distant relative we have never gotten to know. It is surely our loss. Kohlrabi is one of the numerous vegetable members of the cabbage family. Its Latin variant name, *caulorapa*, translates as "stem turnip," an accurate but unflattering description. Don't be put off by name or unfamiliarity. This is a wonderful winter vegetable.

There are both purple and green varieties of kohlrabi. The purple certainly looks snazzier in the fall garden and is slightly hardier, but under good growing conditions, they both taste about the same. Kohlrabi starts out like any other cabbage family seedling, but instead of growing buds, flowers, or heads, it begins to look pregnant. The swollen stem is the food-storage organ for kohlrabi. Kohlrabi can be pickled, grated raw in salads or coleslaw, cut in sticks or thin slices as a base for hors d'oeuvres, added to soups and stews, or baked whole. The standard purple and green varieties are at their best when the bulb is the size of a tennis ball or smaller. Giant winter varieties produce tender storage kohlrabi in the grapefruit- to volleyball-size range.

We limit our production of kohlrabi to fall and winter because it tastes better and grows to a dependable harvest size at that time of year. In the cool temperatures and shortening fall days, kohlrabi slows its growth naturally and remains crisp and tender for a long time. Grow kohlrabi outdoors in the garden until hard freezes begin. Then harvest the remaining bulbs, trim off the leaves and stem, and store them in the cellar. Well-grown plants will store for the whole winter. Kohlrabi is hardy enough to be left in the garden in Zone 6 and south. Even in those climates, the slight protection of a cold frame or plastic tunnel will keep the plants in better condition.

Kohlrabi can be sown directly or planted in a seedbed for transplanting. Sow from late July through mid-September depending on your climate. The advantage of transplants is that the preceding crop can remain in the garden for a few weeks longer. Leaf mold mixed into the top few inches of soil is the best possible preparation for kohlrabi, especially if you have had difficulty with fall crops of other cabbage family members. Otherwise, a light top dressing of compost before transplanting or after the seedlings are established will do just fine. We space kohlrabi about 8 inches apart in 8-inch rows.

LEEK   *Allium porrum*

Planting Distance: 3 rows per 30-inch-wide bed; plants 6 inches apart.

Crop Rotation: Related to onions, shallots, garlic, and chives.

Growing Tips: Extra compost and adequate water will result in the finest leeks.

Storage Tips: Leave in the soil over the winter with protection; dig as needed.

Variety Tips: Winter—'Tadorna'
Early—'King Richard'
Main season—'Upton'

Leeks are a foundation crop of the winter garden because they are so hardy. They also are a classic ingredient for a good meal. You should feel like a participant in a culinary ceremony when you parade into the kitchen with freshly dug leeks snuggled in a basket. Leeks braised in butter can be a dinner dish all their own. They also form the basis for many hearty winter soups. The word *porridge,* which initially meant a thick vegetable soup, is derived from *porrum,* the Latin word for leek.

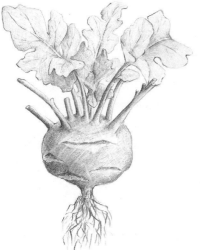

Kohlrabi.

This is a long-season crop. Start winter leeks in early spring in a cold frame seedbed. Transplant pencil-sized seedlings to their permanent home. You can cut back some of the roots and leaves to make them easier to handle when transplanting. Use a right-angle trowel to make deep holes for the young leeks. Press the trowel into the soil to the full depth of the blade and pull toward you slightly. Drop a young leek in behind the trowel and release. Water the area when you finish. Let the holes fill naturally over time from rain or watering. Planting in deep holes in this fashion will guarantee you at least 6 inches of blanched white stem without having to hill the leeks. That white portion is the most tender. Make the holes 6 inches apart in rows 10 inches apart. At that close spacing you can't hill up soil to blanch the stems further, so you must fill in between them with leaves or leaf mold if you want a longer blanched portion. We don't usually bother. We consider the 6 inches of underground stem to be sufficient.

For winter harvest, sow a hardy winter variety and transplant the seedlings to the edge beds of a tunnel or to a cold frame. With tunnel or frame protection, the leek harvest can be extended right through winter. In the coldest climates, the double coverage of tunnel and inner layer keeps the soil from freezing and makes for a much easier leek harvest.

If you want to enjoy leeks all year-round, direct-sow a bunching leek variety early in the spring. These varieties are grown and harvested as if they were bunching onions. They grow to fountain pen size in eight weeks or so. A few succession plantings will supply you with baby leeks right up to the time you start harvesting the summer crop.

There is one final bit of leek lore you may wish to explore. If you still have wintered-over leeks remaining in the spring and they start to go to seed, you can get an extra meal out of them. We haven't yet had the opportunity to try this because we are such enthusiastic leek consumers there are never any remaining. The seed company Sutton and Sons in their 1910 book *The Culture of Vegetables and Flowers* gives the only mention we have ever seen of this option for additional leek enjoyment:

> Any that remain over in spring can be turned to account to supply a delicate and comparatively unknown vegetable. As the flower stems rise nip them out; not one should be left. The result of this practice will be the formation on the roots of small roundish white bulbs, which make an excellent dish when stewed in gravy, and may be used for any purpose in cookery for which Onions or Shallots are employed. They are called "Leek Bulbs," and are obtainable only in early summer.

Now there is a classic seasonal vegetable treat.

LETTUCE   *Lactuca sativa*

Planting Distance:
Head—3 rows per 30-inch-wide bed; plants 10 inches apart.

Leeks.

Leaf—Rows as close as 2 inches apart across bed; sow seeds ½ inch apart.

Crop Rotation: Related to endive, escarole, chicory, and dandelion.

Growing Tips: Always use your best compost for growing tender leafy crops such as lettuce.

Storage Tips: Harvest fresh from garden or cold frame.

Variety Tips: Early—'Black Seeded Simpson', 'Akcel'
Bibb—'Buttercrunch'
Butterhead—'Nancy', 'Sangria'
Leaf—'Waldmann's', 'Red Sails'
Cutting—'Lollo Rossa', 'Matchless'
Head—'Crispino', 'Calmar'
Romaine—'Winter Density', 'Romulus', 'Little Gem'
Winter—'Brune d'Hiver', 'Blonde d'Hiver', 'D'Hiver de Verrières'

Red or green, frilly or smooth, leaf or head—the lettuce family embraces enough colors and textures to decorate anyone's salad bowl. Boston, bibb, butterhead, iceberg, romaine—the names evoke the annual lettuce parade from spring to fall. The specifics of 'Simpson', 'Red Sails', 'Buttercrunch', 'Rouge d'Hiver', 'Crispino', 'Lollo Rossa', and 'Little Gem' ring like exotic place names along the route. In backyard trials over the years, we have grown at least one hundred varieties of lettuce. Whenever traveling or visiting gardeners, we buy or borrow seeds of new varieties. They are fun to test, taste, and compare.

A full-grown lettuce in the garden or on the table is like a large rose, beautiful and decorative. The fact that a plant this lovely is also the foundation for three seasons of salads is proof that nature is benign and generous. Those three seasons are spring, summer, and fall in Zone 5. In more southern areas the seasons are reversed—fall, winter, and spring. Heat-

tolerant lettuce varieties may extend that period in some southern climates. We search for more cold-tolerant varieties to extend the winter season here.

The difficult period for lettuce in Zone 5 coincides almost exactly with official winter—December 21 to March 21. Lettuces that have reached harvestable size in late fall can take the freezing and thawing only so long before they succumb, even in the protection of a cold frame or tunnel. Young lettuce plants of the winter varieties, although they will survive under protection and reach a decent size by around the third week in March, don't always provide a dependable harvest from mid-December to mid-February. Mâche, the cold-weather wonder, is our salad staple for the winter months and a delightful complement to lettuce in late fall and early spring. When the mâche season ends in April, the lettuce season is well established again.

The easiest way to grow lettuce is to harvest young leaves. Plant leaf lettuce in short rows across the bed starting as early in the spring as you can. Make the rows as close as 2 inches apart and sow one seed every ½ inch in each row. Cut the leaves with a knife or scissors an inch above the soil starting when they are three inches high. Water well, and the leaves will continue to grow for a second and third harvest.

Butterhead lettuces in a cold frame.

Alternatively, you can sow in succession every week or ten days and replace the lettuce with some other crop after a once-over harvest.

It is not much more difficult to grow full-size lettuce if your soil is fertile. Always save your best compost for this crop. We prefer to transplant lettuce for full-sized heads, but you can direct-seed. Sow every week in potting soil in the corner of a cold frame and transplant the seedlings to the garden 10 inches apart in rows 10 inches apart. Nothing is prettier than the look of tidy lettuce beds of different ages and varieties.

In order to maintain the lettuce harvest into the fall and winter months, the early fall plantings are crucial. The weekly succession plantings that provide fresh salads all summer no longer apply because lettuce growth slows down in the fall as the days shorten. We sow fall cold frame lettuce from mid-August through September with planting dates for the double-protected tunnel lettuce extending into early October. Any lettuce sown later than that does not have enough time to get established before winter.

For the earliest spring harvest you will want to transplant some of those late sowings to winter over as small plants. Sow seeds around September 25 and again five to seven days later in case the fall is especially warm and the first planting grows too large. During the shortening fall days, that brief delay between plantings has a major effect on the eventual growth before winter. Transplant the young lettuce plants (ideally no more than 3 inches in diameter) to the protected garden in late October at a 6-by-6-inch spacing to allow for losses. Put them in both the tunnels and the outdoor frames to extend the harvest season in spring. (The double-covered heads mature first.) We also plant lettuce seeds in the tunnel frames in January and February, and by early May, when the overwintered crop is finished, we're eating the first of the new spring crop.

MÂCHE
or CORN SALAD   *Valerianella locusta*

Planting Distance: Rows 2 inches apart across bed; seeds 1 inch apart.

Crop Rotation: Not related to any other vegetable crop.

Growing Tips: Prepare a flat and semi-firm seedbed by tamping lightly with the back of a rake.

Storage Tips: Harvest mâche fresh as you need it.

Variety Tips: 'Vit'

Mâche is to winter what sweet corn is to summer—a plant adapted to its season. The mâche plant is not imposing like corn; it's just a small rosette of tender leaves each about the size of your thumb. But it is so cold resistant that it deserves coronation as the queen of vigor and robustness. Mâche is truly the winter wonder green.

It is not only delicious to eat but will survive and continue to grow in colder weather than any other vegetable. Like lettuce, it is a staple green around which the rest of a salad can be created. Most people use the French name mâche for this crop because it is a staple of French winter salads. In England, it's known as corn salad or lamb's lettuce, in Germany it's *Feldsalat,* and in Switzerland, *Nusslisalat.* Originally, it was a winter weed in grain fields and was harvested wild for salads long before it was domesticated.

Mâche can be grown in spring and summer if you insist, but germination will be poor because it is a true winter crop and germinates and grows best in the cooling and shortening days of fall. We plant mâche in a cold frame and our tunnel from early September through early November. Mâche seeds can be planted in rows or broadcast lightly wherever there is an open space. Mâche grows an extensive network of very fine sodlike roots that stabilize the soil and make mâche almost impervious to frost heaving. Mâche also is perfect as a companion crop. For example, in the fall cold frames where lettuce, endive, or radishes are growing, sprinkle mâche seed next to, between, and underneath those crops. It germinates in their shade, and once they are harvested, you'll have a lush bed of mâche to eat through the winter.

Although it can survive outdoors, mâche is best for winter eating when protected by a cold frame or other cover. This is also true in milder climates than ours, if only to keep winter rains from splattering soil on the small plants. Outdoor plantings of mâche will survive the winter to extend the harvest into April after the mâche in the frame is harvested or has begun to go to seed.

The mâche growing under protection will provide salads throughout the winter. No matter how cold the climate, any day that the temperature in the frame goes above freezing, mâche is ready to harvest—even if it was -20°F the night before. You can even harvest mâche when the leaves are frozen if you don't mind them wilting a little in the salad bowl. The preferred harvesting technique is to cut the whole plant at soil level. It is important to smooth and flatten the seedbed before planting mâche so that when you run your knife on top of the soil and under the leaves, you won't be piling lumps of soil onto the newly harvested plants. If you

Harvesting mâche.

harvest progressively along each row, you will open up space for succession plantings of other crops. Before planting a succession crop after mâche, it helps to add some extra nitrogen to the soil. Use some alfalfa meal or fish emulsion at the rate recommended on the container and mix it in. The extensive root system of mâche leaves a lot of fiber in the soil. Some extra nitrogen will allow the new crop to grow while the soil is simultaneously breaking down the mâche roots.

After harvesting, wash the mâche lightly and remove any remaining roots. (There shouldn't be any roots if you harvested right at soil level.) Mâche plants are usually served intact in a salad without being cut up. You can harvest them at any size. Smaller plants are usually more tender but not enough so to make a major difference. A mâche plant generally won't get any bigger than four inches in diameter, so don't postpone harvesting in anticipation of something the size of a head of lettuce. Since mâche is small, you can plant it in close rows or even broadcast the seeds. Cover the seeds lightly, with about ¼ inch of soil. Ideally, you want to plant one seed every inch in the row. Mâche is so vigorous that it will produce well even if you plant closer, but overcrowding will cause the lower leaves to yellow due to lack of light.

Mâche is the most dependable salad ingredient during cold winters. You can mix mâche with any of the additions usually incorporated in your salads, or you can explore the unique culinary possibilities of mâche itself. Our favorite is the way it is enjoyed in France—small, whole mâche plants mixed with slices of cold cooked beets, whole leaves of Belgian endive, and a light vinaigrette. Accompany that salad with an omelet of fresh duck eggs and a homemade hard cider from the apple orchard behind the garden, and you have the makings of a memorable peasant feast.

MELON   *Cucumis melo*

Planting Distance: 1 row per 30-inch-wide bed; plants 16 inches apart.

Crop Rotation: Related to cucumbers, watermelon, and squash.

Growing Tips: Melons need rich soil. Use plenty of compost and some dried seaweed. Warm the soil with infrared-transmitting plastic mulch.

Storage Tips: You can store ripe melons for two weeks in the refrigerator.

Variety Tips: Cantaloupe—'Gold Star' Charantais—'Edonis', 'Savor'

It is easy to commit excesses when it comes to melons. I can remember entire days in August and September when my diet consisted wholly of melons, plucked fresh from the vine and eaten gluttonously, teeth nibbling flesh off of thin slices and juice dripping down my chin. Garden-ripe melons are the quintessential nectar of the gods.

We probably appreciate melons all the more because they are not easy to grow on the Maine coast. They are heat lovers, and the New England maritime climate can be cool even in summer. Thus, we start melons indoors about three weeks before the frost-free date. We prewarm the soil in the melon bed by covering it with infrared-transmitting plastic (see appendix D) at this time. The plastic allows the sun to warm the soil as much as possible, but it does not permit weed growth. We cut a small hole in the plastic at each spot where the melon transplants will be set out.

After transplanting, the bed is covered with a lightweight floating cover (see appendix D) to provide the warmest growing conditions. We pay close attention to plant growth in the following weeks, and when the female blossoms begin to open and need to be pollinated by bees, we remove the cover. The melons then grow uncovered for the rest of the season.

We recommend both the standard American cantaloupe and the smaller, more aromatic French Charantais melons. They grow similarly, but harvesting is different. Cantaloupes are picked at what is called *full slip*—that is, when the end of the stem slips away from the melon under slight thumb pressure. If you wait that long with the Charantais, they will be too ripe. They must be picked at *leaf turn*—when the small leaf at the end of the stem next to the melon fades from green to pale tan.

Our love affair with ripe melons is a metaphor

Melons on black plastic.

for the seasonal garden. Melons are available at their vine-ripened best for only six weeks of the year in Zone 5, but they are the best-tasting melons anyone could imagine. We have melon memories from those six weeks that last until melon harvest comes around. Against those memories, the green-picked, hard-fleshed, out-of-season supermarket melons offer nothing but disappointment.

MINUTINA   See Salad Greens

MIZUNA   See Salad Greens

MUSTARD   See Salad Greens

NEW ZEALAND SPINACH   See Spinach

ONION   *Allium cepa*

Planting Distance: 3 rows per bed 10 inches apart; seeds 1 inch apart; thin to 4 inches apart. Multiplants (see p. 100) are set 3 rows per bed, plants 12 inches apart.

Crop Rotation: Related to leeks, garlic, and chives.

Growing Tips: Spread lime to counteract soil acidity. Keep well weeded when young.

Storage Tips: Harvest promptly at maturity. Cure as instructed. Store in cold (32°–35°F), dry place. Protect from freezing.

Variety Tips: Main crop— 'Copra', 'Mars' Over-winter—'Walla Walla Sweet', 'Olympic' Perennial—'Egyptian' or 'Top Set Onion' Scallion—'Evergreen Hardy White'

The gardener has three options for planting onions—seeds, transplants, or sets. We prefer to sow onion seeds during March in a cold frame and then transplant the seedlings to the garden. Growing from seed allows us access to the full range of varieties available—red, yellow, or white; sweet or snappy; round or long. In addition, this process ensures the greatest harvest and best storage qualities. Seeds also can be sown directly in the garden if you use one of the shorter-season varieties like 'Buffalo'. Some gardeners purchase transplants from the southern plant growers who advertise in garden magazines every spring. Onions transplant well, so this option is popular. Selection, however, is limited. The third and easiest option is onion sets. These are miniature onions about the diameter of a nickel or dime that were grown the year before under crowded conditions that temporarily stunted their growth. They are easy to plant and they start growing again quickly to produce full-sized onions. The variety selection with sets is even more limited than with transplants. Also, most set onions have a flattened globe shape. This shape, compared with round onions, results in fewer slices for the effort of peeling.

Onions, it is often said, want the richest soil in the garden. That is true up to a point. Onions want a very fertile soil, but they thrive on balance rather than excessive richness. Finished compost with attention to soil minerals and pH are the keys to that balance. The onion crop is a good measure of your soil-building progress. When your soil fertility is on the right track, onion foliage has a fresh look with a blue-green bloom, and the bulbs dry consistently after harvest to a tight top and well-colored skin. It may take three to five years to achieve that balance, depending on the condition of the soil when you begin. You will agree the effort is worthwhile once you see how well onions can grow.

Onions do best when planted where lettuce, squashes, or melons grew the year before. Onions are seriously disadvantaged by a preceding cabbage family crop. Both our experience and fifty years of crop rotation studies at the University of Rhode

Island confirm that observation. Onions and their relatives have a beneficial effect on all crops following them in the rotation.

Onions need to be cured at harvest for successful storage. Pull the bulbs when the tops fall over and leave them to dry in the sun for a day with the roots up. Place them on a drying rack (see Garlic) until the neck is tight and the outer skin is dry and rustling. Cut the tops an inch above the bulb and place the bulbs in net bags. If you keep them in a cold, dry place where they won't freeze (such as an unheated porch or attic), they will remain in good condition right through until spring.

You can bridge the gap between the last of the stored onions and the new crop in a number of ways. First, you can eat the sprouts that grow on onions toward the end of their storage period. They are just as tasty as green onions, so there is no sense discarding them. Second, you can maintain a patch of the perennial 'Egyptian' or 'Top Set Onion' variety *(Allium cepa proliferatum)* and in fall plant out the small onion bulbs or top sets that are found on the stalks. They are hardy and will produce green onions early the following year. Third, you can plant a hardy perennial scallion such as 'Evergreen Hardy White', which will survive the winter. Fourth, you

Curing onions.

can purchase onion sets as soon as they are available in the spring and plant them to use as green onions. Plant some under protection and more in the outdoor garden for a continuous harvest. Fifth, you can sow an overwintering onion such as 'Walla Walla Sweet' or 'Buffalo' in August. If you live where winter temperatures are colder than -10°F you will need to provide the protection of a frame or tunnel. Thin them progressively to a 4-inch spacing in late winter and use the thinnings as green onions. The remaining plants produce large bulbs in June and July, well ahead of normal onion harvest.

ORACH   *See Salad Greens*

ORIENTAL VEGETABLES

The early botanists who roamed the deserts and mountains looking for new plant varieties were referred to as plant explorers. You can become a plant explorer without even leaving home if you grow Oriental vegetables. It is inspiring to look through a manual on the full range of Oriental vegetables. You will be amazed by the variety of crops Oriental gardeners have cultivated for centuries. It's like discovering another galaxy of vegetable crops in parallel with the mostly Occidental crops with which U.S. gardeners are familiar.

When you grow a new crop, it is mainly a trial-and-error operation. The experience of putting the crop in the ground and watching what happens is your best teacher. Begin with common sense and intuition. If the crop is related to one of the plant groups with which you are familiar, assume it will benefit from similar conditions. If it's an herb, obviously don't plant as much as you might for a main crop. If it's a vine, try to find a spot in a trellised row. Sometimes there is no clue. In that case sow them here and there around the garden and wait to see what happens. Use compost to enrich the soil. Plant short rows. If they fail, it's no loss; just replant to something else. Even then, if there are seeds left in the packet, try the crop again next year just in case the failure was an anomaly.

Many lesser-known Oriental crops may be valuable additions to the winter garden. We do not have sufficient experience with them yet to do more than encourage you to experiment. But there are two very hardy leaf crops we recommend enthusiastically, tatsoi and pac choi. Sown in September and given the double protection of tunnel and inner layer they have survived the coldest weather. Tatsoi has become a particular favorite not only for its delicious flavor but also because its dark green shiny leaves just plain look nutritious.

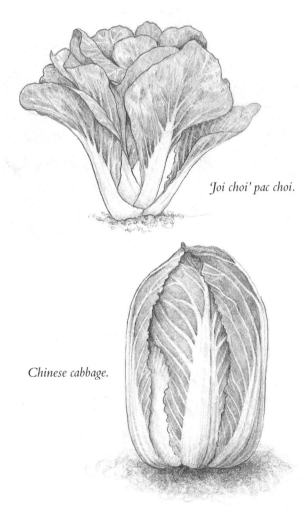

'Joi choi' pac choi.

Chinese cabbage.

PARSLEY   *Petroselinum crispum*

Planting Distance:
Cold frame crop—Rows 6 inches apart; plants 6 inches apart.
Main crop—Rows 8 inches apart; plants 8 inches apart.

Crop Rotation: Related to carrots, celery, and parsnips.

Growing Tips: Parsley can be transplanted if started in small pots.

Storage Tips: Dried parsley has many uses.

Variety Tips: 'Forest Green', 'Titan'

Parsley is a first-rate food and should be considered as more than a garnish. I have always liked it so much that I graze on parsley while working in the garden. Parsley is the essence of garden green: it settles the stomach, cleanses the blood, refreshes the palate, and piques the taste buds. Parsley is a chlorophyll tonic and a carotene powerhouse all rolled into one delightful nibble. When grown in a fertile, humus-rich soil and given adequate moisture, parsley will be sweet and tender, with no biting aftertaste.

I once visited an organic farm in Holland that grew ten acres of parsley for a company producing dried seasonings. The company chose this farm because its fertile soil grew such a sweet parsley. How does one harvest ten acres of parsley? The Dutch farmer had a special machine similar to a grain combine that cut and collected the parsley as it moved down the field. You may not need ten acres of parsley in your home garden, but when it's well grown, you will agree that it deserves more than just an out-of-the-way spot. You can harvest leaf parsley a sprig at a time or by cutting the whole bunch. Either way, the plant will continue to grow.

We aim to have parsley available year-round. We

plant it in both the outdoor garden and winter garden. We also pot up some plants in the fall to grow in a sunny window. Parsley seeds are slow to germinate so it's a good idea to plant a few seeds every so often in cold frames or corners of the garden whenever sowing other crops. That way, this delightful grazing green is always nearby.

Parsley Root (Hamburg Parsley)—A close relative is parsley root (or Hamburg parsley), a root crop bearing the same relation to parsley as celeriac does to celery. It responds to the same cultural conditions as parsley and is grown as easily as carrots or parsnips. Parsley root complements or substitutes for other root crops in any recipe. It can be grated raw in salads, baked whole in a covered dish, added to a shish kebab, cooked tempura style, or, the children's favorite, sliced thinly and fried for some of the best-tasting "chips" you will ever eat. In winter, if there is no other source of parsley, you can bring a few parsley roots up from the basement and force them in a pot on the windowsill. They will produce a continuous harvest of flat-leaved parsley for six weeks or more before needing to be replaced.

Plant root parsley in rows 10 to 12 inches apart and thin the plants to 6 to 8 inches apart. Dig the root parsley in the late fall and store it in the cellar.

Parsley root being forced in winter.

You also can leave the plants in the ground with protection so they can be dug fresh in the spring.

PARSNIP   *Pastinaca sativa*

Planting Distance: Rows 12 inches apart across beds; seeds 1 inch apart; thin plants to 4 inches apart.

Crop Rotation: Related to carrots, parsley, and celery.

Growing Tips: Be sure to plant early enough to get good-sized roots. Fertilize with leaf mold.

Storage Tips: Leave in garden over the winter. Harvest when soil thaws in the spring.

Variety Tips: 'Andover'

Parsnips are the hardiest of root crops. They are traditionally planted in early June for consumption the following spring. They will winter over in the soil with no protection in even the coldest climates. You can dig them once the soil thaws sufficiently. Parsnips taste very sweet in spring because the cold winter temperatures cause the roots to change some of the starch to sugar.

Parsnips are a surprisingly versatile vegetable and far more interesting eating than their pedestrian reputation may suggest. What makes them exciting is that they are suddenly available at the lowest ebb of the vegetable year—the end of winter. Our favorite recipe is an equal mix of puréed parsnips and carrots with cream and a hint of nutmeg. Everyone will come back for seconds.

One spring I was inspired to celebrate the potential of this vegetable by making an all-parsnip meal. It began with an appetizer of some thinly sliced parsnips cooked like potato chips and served with a dip. That was followed by a dish using parsnips instead of potatoes in a scalloped potato recipe. Next came a palate cleanser of very thin slices (from the top of a large parsnip) fried lightly in butter to

Parsnips are traditionally left in the soil all winter and harvested in spring.

soften them and then rolled around a layer of raspberry sorbet. The main course was a vegetarian nut cutlet with cooked parsnips as a major ingredient. The meal was topped off with a parsnip pie (using mashed parsnip instead of pumpkin in a standard pumpkin pie recipe). The only thing missing was the delicate golden parsnip wine so prized by home vintners. Everyone agreed that if my culinary skills had matched my imagination, it could have been a masterpiece.

Plant parsnips in early June in rows 12 inches apart across the bed and thin the plants to 4 inches apart. A small section at the end of a bed will yield enough for spring meals. If the rest of the bed is planted to other wintered-over crops such as dandelion, salsify, sorrel, and spinach, you could place a movable cold frame over the entire bed in early spring to advance the harvest. Parsnips grow well given the same conditions as carrots. In fall, you don't have to do anything but let the tops die back naturally as the weather gets colder.

PEAS *Pisum sativum*

Planting Distance: 2 rows, 4 to 6 inches apart, down the center of a 30-inch-wide trellised bed.

Crop Rotation: Related to other legumes of the pea and bean family.

Growing Tips: Spread compost the fall before. Sow early and mulch before the weather gets hot.

Storage Tips: Don't store. This is a classic fresh vegetable.

Variety Tips: Early—'Strike'
Main crop—'Lincoln'
Fall—'Maestro'
Sugar snap—'Sugar Ann', 'Sugar Snap'

If you have never picked a plump, green pea pod, zipped it down the seam, and popped the sweet peas into your mouth, that is reason enough to start a garden. Fresh peas are truly the king of vegetables. Even if you limit yourself to the standard round green peas (English peas to a southerner), they are regal. If you branch out into sugar snaps and snow peas, you have a whole royal family. No other crop, not even sweet corn, so perfectly defines the advantages of the home garden: food at its best when picked immediately before eating and available to snack on whenever you walk by.

We start the earliest peas in a cold frame, where we harvested the previous crops selectively so as to open up a 10-inch-wide strip along the inside back wall. We plant the peas in that strip in two parallel rows about 4 to 6 inches apart. In frames, you can plant a month or two earlier than you could outdoors. By the time the peas grow tall enough to reach the glass, the weather is usually safe to slide the frames back and let the peas grow through. We then build a 3-foot-tall version of the trellis described in chapter 6 with an upright at either end and a crossbar holding the netting. If for some reason it is necessary to close the frame after this point, you can lean the lights against the crossbar, then cover the back side with plastic or any other temporary protection. For the earliest harvest plant one of the extra-early sugar snap varieties such as 'Sugar Ann'. We plant under the inner layer of the tunnel as early as February. Since sugar snaps are usable at all stages, you can eat the pods like snow peas almost as soon as they form.

The main crop of peas in the outdoor garden is planted in two parallel rows 4 to 6 inches apart down the center of one of the trellised beds. "As early as the ground can be worked" is an old refrain in garden jargon, but it's good advice. Peas are a cool-weather crop, and the yield and quality are best from an early-spring planting. If you have mixed some compost into the soil the fall before, all that's left to do in early spring is to drop in the seeds. When the peas are up and growing well, mulch the bed 4 inches deep with hay or straw. That keeps the soil cooler and moister, lengthening the pea harvest.

The traditional advice for spacing rows of trellised peas is to put them as far apart as the peas are tall. For peas with 6-foot-tall vines, that means a

Peas.

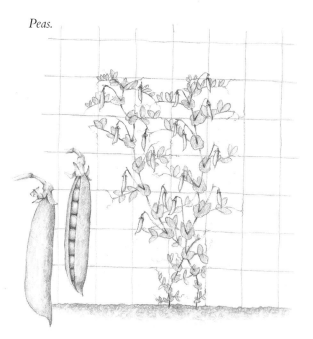

6-foot row spacing. Those spacings are sound advice on a commercial basis, but the home gardener can close things up somewhat. In our garden, the 30-inch-wide bed is perfectly fine for even the tallest peas if we keep the vines from billowing out too far. You control billowing by running garden twine horizontally outside the vines to hold them against the trellis netting. Put up a new strand every foot or so as the peas grow. You also can reduce billowing by planting the seeds farther apart in the parallel rows so there is less plant mass looking for growing space. English gardeners have traditionally planted pea seeds farther apart than Americans. You will determine the best seed spacing for specific varieties by experience, but most peas (especially 'Lincoln', our favorite) grow very well at 2 inches apart in the row, and some of the taller ones grow well at up to 4 inches apart.

In addition to green shell peas, we also grow sugar snaps. If you pick the sugar snap pods when young and flat, they make very acceptable snow peas. For the sweetest sugar snaps, let them grow until the pods are well filled out. We grow the original tall 'Sugar Snap' variety because we like its quality, but some of the new lower-growing varieties also are acceptable.

The most impressive peas I ever saw were the result of too much of a good thing: horse manure. The pea field had been manured twice by mistake. The peas were awesome. The result was a surprise because peas are considered to be self-feeders for nitrogen, since they are legumes. Nevertheless, peas appreciate generous manuring. The same goes for dry beans. Extra organic matter results in absolutely impeccable quality. If you apply a healthy dose of rough compost to the pea beds the fall before planting, it will finish its decomposition in the soil. You should also inoculate the peas with the proper legume bacteria which you can purchase from the same seed catalog that the peas came from.

Whereas sugar snaps are sweetest when the pods are completely filled, we like to pick regular peas at 75 to 90 percent full. If you let them fill completely, they taste starchy and are harder than young peas. When peas are at their prime, they are the most irresistible vegetable in the garden. It's difficult to get them to the kitchen because they are so delicious to eat while picking. Most gardeners just give up all pretense and hunker down in the pea patch to do some serious munching. In fact, until the raw sweet corn is available, raw peas are the finest summer treat.

You can extend the season into the fall by making a midsummer planting of peas. Our traditional date for fall pea planting has been July 12 to 20. That's about sixty days before the average first light frost. Although peas are known as a hardy spring crop, only the leaves and vines are really hardy, not the pods. The first light fall frosts are no problem, but a few degrees of freezing will damage the pods. Grow the fall peas on a trellis, where you can cover them with a plastic sheet to make a temporary A-frame greenhouse as necessary (see page 61). That way, the harvest can be extended by three weeks or a month. 'Maestro' is an excellent fall variety. One of the lower-growing sugar snap types also will fit in well here. Either way, be sure to choose a variety with resistance to pea diseases. The stress of hot weather at planting time makes peas more disease prone in fall than in spring.

PEPPER *Capsicum annum*

Planting Distance: 2 rows per 30-inch-wide bed; plants 18 inches apart.

Crop Rotation: Related to eggplant, potatoes, and tomatoes.

Growing Tips: Mulch with stones or infrared-transmitting plastic in cool climates.

Storage Tips: Sweet peppers will keep for two to three weeks in the refrigerator. Hot peppers are easily dried.

Variety Tips: Earliest—'Ace'
Dependable—'Yankee Bell'
Tasty—'Carmen'

Recently, plant breeders have lent their talents to liberating the range of colors that exist in pepper genes. Whereas most peppers are green when immature, the rainbow of colors starts as they ripen. Catalogs now offer brown, yellow, purple, orange, white, and tan, as well as the traditional red. Hot pepper lovers have always sought to liberate the wide range of hot, hotter, and hottest that peppers can attain. All those options are available in the specialty seed catalogs. Most sweet and hot peppers can be grown with success even in the upper latitudes.

If you live in a cool coastal or northern climate, you may wish to grow sweet and hot peppers under the mobile tunnel. The four varieties listed above are all adapted to greenhouse culture. Greenhouse peppers are common in Europe and are pruned like tomato plants, with the stems tied to overhead supports for vertical growth. We save work by using the same 6-inch-square mesh material that supports climbing peas to support pepper plants. Only in this case we use the mesh horizontally rather than vertically. We drive wooden stakes along the edge of the pepper bed and attach a mesh layer at 12, 24, and 36 inches above the ground. With a little encouragement the peppers grow up through the mesh and the plants are well supported with their fruits held above the ground. The eventual production is enormous.

In the outdoor garden, growth can be enhanced through making the soil warmer, either with infrared-transmitting plastic mulch or by using the same flat stone mulching technique that conserves soil

Peppers.

moisture around celery. The stone mulch absorbs sun heat during the day and releases it to warm the soil and air around the peppers at night. Once the plants are large enough to shade the mulch or the stones, the extra heat is no longer needed. The moisture-conserving properties continue to operate for the entire season.

If you start your own pepper plants, prune off any blossoms that form while they are still in pots. You will lose a little early production, but the plants will be much more vigorous. You can increase total yield by continuing that pruning technique after the peppers are in the garden. If you continue to snip off the earliest blossoms before the fruits form, thus allowing the plant to become established before it has to support fruits, the eventual yield will be higher because later production will increase. In a New England trial, the highest total pepper yield came from plants whose blossoms were removed until July 1. Those plants were able to put all their early energy into growing a vigorous root system, which then supported greatly increased pepper production for the rest of the summer.

Set out pepper plants 18 inches apart in two rows 18 inches apart. Fertilize the bed with well-decomposed compost. Don't use leaves or leaf mold. The extra nitrogen they supply encourages pepper plants to go more to leaf than to fruit, and the yield will be greatly reduced even though the plants may look spectacularly large.

Sweet peppers are eaten fresh while the season lasts. Late fruits picked before the first frost will remain in edible condition for two weeks or more if kept cool (50°F) and moist. The tunnel-grown plants can extend the season by a month or more, especially if you add a layer of fabric over them for extra protection on cold nights. Hot peppers are a natural crop for drying. The whole plant can be pulled and hung by the stem in a sunny shed. If the weather is too moist for outdoor drying, hang them from the beams in the kitchen along with the herbs.

POTATO   *Solanum tuberosum*

Planting Distance: 1 row per 30-inch-wide bed; plants 12 inches apart.

Crop Rotation: Related to tomatoes, peppers, and eggplant.

Growing Tips: Plant 3 inches deep. As soon as shoots emerge, spread 1 inch of rough compost and mulch 6 to 8 inches deep with straw.

Storage Tips: Always store in darkness. Potatoes keep best at 40°F. Below 38°F, they tend to become undesirably sweet.

Variety Tips: White—'Charlotte', 'Kennebec' Red—'Rose Gold', 'Red Gold'

Potatoes have not been as common a home garden crop as one would expect. There seems to be an assumption that they belong on a farm. Fortunately, that misconception is changing. Home gardeners have learned that potatoes are easy to grow and very productive. But there is one serious problem with growing your own. Potatoes grown in a fertile, well-composted soil will taste so good that you will never again be satisfied with store-bought potatoes. It's just like with carrots. Homegrown potatoes seem like a whole new vegetable.

A lot of potatoes can be grown in a very small space. The home garden yield from a 30-foot row should be about sixty pounds (one bushel). That's pretty good, since the average per capita per year consumption in the U.S. is two bushels. Even if you can't find the space to grow all your potatoes, at least grow some for the joy of tasting a real potato. You may then be inspired to search out a local organic farmer from whom you can buy extra potatoes every fall.

Another delight of growing your own is the wide variety available. One outgrowth of the present interest in preserving old vegetable seeds has been an increased availability of old-time potatoes. Catalogs now list more than one hundred cultivars, covering every conceivable skin color, flesh color, texture, flavor, and use (see appendix D). It is definitely worth trying a number of potatoes to find the ideal variety for your soil and taste preference. But be sure to buy your seed potatoes from catalogs that guarantee certified seed.

Growing potatoes couldn't be easier. What you eat is what you plant. You can purchase seed potatoes to plant or, if you have healthy crops, you can plant your own. If after a year or two yields decline or the foliage looks odd there may be a virus problem and you will again want to buy new certified seed potatoes from the specialty growers in northern areas.

There are many systems for growing potatoes. We use a combination of practices for the best results. We plant small, whole seed potatoes 3 inches deep and 12 inches apart in a single row down the center of a 30-inch-wide bed. When the first sprouts poke through the soil, spread an inch of rough compost and mulch the entire bed 6 to 8 inches deep with straw. Renew the mulch as needed during the summer if it looks thin.

Mulching benefits potatoes by keeping the soil cooler and moister. We have found that the major potato pest, the Colorado potato beetle *(Leptinotarsa decemlineata),* can be controlled more simply and successfully by mulching than by any other single practice. The major stresses on potatoes during growth seem to arise from inadequate moisture and excessive soil temperature. A thick mulch is the most effective way of lessening temperature and moisture stress, thus enhancing the plant's resistance to pests.

We often plant a few potatoes for extra-early harvest in one of the cold frames or the tunnel. Put the seed potatoes in a warm room for a month before planting to encourage them to begin sprouting. The early sprouting results in faster growth after planting and earlier harvest. If you are hungry for early potatoes and don't wish to dig the whole plant, you can sneak your hand into the soil around the roots and steal a potato or two. The traditional name for this practice is "grabbling."

Potatoes.

We grow potatoes in the same garden with the rest of the vegetables. We don't segregate them to an acidic soil to minimize the potato scab problem, as so many gardening books recommend. A potato adapted to your soil and carefully tended will grow exceptional crops with little or no scab at a pH of 6.5 to 6.8. With potatoes, as with other crops, the optimal soil levels of organic matter, minerals, moisture, and aeration are the keys to successful culture.

PUMPKIN   See Squash Family

PURSLANE   See Salad Greens

RADICCHIO   See Chicory Family

RADISH   *Raphanus sativus*

Planting Distance:
Small—Rows 4 inches apart across bed; seeds 1
   inch apart.
Large storage-type—Rows 10 inches apart; seeds
   1 inch apart; thin to 6 inches apart.

Crop Rotation: Related closely enough to the cabbage family that it is best not to precede or follow those crops with radishes.

Growing Tips: Best if grown quickly. Amend soil with compost and leaf mold. Keep well watered.

Storage Tips: Winter types store until spring at 32°F. Small radishes will keep for a few weeks in the refrigerator, but they are best fresh.

Variety Tips: Small—'Cheriette', 'D'Avignon'
Specialty—'Shunkyo Semi-Long'
Daikon—'Miyashige'
Winter—'Nero Tondo'

The snack value of radishes was emphasized during a 1989 visit with one of Germany's best organic growers. On the table were platters of red and white radishes in different shapes and sizes in-terspersed with curly green parsley, thick slices of yellow cheese, and brown bread. The platters were surrounded by steins of a local organic dark beer. The warm browns, yellows, and reds not only set a beautiful table but also enhanced the warmth and camaraderie of the discussion that followed.

Another radish scene from that trip is also memorable, this time at a small intensive market garden south of Paris. It was a misty day, and two workers were harvesting and bunching 'French Breakfast' radishes (lovely, oval-shaped bright red radishes with a white tip). They laid each bunch on the soil alongside them as they proceeded. The artistic trail of radish bunches with bright green tops and red and white roots looked like a French Impressionist painting. And well it should have. Radishes provide not only good eating but also culinary art. They decorate the table with a beauty that aids digestion.

The radish is a far more versatile vegetable than many people imagine. It is traditionally the first crop harvested from the earliest spring planting and the last that can be sown for a late-fall harvest. Radishes vary in size from the small red radishes common

'French Breakfast' radishes.

in stores to the massive round or tubular Oriental types. They span every color in the chromatic range, including white and black. They can be eaten raw, cooked, or pickled. When they go to seed, the seed-pods are delicious, and the seeds can be sprouted for a snappy addition to midwinter salads.

Radishes grow best in cool, moist conditions. That makes them a fall, winter, and spring vegetable in most of the country. For crisp, sweet roots, they must be grown quickly to prevent any check to their growth. First, make sure the soil has plenty of organic matter. Second, water them before the soil gets dry. Radishes like full sun, but they will grow well as an interplanted crop.

If your soil is not yet fertile enough to liberate nutrients at the rate radishes need them, you may find radishes difficult to grow well. There are a number of simple solutions. First, you can plant radishes following a leguminous cover crop such as clover. This gives them extra nitrogen from the nodules and decomposing foliage of the clover. Second, you can use alfalfa meal as a fertilizer. Its rate of release seems to work well for radishes. Third, you can spread autumn leaves up to 4 inches deep where you want to grow radishes the next spring. (If your soil pH is below 6, add lime.) Till the leaves into the soil or chop them in with a hoe. In the spring, till or chop again before planting. They should look fairly well decomposed. The leaves begin to break down in the soil over the winter, and by spring their nutrient release is perfect for radishes. The late-summer plantings of radishes will benefit from an inch or two of leaf mold worked into the top few inches of the soil. When soil nutrient release is ideal for radishes, you should have no problem with root maggot. If this still doesn't work for you, grow your spring and fall radishes under the protection of one of the floating fabric covers (see appendix D) that has holes small enough to prevent the entry of the fly that lays the maggot eggs.

We plant small radishes in odd spots around the garden. Any open area or gap in a row is waiting for radish seeds. The rows can be as close as 4 inches apart with the plants 1 inch apart. For best quality, harvest as soon as they are ready. Plant the larger radishes in 10-inch rows at whatever spacing is appropriate for their eventual size (about 6 to 8 inches for the daikon and winter types). At harvest, treat storage radishes like any other root crop: pull them, top them, and store them. They keep well until May.

RUTABAGA   *Brassica napus*

Planting Distance: 2 rows per 30-inch-wide bed; seeds 1 inch apart; thin to 4 to 6 inches apart.

Crop Rotation: Related to the other cabbage family members.

Growing Tips: Sow after June 21. Leaf mold is an ideal soil supplement. Alfalfa meal is a great fertilizer.

Storage Tips: Leave in the ground until hard frosts threaten. Store in root cellar.

Variety Tips: 'Pike', 'Gilfeather'

This is a sturdy vegetable. It is not fancy, and there is no use trying to pretend that it is other than a dependable winter staple. But it's good at what it does. In addition to serving as an ingredient in soups, stews, and boiled dinners, we favor it most when mashed in a half-and-half combination with potatoes. The yellow-orange of the rutabaga and the white of the potato blend well. Serve the mash with a couple of fried eggs on top and accompanied by a carrot salad. It's real peasant food, and you will love it. You also can turn rutabagas into hash browns or chips if you need to tempt recalcitrant children. Make a point of getting to know this dependable food. You'll be pleasantly surprised.

Plant rutabagas a few weeks after the summer

solstice, around the Fourth of July. Choose a spot that has not recently grown another cabbage relative. If you have harvested a patch of early onions or scallions, rutabagas are the perfect succession crop. Mix in some compost or leaf mold before planting and keep the rows moist until the seeds germinate. We plant in rows 16 inches apart and thin the seedlings to 4 to 6 inches in the row. You should harvest rutabagas later than other root crops because cold is an important ingredient in their flavor. There is no need to wax them, as with the flaccid specimens in the supermarket. They store perfectly in open containers in the root cellar.

SALAD GREENS   Mixed species

Planting Distance:
Arugula—Rows 6 inches apart; seeds 1 inch apart.
Claytonia—Rows 6 inches apart; seeds 1 inch apart.
Minutina—Rows 6 inches apart: seeds 1 inch apart.
Mizuna—Rows 6 inches apart; seeds 1 inch apart.
Sorrel—Rows 12 inches apart; plants 12 inches apart.

Crop Rotation: Arugula and mizuna are related to the cabbage family. Claytonia, minutina, and sorrel are not closely related to any other vegetable crops or to each other.

Growing Tips: Add mature compost to the soil in the winter cold frames.

Storage Tips: These will all keep in covered containers in the refrigerator for a few days, but it's best to harvest them fresh daily.

Variety Tips: There are few distinctive varieties, so most catalogs offer these plants by name only.

This category comprises five principal crops in our garden: arugula, claytonia, minutina, mizuna, and sorrel. There are many other possibilities. They are grouped together here because they are probably unfamiliar to many gardeners. If you are one of the unacquainted, give them a try. They are jewels of the winter garden. Once you try them, you will share our enthusiasm.

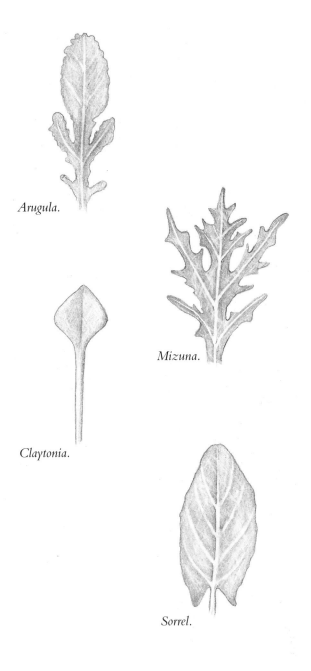

Arugula.

Mizuna.

Claytonia.

Sorrel.

Arugula *(Eruca sativa)* has long been a popular salad crop in Europe. Although often too strongly flavored from the summer garden, when grown under cool conditions it has a mild but distinctive flavor. Arugula is often included as an ingredient in seed mixes for baby leaf/mesclun salads because it does well as a cutting green. We prefer to sow all these salad ingredients individually so we can mix and match the salad at will. Sow arugula in rows 6 inches apart and place 1 seed per inch. Cut the leaves with scissors or a knife. Here in Zone 5, September plantings under protection will yield until really cold weather. After that, September plantings of its hardier wild relative 'Sylvetta' (*Diplotaxis tenuifolia*) are harvestable through the winter months. From Zone 6 south, the regular arugula should be adequately hardy all winter.

You can begin making new sowings in the cold frames and tunnel in February, and the first thinnings will be large enough to start picking by late February.

Claytonia *(Montia perfoliata)* should win the winter salad sleeper award for being both unknown and irresistible. Claytonia was originally a native west coast weed known as miner's lettuce. Recently it has come back across the Atlantic from Holland and Germany, where it was transformed into a popular green they call winter purslane. In the United States, it is called claytonia after John Clayton, an early American botanist. Along with mâche, we find it the hardiest and most delightful of winter salad crops. This almost ornamental plant will keep growing delicious salad leaves all winter under double protection here in Zone 5. In spring, it becomes twice as beautiful in the salad bowl when small white blossoms appear in the center of each leaf.

We aim to sow claytonia seeds an inch apart in 6-inch rows. The seeds are so tiny that is hard to do but the plants don't seem to mind being crowded.

We never thin them. The leaves grow upward on 4-inch stems. To harvest, grasp the leaves and cut the stems below them. The plant will keep producing new leaves throughout the winter.

Minutina *(Plantago coronopus)*, also known as buckshorn plantain, has long, pointed, crunchy-tasting leaves which compliment the succulent round leaves of claytonia. Minutina is related to the plantain that often appears as a weed in lawns but it has none of the fibers of its weedy relative. It is tender, delicious, and productive right through the winter under the double protection of tunnel and inner cover. Sow again from February through April to have new young plants coming along for spring.

Mizuna *(Brassica rapa)* is a mild and delicate Oriental plant with a slight mustard flavor. Its deeply cut fringed leaves are as lovely in a salad mix as they are delicious. It will grow to the size of a large lettuce plant and yield over a long period if cut back to encourage new leaf production. We prefer to harvest it at the seedling stage. We sow mizuna in succession under protection during the fall and winter and cut the leaves when they are about three to four inches tall to serve whole in salads. Mizuna can be transplanted, but it is much simpler to sow the seeds directly in 6-inch rows with seeds 1 inch apart. Fall sowings will yield through the cold months. A January sowing is ready to begin thinning in late February.

Sorrel *(Rumex acetosa)*, also called garden sorrel, shares the lemon piquancy and tang of the common weed from which it was developed, but it has larger leaves and is much more productive. Sorrel holds a unique place among salad greens because it is a perennial. Only one seeding is necessary. In subsequent years, you just select the plant with the nicest leaves, divide it, and transplant the clumps to the cold frames or tunnel in the fall. Half a dozen plants spaced 12 inches apart will provide plenty of leaves for salads and classic sorrel soup throughout the entire winter.

The best salads are patterns of mixed greenery. These crops enhance that mix by adding new shapes, textures, and flavors. For fresh salads throughout the winter, you will find arugula, claytonia, minutina, mizuna, and sorrel, plus mâche and spinach, to be almost unbelievably productive and dependable without any added heat in cold frames and tunnels. These hardy crops are available every day all winter here in Zone 5. Once they are planted, all you do is pick and eat. These crops are also useful replacements for a winter crop that didn't get planted or didn't germinate. Arugula, claytonia, and mizuna, along with mâche and spinach, will germinate and grow anytime during the winter under protection. Use them to replant any gaps in your winter garden.

A number of other salad ingredients should be mentioned to add variety to seasonal salads. Cress, purslane, red mustard, chervil, and orach are some of the lesser-known possibilities available in specialist seed catalogs. They may fit your growing conditions and salad preferences better than our favorites. You can sow them in short rows and cut them with scissors when they are four inches high to use as part of your signature mesclun mix. Whichever ones you choose, a soil amended with mature compost (and limestone where necessary to maintain a pH of 6.5 to 6.8) will grow the tastiest and healthiest specimens.

SORREL   See Salad Greens

SPINACH   *Spinacia oleracea*

Planting Distance: Rows 8 inches apart; seeds 1 inch apart; thin to 4 inches.

Crop Rotation: Related to beets and Swiss chard.

Growing Tips: A fertile soil, plenty of moisture, a neutral pH, and cool temperatures will grow the best crop. Spinach is more resistant to warm weather bolting in heavier than in lighter soils.

Storage Tips: Will store for a week in the refrigerator but always best eaten fresh.

Variety Tips: 'Space'

Spinach is a key contributor to the fall, winter, and spring harvest. This hardy green will germinate and grow at temperatures only slightly above freezing. Spinach is at its best when grown in a well-composted soil. The balanced nutrient release from mature compost makes a difference in its flavor and nutritional value. Spinach grown with excessive nitrogen from imbalanced fertilization has a flat, metallic flavor and often has high levels of nitrates.

The spinach season begins in the fall. In Zone 5, we start planting between August 1 and 15. The first spinach is ready to harvest in September, and the cool temperatures and short fall days keep it in prime condition until hard freezes. We continue planting for continuous harvest according to the schedule in table 15.

Spinach.

TABLE 15
Spinach Planting Dates

Date	Site	Use
September 15	Cold frame	For late-fall eating.
September 25	Outdoors	For wintering over, cover with straw in late November.
October 1	Cold frame	For wintering over.
October 15	Under double coverage	For winter consumption.
January 15 to March 1	Under double coverage	For an early spring crop.
April 15	Outdoors	For an outdoor crop.

Since young spinach thinnings are a delicious addition to green salad mixtures, we sow the seeds 1 inch apart in rows 8 inches apart and get many salad servings by progressive thinning before the leaves reach cooking size.

During the dog days of summer when spinach goes to seed quickly (especially in our sandy soil), we plan to enjoy other greens until the fall crop begins. Some of those other greens have "spinach" in their names, even though they are not related. New Zealand spinach *(Tetragonia expansa)* and Malabar spinach *(Basella alba)* are excellent warm-weather vegetables for those who wish a spinach-type leafy green. Even in cool climates you can grow them on trellises in the tunnel during the summer, since they are vinelike and appreciate the extra heat.

SQUASH FAMILY *Cucurbita* spp.

Planting Distance:
Winter squash—1 row per 30-inch-wide bed; plants 30 inches apart.
Summer squash—1 row per 30-inch-wide bed; plants 24 inches apart.

Crop Rotation: Related to melons, cucumbers, and pumpkins.

Growing Tips: The trace minerals in dried seaweed added to the soil will improve pest resistance in squash crops.

Storage Tips: Winter squashes store best at 50°F in a fairly dry atmosphere.

Variety Tips: Zucchini—'Zucchini Elite'
Climbing—'Zucchetta Rampicante'
Yellow—'Sunray'
Winter—'Buttercup', 'Butternut'

If you think zucchini has a reputation as an overzealous producer, wait until you meet 'Zucchetta Rampicante', a climbing zucchini that grows fruits on long vines. Its rampant growth makes it suitable for a sci-fi feature titled "The Zucchini That Ate Manhattan." But when something tastes this good, it can do all the growing it wants. We train a few 'Zucchetta' plants on one of our trellises, where the long, curved fruits can hang from the vines. The flesh is firmer and not as watery as that of regular zucchini. Both flavor and texture are superb when the squash is cooked alone or in any standard recipe.

We think regular green zucchini as well as yellow summer squash are best picked very small when the fruits are only four inches long and the blossom has just been pollinated. This is the size called *courgettes* in France and when lightly steamed or sauteed these small squash will make believers out of even the most jaded zucchini haters.

Winter squash are vine crops. They are the one common vegetable that doesn't fit neatly into the spacing of 30-inch-wide beds. Pumpkins wouldn't fit either, but we don't grow them since Buttercup squash makes a better "pumpkin" pie. One solution to long vines is to grow them at the edge of the garden and encourage the vines to run through the fence and out onto the lawn. Their forays outside the garden confines have not been a problem. Once the first fall frost nips the vines, harvest the fruits and drag the vines to the compost heap. A second solution is to grow them up a trellis or train them to a garden fence by tying the vines every few feet for support. The 7-foot-tall lattice fence around our garden, which also serves as deer protection, is transformed in late summer and fall into a vertical squash field. Buttercup and Butternut squashes can hang from the vines safely but larger, heavier squashes like

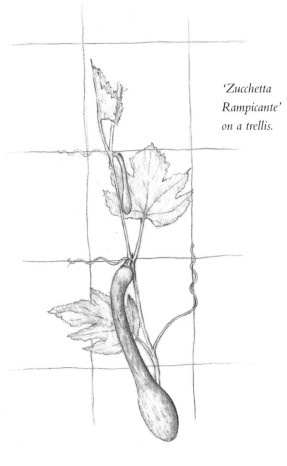

'Zucchetta Rampicante' on a trellis.

Hubbards will need the extra support of a net bag or something similar to keep them suspended.

We have always cured winter squashes, to harden the skin before storage, by leaving them on a sunny porch for a few weeks and providing frost protection when necessary. According to the latest information from the storage experts, that step is not necessary. It has been accepted for a while that curing is not required for the acorn and delicata types, which are *Cucurbita pepo*. But for the other winter squashes, most of which are *Cucurbita maxima*, we plan to keep curing them as we always have. We are reluctant to give up a system that has served us well. We also think they look pretty on the porch.

All of the squash family grow well in soil amended with compost. They germinate best in a warm soil. For an extra-early harvest, you may wish to start them about three weeks ahead and transplant the seedlings after the danger of frost has passed. We do succession planting with zucchini to keep them under control. We sow a few zucchini seeds on May 21, June 21, and July 10. We remove the large plants from the previous sowing and put them on the compost heap once the new plants start to bear. Older, overgrown zucchini plants tend to take over the garden paths, making it harder to move about. They also are more likely to hide their fruits. The younger plants are more productive and the fruits easier to pick.

SWISS CHARD   *Beta vulgaris cicla*

Planting Distance: 3 rows per 30-inch-wide bed; plants 10 inches apart.

Crop Rotation: Related to beets and spinach.

Growing Tips: Occasional top dressing with compost will maintain production.

Storage Tips: Eat fresh.

Variety Tips: Hardiest—'Argentata' Red-leaved—'Ruby Red'

Swiss chard.

Swiss chard is a beautiful, dependable, and under-appreciated vegetable. One could attribute the lack of fans to its undistinguished name. Switzerland is not the culinary capital of the world, and chard (from the French *chardon,* "thistle") adds little additional appeal. In England, a common name for chard is perpetual spinach, a term that would likely inhibit generations of children from ever trying it at all. However, its French name, *poirée,* makes it sound and taste delicious.

You harvest chard over a long period by picking leaves as they reach the desired size, leaving the heart of the plant to continue producing more. Both the protected growing conditions in the cool months and the selective harvesting result in a tender, higher-quality leaf. When chard is grown during the outdoor season, the hot summer climate toughens the leaves. The outdoor grower can achieve more tender leaves by treating chard like beets—making succession plantings and harvesting the whole plant when the size of baby beets and greens.

When grown under the protection of a cold frame or tunnel, chard is a reliable winter producer.

If the seeds are sown in July and the seedlings transplanted in August, chard will produce dependably from October to May. When grown in outdoor, unprotected conditions, chard is hardy enough to keep growing new leaves quite late into the fall. Even in the coldest parts of New England, frozen chard plants in the outdoor garden will come right back during the first midwinter thaw, although they will usually succumb to the next onslaught of cold.

The same growing tips that apply to beets also apply to chard, as they are close relatives. When treated as a long-season, cut-and-come-again crop, however, chard needs some extra care. An occasional top dressing of compost is a tonic for keeping long-season chard tender and tasty. Chard can be transplanted or direct-seeded. When chard is sown as a transplant crop you should set out seedlings in the garden three weeks later. For whole-plant harvest, direct-seed the chard in 10-inch rows and thin the plants to 4 inches apart. For long-season production, transplant the seedlings at a 10-by-10-inch spacing. A bed of well-grown chard, especially the red-leaved varieties, is as decorative as it is delicious. Try chard in any dish where you might use other greens. You won't be disappointed.

TOMATO *Lycopersicon esculentum*

Planting Distance:
Trellis—1 row per 30-inch-wide bed; plants 15 inches apart.
Ground—1 row per 30-inch-wide bed; plants 30 inches apart.

Crop Rotation: Related to potatoes, peppers, and eggplant.

Growing Tips: Use a weekly spray of compost tea to enhance plant vigor.

Storage Tips: Drying beats all other tomato preservation methods.

Variety Tips: Early—'New Girl'
Cherry—'Sun Gold', 'Sweet 100+'
Trellis—'Big Beef', 'Early Cascade'
Drying—'Tuscany', 'LaRossa'

If nothing else can compel you to begin a garden, let us suggest the desire to eat a *real* tomato. In this case, "real" means a tomato bred for eating, not shipping; grown in a fully fertile, humus-rich soil; and picked at the peak of its ripeness and flavor. Even normal tomatoes are a delightful treat; when above average, they are exceptional; when truly well grown, they are beyond belief. Henry David Thoreau said he wanted to live deliberately so as not to come to the end of life and find he had never lived. The tomato lover says you want to grow your own so as not to come to the end of life and find you have never tasted a real tomato.

When the commercial catalogs praise the flavor of a tomato variety, they mean that despite being picked green, gassed to make them turn red, and shipped to a faraway location, the taste is not totally insipid. The tomato flavor of commercial-industrial specimens is best represented by a flat line at the bottom of the graph. Real tomato flavor is a bell curve, barely on the graph if picked green, then ascending through layers of soil fertility, variety selection, cultural technique, sun, and warmth to a

Tomato.

crescendo that is maintained briefly before descending on the other side.

How do you create such delights? Compost, sunshine, and patience are the three main ingredients. But let's start at the beginning. The best tomato transplants for your garden are six to seven weeks old, each in a 4-inch pot. A 4-inch pot? Absolutely. You want plenty of room to encourage a strong root system and plenty of potting soil to feed the young plant. The six-pack of tomatoes sold at the garden center has less soil than is ideal for a single plant. Those plants will eventually produce tomatoes, but never as dependably as good plants.

If you are growing plants at home, start them six to seven weeks before the outdoor transplant date. Keep the newly sown flats warm (70° to 80°F) until they germinate. At ten days, move the seedlings to a wider spacing (about 2 by 2 inches). Don't wait until they get bigger before you move them. It is precisely those crowded conditions that are inhibiting their growth. Another ten days to two weeks later, move them to 4-inch pots. Try to maintain 70°F daytime and 60°F nighttime temperatures throughout the process.

Set the pots in your sunniest window. When the leaves begin to touch, space them farther apart. Move them to a cold frame or tunnel for the last ten days. Provide a little heat if you can. By the time they are seven weeks old, you will have sturdy, well-rooted plants with the first flower clusters ready to open. If your growing conditions are cooler, they will take a little longer.

If you use the standard potting mix suggested in chapter 9, you won't need to feed the plants. There is adequate nutrition in the mix to carry the tomatoes until they are transplanted. If for some reason the plants look hungry (poor color, stunted growth), use a compost tea or one of the liquid seaweed-fish products as an effective temporary food.

When they are ready for the garden, set the

plants 16 inches apart in a single row if you plan to trellis them. We space them 30 inches apart if they are to be grown on the ground. A total of 12 to 24 plants will supply both fresh eating and drying tomatoes. If you want to give the plants a boost at setting-out time, fill the planting holes with the same dilution of compost tea or seaweed-fish emulsion used earlier and let it soak into the soil before setting out the plants.

The description in the seed catalog will tell you whether your tomatoes are determinate or indeterminate. The determinate varieties are best grown on the ground or in low cages because they don't grow much after the fruits form. Most early varieties are determinate. Indeterminate varieties such as 'Gardener's Delight' and 'Carmello' are suitable for trellis culture, as they continue to grow and ripen fruits simultaneously.

We prefer to grow fresh tomatoes vertically in tall cages made from 6-inch mesh reinforcing wire. Vertical tomatoes are not only twice as productive and form a beautiful red and green hedge, but they also ripen up to two weeks earlier and are less prone to rot, since the fruits have no contact with the soil. The cages are 16 inches in diameter. We prune off the two lowest suckers. After that we let everything grow but encourage the stems to stay in the confines of the cage as the plant grows upward.

If your tomatoes have been troubled by tomato blight, we recommend spraying the foliage once a week with compost tea. European studies have found a tea made from soaking well-decomposed compost in water for four days to be a very effective treatment for strengthening the plant's resistance to blight. Adding seaweed to the soil has also been shown to help. Don't mulch your tomato plants until both the weather and the soil have warmed up. Whereas early mulching will cool the soil and slow them down, later mulching will help retain moisture for the rest of the summer.

One final note on the proper pronunciation of the word, *tomato*. When speaking of the mediocre, run-of-the-mill, commercial-industrial tomato, we happily call it a *tom AY toe*. But when speaking of a compost-fertilized, sun-ripened, full-flavored, homegrown beauty, the proper pronunciation is definitely *tom AHH toe,* with the emphasis on the *AHH!*

TURNIP *Brassica rapa*

Planting Distance: 3 rows per bed; thin to 3 inches apart.

Crop Rotation: Related to the cabbage family.

Growing Tips: Can be grown as a spring or summer crop but best in the fall. Cooler growing temperatures make for sweeter turnips.

Storage Tips: Can be left in the ground all winter under double coverage.

Variety Tips: 'Hakurei', 'White Doll'

Turnips are a delightful example of a peasant vegetable that has attained gourmet status. They had a long way to go, since turnips were best known in the 18th century as livestock food due to their key position in the farmer's crop rotation of wheat, oats, clover, and

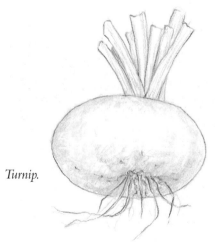

Turnip.

turnips. In addition, Yann Lovelock in *The Vegetable Book* tells us it was a "country tradition for a girl to give a young man a turnip when she tired of his favors." Now chefs in fancy restaurants are increasingly using small turnips as garnishes, in sauces, and to surround meat dishes. And why not? Ever since Japanese seed breeders began hybridizing turnips in the late 1950s with an emphasis on eating quality, the humble turnip has been transformed. Seed catalogs now use phrases like "sweet and fruity" or "crisp and tender" in their descriptions with no exaggeration. The turnip revolution is in full swing.

Turnips are also treasured for their edible leaves. "A mess of greens" more often than not either means or includes turnip greens. Like kale, they are an excellent source of calcium and vitamins A and C. When turnips begin to sprout and make flower buds, the greens and buds can be used as a substitute for broccoli raab. We were shown that by a vendor at the Santo Spiritu market in Florence one winter. He was selling both regular raab and the bolting-turnip substitute from a bed of July sown turnips.

The new tender-and-sweet turnip varieties are at their best when they are grown quickly, like radishes, and the same growing tips such as plenty of compost, a nitrogen supplement like alfalfa meal, and generous watering apply. Turnips were traditionally a fall crop on sandy land. Their preference for cool, moist fall weather and light soil inspired the old saying, "turnips like a dry bed with a wet head." For spring and summer crops they should be sown often in succession and only small amounts sown each time so they can be harvested promptly at their best.

WATERCRESS   *Nasturtium officinale*

Planting Distance: In the winter greenhouse we transplant watercress seedlings 6 inches apart in 6-inch rows.

Crop Rotation: Related to the cabbage family.

Growing Tips: Watercress needs plenty of well decomposed compost and a good supply of calcium. If your soil is acid, add extra lime. On some soils an application of gypsum (calcium sulfate) may be beneficial.

Storage Tips: Highly perishable after harvest. The perfect crop for eating fresh.

Variety Tips: Most seed catalogs list a generic 'watercress,' although some specify 'Dutch Broadleaf'.

Some watercress seedlings, left over after transplanting watercress to a stream bed years ago, gave the first hint that watercress could be grown without running water. The leftovers thrived in the cool greenhouse conditions and the crop they produced was delicious. Since then watercress has become a standard and dependable winter greenhouse crop. It's not surprising really. Watercress thrives where the conditions are moist and cool with filtered light. That's a lot like the conditions existing naturally under the inner layer of the winter tunnel.

If you have watercress growing in a stream nearby you can transplant cuttings from there to the

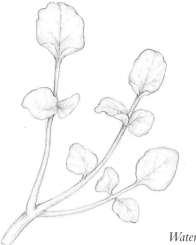

Watercress.

tunnel in October. It is also possible to root the commercial watercress you buy at the market. Or you can sow seeds in a flat in September and transplant the seedlings a month later. If the cress wilts or looks unhappy you have probably started it too early for your area. We usually sow a second flat a few weeks after the first to cover ourselves in case the fall is unusually dry and warm.

This is the one crop we water in the winter greenhouse even during the Persephone months when we are not watering any others. The extra moisture seems to make it more cold hardy. In Zone 6 and south watercress will produce all winter with two layers of protection. In Zone 5 and north you will want to put another smaller tunnel covered with bubble plastic under the inner layer for extra protection. Give your watercress bed a top dressing of compost after picking to encourage the stems to root and regrow. Or you can occasionally transplant your own cuttings to a new bed. We think our homegrown watercress crop is worth a little extra effort. It is a health food par excellence and one of the gourmet delights of the winter garden.

CLIMATE RESOURCES

THE RESOURCE MATERIALS that follow enable comparisons between many factors of the climate in different regions of North America and Europe. I have included these charts and maps to help convince gardeners all across the country to give the winter harvest a try. Not many places have longer winters than we have here in Maine, but during the 1980s, in the early stages of developing these ideas, I was living in Zone 3 on a farm in the mountains of Vermont. The winter harvest worked just fine there also. Every year in the late summer, when we start sowing seeds for the winter harvest crops, we don't do it with some naïve hope that we will have a mild winter. We do it with confidence that the four-season harvest has proven to be resilient and dependable whatever the weather.

1. Effects of Temperature on Plants: An Outline. Page 204.

2. Planting Dates for an Extended Harvest. On pages 206–207 is a table listing garden crops with a timeline for planting correlated to fall frost dates. An explanation of how to use this information is given on page 205.

3. USDA First Fall Frost Dates for All Regions of the United States. Page 208. This map is used in conjunction with the Planting Dates for an Extended Harvest table on pages 206–207.

4. USDA Plant Hardiness. Page 209. This standard map divides the country according to minimum temperatures reached during the winter. Our garden in Maine is rated as Zone 5. The zone map is of some use in comparing different parts of the country vis-à-vis the winter harvest, but it does not take into consideration how long the winter goes on.

5. Mean Annual Number of Days Minimum Temperature 32°F and Below. Page 210. This map gives a good idea of the length of the winter period. We are located two-thirds of the way up the Maine coast on the 150-day line. A garden in northeastern Missouri with a similar Zone 5 rating from the USDA map would be on the 90-day line, quite a difference in length of winter.

6. Average Depth of Frost Penetration. Page 211. This map offers another way to look at the severity of the winter. Although it only covers the years 1899–1938, the data is still useful. At our location on the coast of Maine the average frost depth is 48 inches. That imaginary garden in northeastern Missouri mentioned above experiences an average frost depth of 20 inches, again quite a difference in severity of winter.

7. Mean Annual Number of Days Maximum Temperature 90°F and Above. Page 212. This map is useful for deciding between a "mobile" or a "convertible" greenhouse. In my opinion those gardeners in areas with more than ten to twenty days above 90°F may be better off with a convertible-style greenhouse that can be uncovered during the warm season to prevent overheating.

8. A European Zone Map. Page 213. This map is included to satisfy the curiosity of those gardeners who wonder how the European continent compares to the North American continent when divided up by the same temperature classifications as the familiar USDA zone map. Even though Europe is farther north on the globe than most of the U.S., the effects of the Gulf Stream extends a maritime climate for quite a distance across the continent.

Effects of Temperature on Plants: An Outline

Temperature	
120°	
115°	< Upper limit. Plants die.
110°	
100°	
95°	< Maximum photosynthesis. Too hot if continued too long.
90°	
80°	
75°	< Optimum photosynthesis and plant growth.
70°	
60°	
55°	< Average daytime greenhouse temperature during coldest months.
50°	
40°	
35°	< Ideal minimum greenhouse air temperature. No freezing of crops.
30°	
20°	
15°	< Lower limit for quality harvest of most winter salad crops.
10°	
0°	

Temperature factors that affect winter salads in protected cultivation:

1. Rate of temperature drop.
2. Depth of temperature drop.
3. Duration of temperature drop.
4. Frequency of temperature drops.

TABLE 16

Planting Dates for an Extended Harvest

The information on the following pages is compiled from USDA publications with modifications based on my experience. The dates given indicate when you should ideally plant vegetables in the open for a late-season harvest, for all sections of the country. You can adapt these tables for cold frame and tunnel planting. First find the column for the approximate first fall frost date for your area. (Find the date on the USDA map nearest to the place you live if you are unsure of your frost dates.) Then read 2 or 3 columns to the right of this date for when to plant in the cold frame, and 4 to 5 columns to the right for when to plant in the tunnel-protected cold frames.

These dates are your guidelines. They are subject to the variability of local conditions but will give you a place to start. Your experience and observations will be needed to refine this general information into a precise planting schedule for your specific garden climate.

TABLE 16
Planting Dates for an Extended Harvest

| Crop | *First Fall Frost Dates* | | | | | |
	Aug. 30	Sept 10	Sept 20	Sept. 30	Oct. 10	Oct. 20
Asparagus					10/20-11/15	11/1-12/15
Bean	5/15-6/15	6/1-7/1	6/1-7/1	6/1-7/10	6/15-7/20	7/1-8/1
Beet	5/15-6/15	ditto	ditto	ditto	6/15-7/20	7/1-8/5
Broccoli, Sprouts	5/1-6/1	5/1-6/1	5/1-6/15	6/1-6/30	ditto	7/1-8/1
Cabbage	ditto	ditto	ditto	6/1-7/10	6/1-7/15	7/1-7/20
Cabbage, Chinese	5/15-6/15	5/15-6/15	6/1-7/1	6/1-7/15	6/15-8/1	7/15-7/15
Carrot	ditto	ditto	5/1-8/1	6/1-8/1	6/1-8/1	7/15-8/15
Cauliflower	5/1-6/1	5/1-7/1	5/1-7/1	5/10-7/15	6/1-7/25	7/1-8/5
Celery, Celeriac	ditto	5/15-6/15	5/15-7/1	6/1-7/5	6/1-7/15	7/1-8/1
Chard	5/15-6/15	5/15-7/1	6/1-7/1	ditto	6/1-7/20	ditto
Chicory, witloof	5/15-6/15	5/15-6/15	ditto	6/1-7/1	6/1-7/1	6/15-7/15
Chicory, green	6/1-6/15	6/1-7/1	6/1-7/1	6/15-7/15	7/1-8/1	7/15-8/15
Cornsalad (mâche)	ditto	5/15-7/1	6/15-8/1	7/15-9/1	8/15-9/15	9/1-10/15
Corn			6/1-7/1	6/1-7/1	6/1-7/10	6/1-7/20
Claytonia	6/15-7/1	6/15-8/1	7/15-9/1	8/15-9/15	8/15-9/15	9/1-10/1
Cucumber		6/1-6/15	6/1-7/1	6/1-7/16	6/1-7/1	6/1-7/15
Dandelion	6/1-6/15	6/1-7/1	6/1-7/1	6/1-8/1	7/15-9/1	8/1-9/15
Eggplant				5/30-6/10	5/15-6/15	6/1-7/1
Endive, Escarole	6/1-7/1	6/1-7/1	6/15-7/15	6/15-8/1	7/1-8/15	7/15-9/1
Garlic	10/10	10/10	10/15	10/15	10/20	10/30
Kale	5/15-6/15	5/15-6/15	6/1-7/1	6/15-7/15	7/1-8/1	7/15-8/15
Kohlrabi	ditto	6/1-7/1	6/1-7/15	ditto	ditto	ditto
Leek	5/1-6/1	5/1-6/1	5/1-6/15	5/1-6/15	5/1-6/15	6/1-7/1
Lettuce	5/15-7/15	5/15-7/15	6/1-8/1	6/1-8/1	7/15-9/1	7/30-9/10
Melon			5/1-6/15	5/15-6/1	6/1-6/15	6/15-7/20
Mizuna	5/15-7/15	5/15-6/1	6/1-8/1	6/15-8/1	7/15-8/15	8/1-9/1
Onion, bulb	5/1-6/10	5/1-6/10				
Onion, green	5/1-6/1	5/1-6/10	6/15-7/15	6/15-8/1	7/15-8/15	7/15-9/1
Parsley, Parsley root	5/15-6/15	5/1-6/15	6/1-7/1	6/1-7/15	6/15-8/1	7/15-8/15
Parsnip	5/15-6/1	ditto	5/15-6/15	6/1-7/1	6/1-6/10	
Peas	5/10-6/15	5/1-7/1	6/1-7/15	6/1-8/1		
Pepper			6/1-6/20	6/1-7/1	6/1-7/1	6/1-7/10
Potato	5/15-6/1	5/1-6/15	5/1-6/15	5/1-6/15	5/15-6/15	6/15-7/15
Radicchio	9/1-10/1	9/15-10/15	9/15-10/1	10/1-11/1	10/15-11/15	10/15-11/1
Radish	5/1-7/15	5/1-8/1	6/1-8/15	7/1-9/1	7/15-9/15	8/1-10/1
Rutabaga	5/15-6/15	5/1-6/15	6/1-7/1	6/1-7/1	6/15-7/15	7/10-7/20
Salsify	5/15-6/1	5/10-6/10	5/20-6/20	6/1-6/20	6/1-7/1	6/1-7/1
Sorrel	5/15-6/15	5/1-6/15	6/1-7/1	6/1-7/15	7/1-8/1	7/15-8/15
Spinach	5/15-6/1	6/1-7/15	6/1-8/1	7/1-8/15	8/1-9/1	8/1-9/15
Spinach, New Zealand				5/15-7/1	6/1-7/15	6/1-8/1
Squash, summer	6/10-6/20	6/1-6/20	5/15-7/1	6/1-7/1	ditto	6/1-7/20
Squash, winter			5/20-6/10	6/1-6/15	6/1-7/1	6/1-7/1
Tatsoi	5/15-6/1	6/1-7/15				
Tomato	6/20-6/30	6/10-6/20	6/1-6/20	6/1-6/20	6/1-6/20	6/1-7/1
Turnip	5/15-6/15	6/1-7/1	6/1-7/15	6/1-8/1	7/1-8/1	7/15-8/15

Crop	First Fall Frost Dates					
	Oct. 30	Nov. 10	Nov 20	Nov. 30	Dec. 10	Dec. 20
Asparagus	11/15–1/1	12/1–1/1				
Bean	7/1–8/15	7/1–9/1	7/1–9/10	8/15–9/20	9/1–9/30	9/1–11/1
Beet	8/1–9/1	8/1–10/1	9/1–12/1	9/1–12/15	9/1–12/31	9/1–12/31
Broccoli, Sprouts	7/1–8/15	8/1–9/1	8/1–9/15	8/1–10/1	8/1–11/1	ditto
Cabbage	8/1–9/1	9/1–9/15	9/1–12/1	9/1–12/31	9/1–12/31	ditto
Cabbage, Chinese	8/1–9/15	8/15–10/1	9/1–10/15	9/1–11/1	9/1–11/15	9/1–12/1
Carrot	7/1–8/15	8/1–9/1	9/1–11/1	9/15–12/1	9/15–12/1	9/15–12/1
Cauliflower	7/15–8/15	ditto	8/1–9/15	8/15–10/10	9/1–10/20	9/15–11/1
Celery, Celeriac	6/15–8/15	7/1–8/15	7/15–9/1	8/1–12/1	9/1–12/31	10/1–12/31
Chard	6/1–9/10	6/1–9/15	6/1–10/1	6/1–11/1	6/1–12/1	6/1–12/31
Chicory, witloof	7/1–8/10	7/10–8/20	7/20–9/1	8/15–9/30	8/15–10/15	8/15–10/15
Chicory, green	8/1–9/15	8/15–10/1	8/25–11/1	9/1–12/1	9/1–12/31	9/1–12/31
Cornsalad (mache)	9/15–11/1	10/1–12/1	10/1–12/1	10/1–12/31	10/1–12/31	10/1–12/31
Corn	6/1–8/1	6/1–8/15	6/1–9/1			
Claytonia	9/15–10/15	10/1–11/1	10/1–11/10	10/1–11/20	10/1–12/31	10/1–12/31
Cucumber	6/1–8/1	6/1–8/15	6/1–8/15	7/15–9/15	8/15–10/1	8/15–10/1
Dandelion	8/15–10/1	9/1–10/15	9/1–11/1	9/15–12/15	10/1–12/31	10/1–12-31
Eggplant	6/1–7/1	6/1–7/15	6/1–8/1	7/1–9/1	8/1–9/30	8/1–9/30
Endive, Escarole	7/15–8/15	8/1–9/1	9/1–10/1	9/1–11/15	9/1–12/31	9/1–12/31
Garlic	10/30	8/1–10/1	8/15–10/1	9/1–11/15	9/15–11/15	9/15–11/15
Kale	7/15–9/1	8/1–9/15	8/15–10/15	9/1–12/1	9/1–12/31	9/1–12/31
Kohlrabi	8/1–9/1	8/15–9/15	9/1–10/15	ditto	9/15–12/31	ditto
Leek	7/1–8/1	8/1–8/15	9/1–11/1	9/1–11/1	9/1–11/1	9/15–11/1
Lettuce	8/15–10	8/25–10/1	9/1–11/1	9/1–12/1	9/15–12/31	9/15–12/31
Melon	7/1–7/15	7/15–7/30				
Mizuna	8/15–10/15	8/15–11/1	9/1–12/1	9/1–12/1	9/1–12/1	9/15–12/1
Onion, bulb		9/1–10/15	10/1–12/31	10/1–12/31	10/1–12/31	10/1–12/31
Onion, green	8/1–10/15	8/1–10/15	9/1–11/1	9/1–11/1	9/1–11/1	9/15–11/1
Parsley, Parsley root	8/1–9/15	9/1–11/15	9/1–12/31	9/1–12/31	9/15–12/31	9/1–12/31
Parsnip			8/1–9/1	9/1–11/15	9/1–12/1	9/1–12/1
Peas	8/1–9/15	9/1–11/1	10/1–12/1	10/1–12/31	10/1–12/31	10/1–12/31
Pepper	6/1–7/20	6/1–8/1	6/1–8/15	6/15–9/1	8/15–10/1	8/15–10/1
Potato	7/20–8/10	7/25–8/20	8/10–9/15	8/1–9/15	8/1–9/15	8/1–9/15
Radicchio	11/1–12/1					
Radish	8/15–10/15	9/1–11/15	9/1–12/1	9/1–12/31	8/1–9/15	10/1–12/31
Rutabaga	7/15–8/1	7/15–8/15	8/1–9/1	9/1–11/15	10/1–11/15	10/15–11/15
Salsify	6/1–7/10	6/15–7/20	7/15–8/15	8/15–9/30	8/15–10/15	9/1–10/31
Sorrel	8/1–9/15	8/15–10/1	8/15–10/15	9/1–11/15	9/1–12/15	9/1–12/31
Spinach	9/1–10/1	9/15–11/1	10/1–12/1	10/1–12/31	10/1–12/31	10/1–12/31
Spinach, New Zealand	6/1–8/1	6/1–8/15	6/1–8/15			
Squash, summer	ditto	6/1–8/10	6/1–8/20	6/1–9/1	6/1–9/15	6/1–10/1
Squash, winter	6/10–7/10	6/20–7/20	7/1–8/1	7/15–8/15	8/1–9/1	8/1–9/1
Tomato	6/1–7/1	6/1–7/15	6/1–8/1	8/1–9/1	8/15–10/1	9/1–11/1
Tatsoi						
Turnip	8/1–9/15	9/1–10/15	9/1–11/15	9/1–11/15	10/1–12/1	10/1–12/31

USDA First Fall Frost Dates for All Regions of the United States

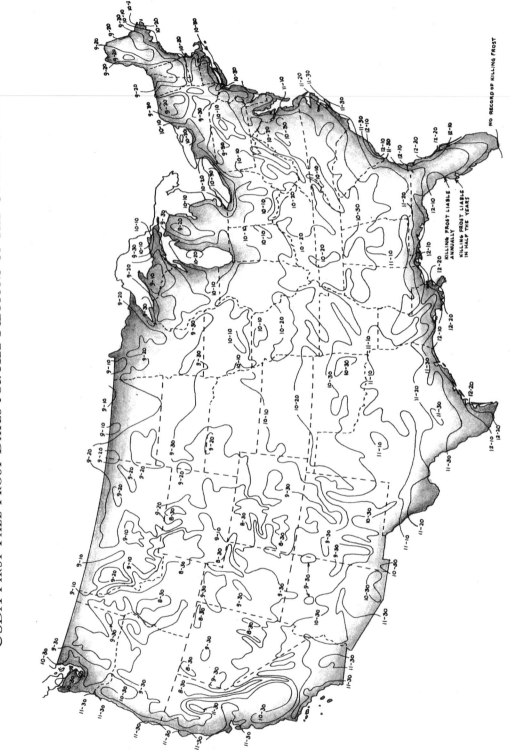

Credit: USDA

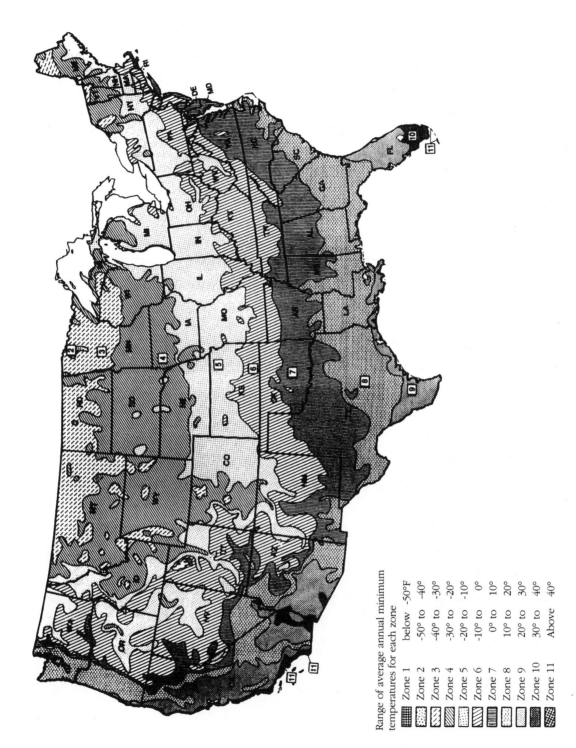

Range of average annual minimum
temperatures for each zone

Zone 1	below -50°F
Zone 2	-50° to -40°
Zone 3	-40° to -30°
Zone 4	-30° to -20°
Zone 5	-20° to -10°
Zone 6	-10° to 0°
Zone 7	0° to 10°
Zone 8	10° to 20°
Zone 9	20° to 30°
Zone 10	30° to 40°
Zone 11	Above 40°

MEAN ANNUAL NUMBER OF DAYS MINIMUM TEMPERATURE 32°F AND BELOW

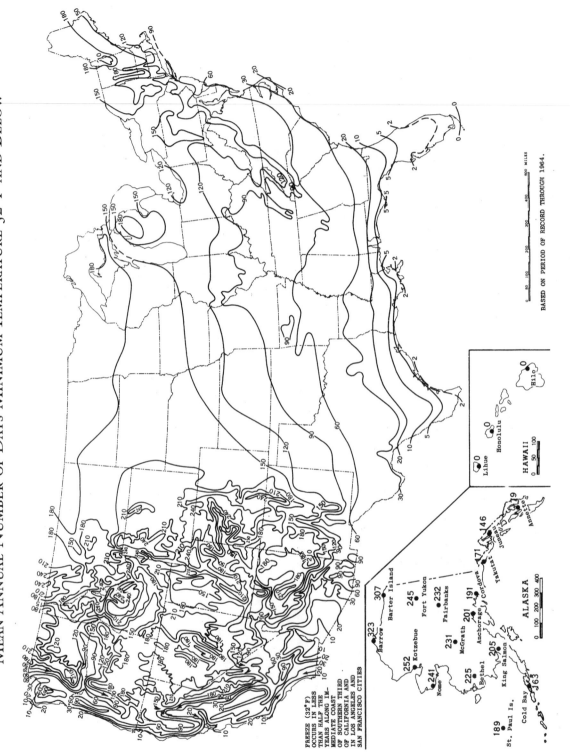

FREEZE (32°F)
OCCURS IN LESS
THAN HALF THE
YEARS ALONG IM-
MEDIATE COAST
OF SOUTHERN THIRD
OF CALIFORNIA AND
IN LOS ANGELES AND
SAN FRANCISCO CITIES

BASED ON PERIOD OF RECORD THROUGH 1964.

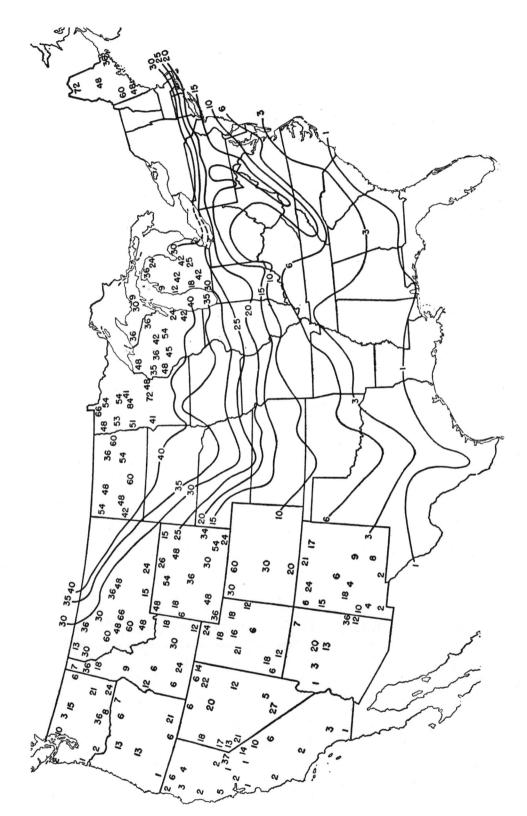

Period 1899–1938. Information collected from unofficial sources.

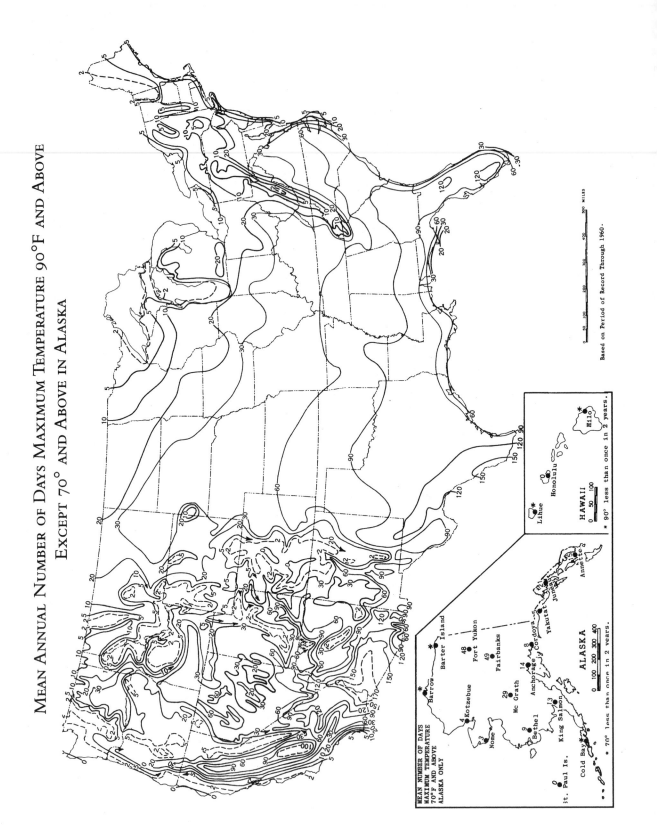

MEAN ANNUAL NUMBER OF DAYS MAXIMUM TEMPERATURE 90°F AND ABOVE
EXCEPT 70° AND ABOVE IN ALASKA

Based on Period of Record Through 1960.

A EUROPEAN ZONE MAP

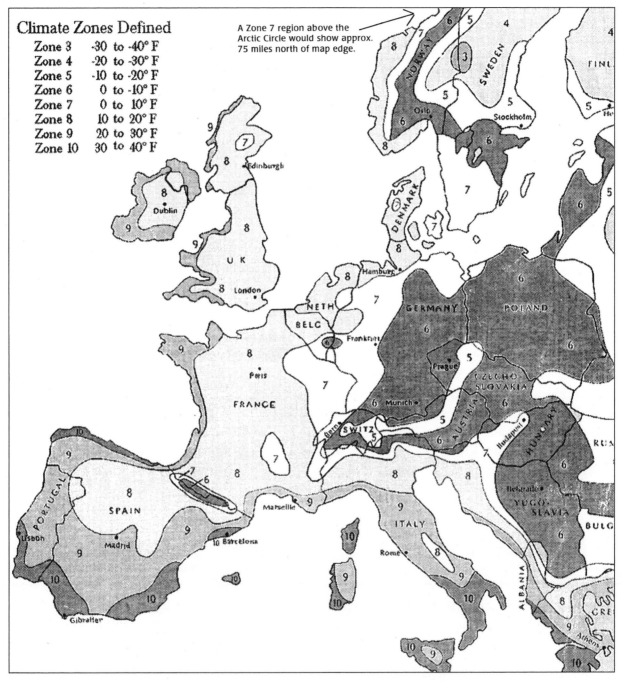

Climate Zones Defined

Zone 3	-30 to -40° F
Zone 4	-20 to -30° F
Zone 5	-10 to -20° F
Zone 6	0 to -10° F
Zone 7	0 to 10° F
Zone 8	10 to 20° F
Zone 9	20 to 30° F
Zone 10	30 to 40° F

A Zone 7 region above the Arctic Circle would show approx. 75 miles north of map edge.

Reprinted from Hardy Enough, *Vol 5, No. 4*

Do We Really Want to Use Plastic?

MOVIEGOERS WILL REMEMBER that moment in *The Graduate* when the avuncular businessman takes the unreceptive young hero aside and advises him that the "one word" for his future should be "plastic." It's easy to laugh at that scene because we all understand the sense of tackiness and artificiality that has come to be associated with the word. Yet, at the same time, it's easy to be fascinated with the ability of plastic, in the form of an inexpensive sheet of polyethylene, to cover a lightweight structure and transform the climate within. But aren't plastic greenhouses sort of unattractive? And what about the energy that goes into making plastic? We have looked into those subjects and present some answers below.

Background

No idea is really new in horticulture. Gardeners are so tirelessly ingenious that someone, somewhere is sure to have visited an idea at a previous time. I'm fond of the passage in Antoine de Saint-Exupéry's *Wind, Sand and Stars,* where he suggests that the most delightful design solutions were not invented by anyone "but simply discovered, had in the beginning been hidden by nature and in the end been found." As we progressed along, investigating our "discovery" of the double-layer solution to producing winter vegetables in the North American climate, we knew that someone must have wandered this route before us. And so, while researching some old abstract journals in the library a few winters ago, we were not surprised to find a reference to a study published in the 1950s by E. M. Emmert, a professor of horticulture at the University of Kentucky. That study, detailing his system for winter vegetable production without supplementary heat, led us to his other publications and into the history of the early use of plastics in horticulture.

The more we learned about Professor Emery Myers Emmert (1900–1962), the more we were impressed by his accomplishments. Although originally a biochemist, respected for his work on tissue analysis and plant hormones, he also worked in experimental horticulture and was almost solely responsible for developing the main applications of plastics in vegetable cultivation. He is acknowledged as the father of plastic-covered greenhouses, having begun trials as early as the 1930s by using the largest sheets he could find of the cellulose acetate material that covers cigarette packages. He stretched and fastened those sheets to lightweight frames, and combined numerous frames on a superstructure to create a greenhouse. Once polyethylene was available after World War II, he built his first plastic-covered house in 1949. He designed and built inexpensive field houses with lightweight wooden frames that are the precursors of the high tunnels of today. He pioneered wire-hoop supported low tunnels as well. He was the first to use black plastic mulch. But the item of most interest to us was his use of an inner layer of plastic inside his plastic greenhouses for unheated winter production.

Drawings in Emmert's pamphlets of his winter greenhouses show an inner layer of polyethylene held about a foot above the soil. Pictures reveal that the plastic was supported by flat-topped wire wickets. Emmert used two separated layers of plastic to cover his field greenhouses and also used two layers of plastic for the inside layer. He noted that a protected lettuce crop didn't freeze inside even when the temperature dropped to 10°F outside. He experimented with blowing air under his sheet plastic inner covers to vent them during the day, a concern we don't share because of the self-venting ability of today's spun-bonded fabrics.

Emmert's efforts were directed toward using plastic covers to get as much as he could for free from the natural world. In addition to the inner layers for his winter greenhouses, Emmert dug ditches one foot wide and three feet deep that ran alongside the inside walls of the greenhouse and extended outside for fifty feet down a slope. He covered the ditches tightly with a semi-circular plastic hood, so that ground heat, warmed by the sun during the day, could flow up into the greenhouse. He recorded as much as 5°F warmer nighttime temperatures with this system.

Reading Emmert's pamphlets one can't help but be impressed by the extent of his ingenuity and imagination. There is hardly an idea he didn't try, and usually successfully. But it is dismaying to realize that few people know of him, even in his home state of Kentucky, and no one seems to have followed up on his inner-layer concept. He was fascinated by plastic because he was interested in low-cost greenhouse options, and it may be that he was too successful. His developments probably seemed so easily homemade, so practical, and so simple for people to do themselves that no one could see a business opportunity in marketing them. Or it may be that

Emmert's ingenious design for venting low tunnels of sheet plastic. Notches in the wickets permit venting and inspection.

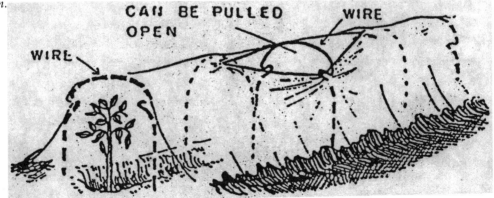

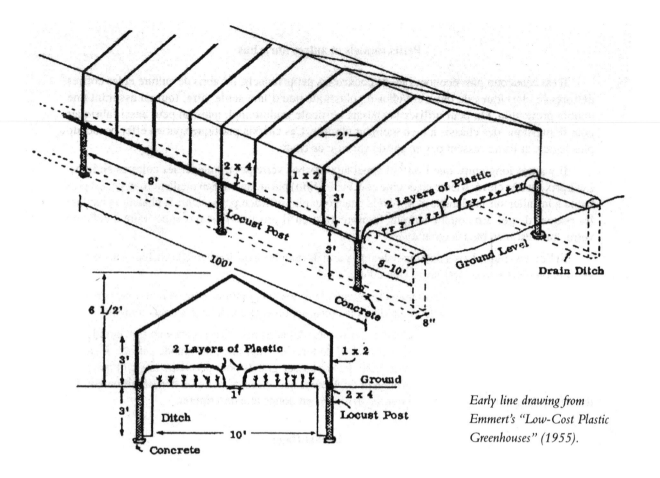

Early line drawing from Emmert's "Low-Cost Plastic Greenhouses" (1955).

there has never been a greenhouse tradition among U.S. gardeners and thus there was no natural audience. Whatever the reason for Emmert's lack of following in the U.S., other countries were not so blasé. One correspondent told us that both Asian and European growers at that time were paying close attention to Emmert's work.

The "Look" of Plastic

We saw many examples of the continued development of tunnels for unheated production on commercial farms across southern France. At first glance, farms with plastic greenhouses seem less industrial-looking than the endless acres of chenilles mentioned in chapter 9. But on closer inspection it is obvious that tunnel greenhouses are not really attractive. Their first fault is the quonset hut shape.

In our backyard we escaped "quonset hut blight" by choosing a high tunnel constructed in a gothic arch design. The pointed top and the gracefully curved sides result in a shape that is far more pleasing to the eye than the rounded quonset look. It is also a roof shape that, because of its steepness, encourages snow to slide off more easily. The second visual fault of plastic greenhouses, what we call the "blob" look, is due to the milky translucence of most greenhouse plastics. For our backyard tunnel we avoided "the blob" by covering it with an extremely transparent plastic. That makes it possible to see through to the supporting structure and the plants on the inside. When you can look into the greenhouse, as with a glass-covered structure, the blob effect mostly disappears.

We have seen a number of attractive plastic-covered greenhouses made with wooden frames. The straight or slightly slanted walls plus the gable roof looks more conventional than a curved shape to begin with. In addition to the more conventional "house" shape, it is then possible to add visual definition in a number of ways. For example, we saw one house where strips of a darker wood were nailed on top of each wooden rafter to hold down the plastic. By dividing the large expanse of the roof into a series of pleasing rectangles, the structure was emphasized and a certain elegance was added to the look.

There is no question that plastic greenhouses can be made very attractive. But even if we were to come up with a plastic greenhouse design that looked as elegant as a glass greenhouse, there would still be a stigma attached. Plastic is the definition of cheap and modern. Does it really have a place in the garden? We did an energy study and our answer to that question is an unqualified, *yes*.

The Energy Equation

Our principal delight in the winter harvest is the freshness and quality of the food. But, in a world of finite resources, we are also interested in the energy savings of producing winter food locally rather than importing food from a warmer climate. But is that actually the case? What about the energy used in building even a simple plastic-covered greenhouse? Isn't that more than the energy used to ship in the same amount of vegetables from a warmer climate? To answer that question we did a little study to compare the energy in a plastic greenhouse with the

energy involved in trucking produce from California. The calculations from which the figures given below were derived are included on the next page.

Let's use a crop of commercial lettuce as an example. If lettuce is planted in a 30-by-100-foot greenhouse at a spacing of 10 by 10 inches, that amounts to 4,200 lettuces (actually 4,320 lettuces, but let's round down for simplicity). It requires a sheet of polyethylene plastic 42 feet by 100 feet (4,200 square feet) to cover that greenhouse. Therefore, we can assign one square foot of plastic to each lettuce.

All the energy used in raw materials, production, and delivery of a manufactured item is defined by the term "embodied energy." The embodied energy in one square foot of 6-mil polyethylene greenhouse plastic (which we are assigning to cover one lettuce planted on a 10-by-10-inch grid in a 30-by-100-foot greenhouse) is 1,221 BTU.

If, on the other hand, the lettuce were grown in California, it would have to be transported 3,200 miles from California to the East Coast. We need to know the energy consumption of a semi-tractor-trailer driven across the country and divide that by the number of lettuces per load. We found three different figures from three different transportation energy data sources. Based on the average from those figures the energy consumption per 12-ounce head of lettuce to transport a semi-tractor-trailer load 3,200 miles from California to the East Coast is 3,034 BTU.

According to those calculations, a head of lettuce grown in a Maine greenhouse requires only 40 percent as much energy as delivering that lettuce from California. However, it is actually a lot better than that. Since the greenhouse polyethylene lasts three years and since the grower could get both a spring and a fall crop each year with no other energy input, six lettuces can be produced over the lifespan of that square foot of polyethylene. Each Maine-

Data for Computing Energy-Use Comparison

Polyethylene Plastic Greenhouse Covering 6 mil

42 ft. x 100 ft. roll of plastic (4,200 sq. ft.) covers a 30 ft. x 100 ft. greenhouse (3,000 sq. ft.)

Lettuce planted at 10 in. x 10 in. spacing gives approximately 4,200 lettuces per 3,000 sq. ft. greenhouse or one lettuce per square foot of plastic cover.

4,200 sq. ft. of 6-mil plastic weighs 122.2 lbs.

4,200 sq. ft. ÷ 122.2 lbs. = 34.4 sq. ft./lb.

Embodied energy of HDPE (High Density Poly-Ethylene) = 42,000 BTU/lb. (Source: A study by
the Society of the Plastics Industry (SPI), "Comparative Energy Evaluation of Plastic Products").
The embodied energy of 1 square foot of 6-mil polyethylene covering one head of lettuce
is:

42,000 BTU/lb. ÷ 34.4 sq. ft./lb. = <u>1,221 BTU/sq. ft.</u>

Transportation of Lettuce

Calculation 1

1,546 BTU/ton-mile for truck transportation

1,546 BTU/ton-mile x 3,200 miles = 4,947,200 BTU to transport 1 ton (2,000 lbs.) of
lettuce from California to Maine.

4,947,200 BTU ÷ 2,000 lbs. = 2,474 BTU/lb.

A 24-count lettuce weighs 12 ounces. To transport one .75-lb. head of lettuce from California to
Maine means .75 lb./head x 2,474 BTU/lb. = <u>1,856 BTU/head</u>.

Calculation 2

22,332 BTU/mile (for tractor trailers) x 3,200 miles = 71,462,400 BTU

One lettuce load of 25 pallets @ 35 cases/pallet @ 24 heads/case = 21,000 heads

71,462,400 BTU ÷ 21,000 heads = <u>3,403 BTU/head</u>

Calculation 3

1 gallon diesel fuel = 138,700 BTU/gal.

Average mileage for semi-tractor-trailer (class 8) = 5.5 miles/gallon

3,200 miles ÷ 5.5 miles/gallon = 582 gal.

582 gal. x 138,700 BTU/gal. = 80,723,400 BTU

80,723,400 BTU ÷ 21,000 heads = <u>3,844 BTU/head</u>

greenhouse-grown lettuce thus consumes only 6 percent of the energy required by each trucked-in lettuce.

For the sake of simplicity, only the energy in the plastic cover and the energy in transportation have been considered. These are the key factors in each system. We have not included the greenhouse pipe frame, nor the truck and its refrigeration unit, nor the highway construction. Nor did we consider the productiveness of the greenhouse for the remainder of the year for out-of-season vegetables. An analysis of those figures would make the ratio even more favorable to the Maine greenhouse. Nor have we considered any pollution from the plastic manufacturing and recycling process compared to the pollution from the burning of the average 582 gallons of diesel fuel used in the cross-country trucking. Those are obviously environmental problems that need to be addressed, but they are outside this locally-grown vs. trucked-in comparison.

At the moment plastic-covered greenhouses are by far the least expensive option for both home gardeners and commercial growers. A comparable glass-covered greenhouse costs ten to twenty times more than a plastic house. Glass also contains ten times the embodied energy of plastic—12,000 BTU per square foot—but can be expected to last ten times as long (making the energy-use comparison given above valid whether the lettuce was grown under glass or plastic). Having said that, do we believe greenhouses covered with plastic made from non-renewable petroleum feedstocks make any more long-term sense than transportation based on those same non-renewable petroleum feedstocks? Obviously not. We need to address the use of non-renewable resources as a factor in any out-of-season produce discussion.

Since greenhouse plastic is made from petroleum feedstocks, the question is whether this useful material can be made from some renewable raw material when our economy's present fixation with petroleum comes to an end. We are assured by friends who understand polymer chemistry that greenhouse plastic can indeed be made from renewable materials and that many plant-based compounds would be suitable feedstocks. Maybe that is an option that could be demanded by gardeners. However, it is more likely an option that will happen on its own someday when dictated by the comparative cost of feedstocks.

Garden Tools and Supplies and Their Sources

Listed below are the sources from which we purchase supplies for use in our garden. I am familiar with these firms, and I know that they stocked these items at the time of publication. This is not meant to be a sole endorsement of the companies mentioned nor an exclusion of suppliers not listed.

Compost and Soil Amendments

These two excellent garden catalogs carry a number of different **compost containers**, including stationary units, tumblers, and worm composters in addition to aerators, thermometers, and activators.

Gardener's Supply Company
128 Intervale Road, Burlington, VT 05401
(800) 955-3370 www.gardeners.com

Lee Valley Tools, Inc.
P.O. Box 1780, Ogdensburg, NY 13669
(800) 871-8158 www.leevalley.com

Lee Valley Tools, Ltd.
1090 Morrison Drive, Ottawa, ON K2H 1C2
Canada (800) 871-8158 www.leevalley.com

If phosphate rock, greensand, dried blood, seaweed-fish emulsion and other **soil amendments** are not available at your local garden center, you can purchase them by mail from the companies listed below. These companies also offer a wide selection of other products.

Gardener's Supply Company
128 Intervale Road, Burlington, VT 05401
(800) 955-3370 www.gardeners.com

Peaceful Valley Farm Supply
P.O. Box 2209, Grass Valley, CA 95945
(888) 784-1722 www.groworganic.com

Nutrite Inc.
25 Sheffield Street, Unit 6,
Cambridge, ON N3C 1C4 Canada
(519) 669-5401 www.nutrite.com

West Coast Seeds, Ltd.
3925 64th Street, Delta, BC V4K 3N2 Canada
(888) 804-8820 www.westcoastseeds.com

Seeds

The following North American **seed catalogs** offer all the varieties we presently grow in our four-season garden plus plenty of yet-to-be-appreciated cultivars we haven't tried yet.

Johnny's Selected Seeds, 955 Benton Avenue,
Winslow, ME 04901 (877) 564-6697
www.johnnyseeds.com

Ornamental Edibles, 5723 Trowbridge Way,
San Jose, CA 95138 (408) 528-7333
www.ornamentaledibles.com

The Cook's Garden, P.O. Box C5030,
Warminster, PA 18974 (800) 457-9703
www.cooksgarden.com

Fedco Seeds, P.O. Box 250, Waterville, ME 04903
(207) 873-7333 www.fedcoseeds.com

Territorial Seed Company, P.O. Box 158,
Cottage Grove, OR 97424 (800) 626-0866
www.territorialseed.com

Renne's Garden, 6116 Highway 9,
Felton, CA 95018 (888) 880-7228
www.reneesgarden.com

Vesey's Seeds Ltd., P.O. Box 9000,
Calais, ME 04619 (800) 363-7333.
In Canada: York, PE C0A 1P0
(902) 892-1048 www.veseys.com

Stokes Seeds, P.O. Box 548, Buffalo, NY 14240
(716) 695-6980. In Canada: P.O. Box 10,
St. Catherine's, ON L2R 6R6 (416) 688-4300
www.stokeseeds.com

Harris Seeds, P.O. Box 24966,
Rochester, NY 14624-0966 (800) 544-7938
www.harrisseeds.com

Thompson and Morgan Ltd., 220 Faraday Avenue,
Jackson, NJ 08527-5073 (800) 274-7333
www.thompson-morgan.com

West Coast Seeds, 3925 64th Street,
Delta, BC V4K 3N2 Canada (888) 804-8820
www.westcoastseeds.com

For **heirloom seeds** the original is still the best.
The Seed Savers Exchange puts out a catalog of their
favorites. The Seed Savers Exchange, 3076 North
Winn Road, Decorah, IA 52101 (563) 382-5990
www.seedsavers.org.

For the **French seed varieties** mentioned in
the text, I am not listing Graines Gautier because
they do not sell by mail to retail customers nor am I
including Jean-Luc Danneyrolles because his small
business is not equipped to handle a flood of overseas
orders. However, almost every variety imaginable
and an inexhaustible supply of others are available
from:

Graines Baumaux, B.P. 100, 54062 Nancy Cedex,
FRANCE. Phone 011 33 383 15 86 86 from 8
A.M. to 4 P.M. (French time) Monday through Fri-
day. www.graines-baumaux.fr

Just to mention a few, the catalog includes 'Bastion' and 'Orus' melons, 'Muscade de Provence'
pumpkin, rampion, scorzonera and scolymus, tu-
berous-rooted chervil, eight pages of French beans,
innumerable French heirloom onions and turnips,
four pages of chicories and radicchios, sea-kale, vi-
olet artichokes, white asparagus, and three African
eggplants that look like a cross between a ribbed
pumpkin and a tomato.

Unless you speak French well enough to order
by phone, the easiest way to purchase seeds from
Graines Baumaux is on their Web site. In recent
years, it appears this company has become less interested in selling outside the European common
market. The easiest way to order seeds would be to
have seeds sent to a friend in the common market
and have your friend transship the seeds to you.

The best **organically grown certified seed
potatoes** are sold by Wood Prairie Farm, 49 Kin-
ney Road, Bridgewater, ME 04735 (800) 829-9765
www.woodprairie.com.

A wide selection of seed potatoes are available

from Irish Eyes, 5045 Robinson Canyon, Ellensburg, WA 98926 (509) 964-7000 www.gardencityseeds.com.

Both Johnny's Selected Seeds and Peaceful Valley Farm Supply are good sources for seeds of the many **green manures.** Your local garden or farm supply store may also stock them.

Garden Tools

A complete selection of garden tools are available from the Johnny's Selected Seeds and Gardener's Supply catalogs. In the course of working with Johnny's Selected Seeds as a garden tool consultant, I have encouraged them to carry my favorites.

1. European-style **scythe** with a folding blade for safe transport and storage. They also sell *The Scythe Book*, by David Tresemer, which will teach you how to use and enjoy using a scythe for mowing grass and weeds.
2. **Curved-tine cultivator**
3. **Broadfork**
4. **Right-angle trowel**
5. A **grading rake** that is the perfect size for smoothing 30-inch-wide beds. It is also an excellent design for raking up the compost material that you mow with the scythe.
6. **Collineal hoe**
7. **Stirrup** or **oscillating hoe**
8. A **watering can** with arched handle and the Wonder Waterer **wand** with the fine rose that makes a gentle spray for seedlings.

In Canada, a similar selection of tools is available from Lee Valley Tools, Ltd. (see address above).

The Cavex hoe is available from A.M. Leonard, 241 Fox Drive, Piqua OH 45346-0816 (800) 543-8955 www.amleo.com.

The trellis netting I use is available from Johnny's Selected Seeds and Gardener's Supply. The natural wood preservative is called Donnos. It is one of a line of natural products distributed by:

The Natural Choice
Plaza Entrada, 3005 South Saint Francis Drive
Santa Fe, NM 87505
(800) 621-2591 www.bioshieldpaint.com

Natural wood preservatives are also available from:

Eco-House
P.O. Box 220, Station A
Fredericton, NB E3B 4Y9 Canada
(877) ECO-HOUSE www.eco-house.com

Frames and Tunnels

The **glass substitutes,** *Polygal* and *Lexan,* for glazing the lights of your cold frames are made in a variety of thicknesses by the following companies (1/8-1/4" should be adequate for the Dutch light model). You can contact the following companies for the name of your nearest dealer:

Polygal—Polygal Inc., P.O. Box 410592, Charlotte, NC 28241 (800) 537-0095

Lexan—General Electric Plastics, One Plastics Avenue, Pittsfield, MA 01201 (800) 323-3783

There are a number of brands and qualities of **temperature-activated automatic venting arms.** The best source is:

Charlie's Greenhouse Supply
17979 State Route 536
Mount Vernon, WA 98273
(800) 322-4707 www.charleysgreenhouse.com

Johnny's Selected Seeds sells a newly redesigned and reasonably priced cedar **cold frame.** It can be equipped with an automatic venting arm and is ingeniously designed to allow maximum light to reach the plants. Gardener's Supply also sells a red cedar cold frame.

A wide selection of the **floating covers** used as season extenders and pest barriers, plus the **infrared-transmitting plastic mulch**, are available from Gardener's Supply, Johnny's Selected Seeds and Peaceful Valley Farm Supply (see addresses above).

My simple **hoop-style tunnel greenhouse** is an easily-erected model usually available in 14- and 17-foot widths from numerous manufacturers. Consult ads in the back of your favorite gardening magazine, phone your local extension service for recommendations, or call Gardener's Supply, which sells a hoop-style greenhouse kit called the Grow House.

For a more professional (but also more expensive) **greenhouse frame** contact the company below and inquire about their line of smaller-size houses made by Harnois in Canada: Greenhouse Supply Inc., P.O. Box 3038, Brewer, ME 04412 (800) 696-8511 www.agrotech.com.

Greenhouse plastic and small spray waterers for watering the cold frame can be purchased through your local greenhouse supply company. You will save money if you buy a 100-foot roll of plastic. Since the plastic lasts three years in use, a 100-foot roll will provide enough to cover your tunnel for six to nine years, depending on tunnel size and how much you use for the ends. If you calculate your cost per year as the total cost of the plastic divided by the years of service, you will see that the greenhouse covering is a minimal expense considering the value of the food to be harvested. The extremely clear plastic mentioned on page 217, which is also high light transmitting (92 percent), is called Patilux. It is available from Growers Requisites Ltd., 1915 Setterington Drive, Kingsville ON N9Y 2E5 Canada (800) 819–8776 www.greenhousepoly.ca. **Fiberglass rods** for the instant tunnel can usually be located by calling the listings under "Fiberglass Products" in the Yellow Pages. Plans for homemade **wooden greenhouses** can be purchased from the following source:

The Department of Natural Resources,
    Management, and Engineering
University of Connecticut
1376 Storrs Road, Storrs, CT 06269
(860) 486-2840 www.nrme.uconn.edu

Northern Greenhouse Sales carries a **heavy-duty plastic**, and can offer innovative ideas on tunnel construction.

Northern Greenhouse Sales
Box 42 EC, Neche, ND 58265
(204) 327-5540 www.northerngreenhouse.com

Northern Greenhouse Sales
Box 1450, Altona, MB R0G 0B0 Canada
(204) 327-5540

Food Dryer

Our **food dryer** is a top-of-the-line *Harvest Maid "Gardenmaster"* purchased from Johnny's Selected Seeds. I highly recommend it. The dried tomatoes alone are worth the price. Addresses for plans to make your own dryer are available from The Department of Natural Resources, Management, and Engineering at the University of Connecticut (see above).

In Canada, write to the following for plans:

Brace Centre for Water Resources Management
Publications Dept.
Macdonald College of McGill University
21111 Lakeshore Road
Ste. Anne de Bellvue, QC H9X 3V9
Canada
(514) 398-7833
www.macgill.ca/brace/

Annotated Bibliography

Garden Books

The New Organic Grower (see below) has an extensive bibliography on the subject of organic gardening. Even though many of the best old books are out of print, your local library should be able to get you a copy of any of them through interlibrary loan.

Bruce, M. E. *Common Sense Compost Making*. London: Faber and Faber, 1946. This was the first composting book I read and I still find it enjoyable, helpful, and delightfully eccentric.

Burr, Fearing. *Field and Garden Vegetables of America*. Chillicothe, Ill.: American Botanist, 1994. This reprint of an 1863 gardening classic is worth reading just to realize that gardeners back then had as much (or more) variety in choice of vegetables for their garden as we do today.

Castelvetro, Giacomo. *The Fruit, Herbs and Vegetables of Italy*. London: Viking, 1989. Translated with an introduction by Gillian Riley. Originally published in 1614. Castelvetro has the soul of a true vegetable lover. Riley's introduction offers much fascinating historical information.

Coleman, Eliot. *The New Organic Grower, Revised, Expanded Edition*. White River Junction, Vt.: Chelsea Green, 1995. Gardeners looking for more in-depth explanations of the soil fertility and garden management practices of *Four-Season Harvest*, plus technical details on tools and greenhouses, will find them in this book.

Damrosch, Barbara. *The Garden Primer.* New York: Workman, 1988. The best general gardening book for beginners and experienced gardeners alike. Everything you could ever want to know is here. The explanations are clear and engagingly written.

Easey, Ben. *Practical Organic Gardening.* London: Faber and Faber, 1955. One of the most comprehensive and reasonable presentations of the ideas and techniques involved in organic gardening.

Evelyn, John. *Acetaria: A Discourse of Sallets.* Brooklyn, N.Y.: Brooklyn Botanic Garden, 1938. This is a reprint of the second-oldest book I consulted, originally published in England in 1699. It appears that Castelvetro's book may have had some influence on English knowledge of vegetables in those days since Evelyn lists seventy-seven different vegetable crops, just for salads alone.

Gerst, Jean-Jaques. *Légumes Sous Baches.* Centre technique interprofessionnel des fruits et légumes (CTIFL), 22, rue Bergère, 75009 Paris, 1993. The title translates as *Vegetables Under Covers.* The contents include every possible vegetable and every imaginable combination of high tunnels, low tunnels, reflective covers, floating covers, and heated and unheated greenhouses. The book is written for commercial growers, but that doesn't make it any less valuable. If you don't speak French it is worth learning the language or marrying a French speaker just so you can read this book. European technical manuals for growers are very complete and practical. This 250-page paperback is worth every penny of its 180 franc price.

Larcom, Joy. *Oriental Vegetables.* New York: Kodansha International, 1991. This is the book we consulted when we began to explore the vast riches of potential Asian crops. Everything you ever wanted to know and more.

Nearing, Helen and Scott. *Our Sun-Heated Greenhouse.* Charlotte, Vt.: Garden Way, 1977. Helen and Scott Nearing were my neighbors, friends, and teachers when I moved to Maine in 1968 and for many years thereafter. Seeing their greenhouse years ago inspired me to investigate further possibilities for harvesting fresh food year-round.

O'Brien, Dalziel. *Intensive Gardening.* London: Faber and Faber, 1956. This book has been a source of ideas for many organic gardeners. Although the author was a commercial grower, her simple and innovative organic methods are applicable on any scale. She provides thorough background material on Dutch lights, composting, and shallow cultivation.

Organ, John. *Rare Vegetables*. London: The Garden Book Club, 1960. Fascinating descriptions of rampion, scorzonera, seakale, King Henry and some fifty others of varying degrees of rarity (sweet corn is rare to an English gardener) will inspire you to try new crops.

Pailleux, A. and D. Bois. *Le Potager d'un Curieux*. Marseille, France: Editions Jeanne Laffitte, 1993. A modern reprint of the 1893 French classic. It includes the history, culture, and uses of two hundred edible plants. A wonderful tour of obscure and not so obscure vegetables for those who read French.

Rodale, J. I. *How to Grow Vegetables and Fruits by the Organic Method*. Emmaus, Pa.: Rodale Press, 1960. This is the first organic gardening book I read many years ago. I found it very helpful. Good information is timeless.

Salter, P. J., J. K. A. Bleasdale, et al. *Know and Grow Vegetables*, Vols. 1 and 2. New York: Oxford University Press, 1979, 1982. Two extremely useful books from the staff of the British National Vegetable Research Station.

Scotto, Elizabeth. *Les Légumes Oubliés*. Paris: Éditions du Chêne, 1995. A book in coffee table format with beautiful color photos and minimal text. Background and recipes for uncommon vegetables. In French.

Vilmorin-Andrieux, MM. *The Vegetable Garden*. London: John Murray, 1865. For those who don't read French, this is an English translation of another 19th century classic. Written by a member of the renowned Vilmorin family of French seed merchants, this six hundred-page book, full of poetic descriptions and excellent line drawings of every imaginable vegetable, will make you determined to increase the size and scope of your garden.

Cookbooks

Madison, Deborah. *Vegetarian Cooking for Everyone*. New York: Broadway Books, 1997. Whether meat eater or vegetarian you'll love this book. It is filled with great cooking tips and fourteen hundred recipes to enhance your enjoyment of homegrown vegetables year-round. When you have the best ingredients, it makes sense to combine them with the best inspiration.

Morash, Marion. *The Victory Garden Cookbook*. New York: Alfred A. Knopf, 1982. If you are wondering how imaginative you can be with both the common and less common winter vegetables, this is the book to consult. Delicious recipes from a very talented garden chef, using every vegetable under the sun.

Waters, Alice. *Chez Panisse Vegetables*. New York: Harper Collins, 1996. Alice Waters is the godmother of the fresh, local, organically grown vegetable revival in restaurants across the country. After you read and taste these recipes from her Chez Panisse restaurant in San Francisco, you'll know why she has been so influential.

INDEX

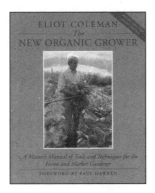

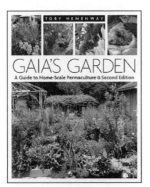
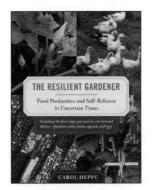

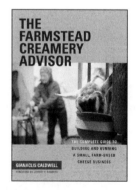
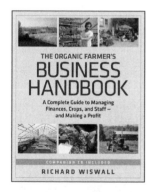